THE VEIL OF PARTICIPATION

Public participation is a vital part of constitution-making processes around the world, but we know very little about the extent to which participation affects constitutional texts. In this book, Alexander Hudson offers a systematic measurement of the impact of public participation in three much-cited cases – Brazil, South Africa, and Iceland – and introduces a theory of party-mediated public participation. He argues that public participation has limited potential to affect the constitutional text but that the effectiveness of participation varies with the political context. Party strength is the key factor, as strong political parties are unlikely to incorporate public input, while weaker parties are comparatively more responsive to public input. This party-mediation thesis fundamentally challenges the contemporary consensus on the design of constitution-making processes and places new emphasis on the role of political parties.

Dr. Alexander Hudson is a Research Fellow in the Comparative Constitutionalism Fellow Group at the Max Planck Institute for the Study of Religious and Ethnic Diversity. His research focuses on the role of citizens in processes of constitutional change, including participatory drafting processes, referendums, and crowdsourcing.

T0384525

COMPARATIVE CONSTITUTIONAL LAW AND POLICY

Series Editors

Tom Ginsburg, *University of Chicago*
Zachary Elkins, *University of Texas at Austin*
Ran Hirschl, *University of Toronto*

Comparative constitutional law is an intellectually vibrant field that encompasses an increasingly broad array of approaches and methodologies. This series collects analytically innovative and empirically grounded work from scholars of comparative constitutionalism across academic disciplines. Books in the series include theoretically informed studies of single constitutional jurisdictions, comparative studies of constitutional law and institutions, and edited collections of original essays that respond to challenging theoretical and empirical questions in the field.

Books in the Series

Redrafting Constitutions in Democratic Orders: Theoretical and Comparative Perspectives
Edited by Gabriel L. Negretto

From Parchment to Practice: Implementing New Constitutions
Edited by Tom Ginsburg and Aziz Z. Huq

The Failure of Popular Constitution Making in Turkey: Regressing Towards Constitutional Autocracy
Edited by Felix Petersen and Zeynep Yanaşmayan

A Qualified Hope: The Indian Supreme Court and Progressive Social Change
Edited by Gerald N. Rosenberg, Sudhir Krishnaswamy and Shishir Bail

Constitutions in Times of Financial Crisis
Edited by Tom Ginsburg, Mark D. Rosen and Georg Vanberg

Reconstructing Rights: Courts, Parties, and Equality Rights in India, South Africa, and the United States
Stephan Stohler

Constitution-Making and Transnational Legal Order
Edited by Tom Ginsburg, Terence C. Halliday and Gregory Shaffer

Hybrid Constitutionalism: The Politics of Constitutional Review in the Chinese Special Administrative Regions
Eric C. Ip

The Politico-Legal Dynamics of Judicial Review: A Comparative Analysis
Theunis Roux

The Invisible Constitution in Comparative Perspective
Edited by Rosalind Dixon and Adrienne Stone

Constitutional Courts in Asia: A Comparative Perspective
Edited by Albert H. Y. Chen and Andrew Harding

Judicial Review in Norway: A Bicentennial Debate
Anine Kierulf

Constituent Assemblies
Edited by Jon Elster, Roberto Gargarella, Vatsal Naresh, and Bjorn Erik Rasch

The Veil of Participation

CITIZENS AND POLITICAL PARTIES IN CONSTITUTION-MAKING PROCESSES

ALEXANDER HUDSON

Max Planck Institute (Göttingen, Germany)

Shaftesbury Road, Cambridge CB2 8EA, United Kingdom

One Liberty Plaza, 20th Floor, New York, NY 10006, USA

477 Williamstown Road, Port Melbourne, VIC 3207, Australia

314–321, 3rd Floor, Plot 3, Splendor Forum, Jasola District Centre, New Delhi – 110025, India

103 Penang Road, #05–06/07, Visioncrest Commercial, Singapore 238467

Cambridge University Press is part of Cambridge University Press & Assessment, a department of the University of Cambridge.

We share the University's mission to contribute to society through the pursuit of education, learning and research at the highest international levels of excellence.

www.cambridge.org
Information on this title: www.cambridge.org/9781108793513

DOI: 10.1017/9781108878685

First published 2021
First paperback edition 2024

A catalogue record for this publication is available from the British Library

Library of Congress Cataloging-in-Publication data
NAMES: Hudson, Alexander, author.
TITLE: The veil of participation : citizens and political parties in constitution-making processes / Alexander Hudson, Comparative Constitutionalism Fellow Group, Max Planck Institute for the Study of Religious and Ethnic Diversity.
DESCRIPTION: [New York] : [Cambridge University Press], 2021. | Series: CCLP comparative constitutional law and policy | Includes bibliographical references and index.
IDENTIFIERS: LCCN 2020047392 (print) | LCCN 2020047393 (ebook) | ISBN 9781108840071 (hardback) | ISBN 9781108793513 (paperback) | ISBN 9781108878685 (ebook)
SUBJECTS: LCSH: Constitutions. | Constitutional law | Political participation. | Political parties – Law and legislation. | Legislation – Citizen participation.
CLASSIFICATION: LCC K3165 .H783 2021 (print) | LCC K3165 (ebook) | DDC 342.02–dc23
LC record available at https://lccn.loc.gov/2020047392
LC ebook record available at https://lccn.loc.gov/2020047393

ISBN   978-1-108-84007-1   Hardback
ISBN   978-1-108-79351-3   Paperback

To Isobel

Contents

Figures

Tables

Acknowledgments

In conducting this research across a number of years and four continents, I have relied on the help of a great many people. In some cases I sought them out, in others, they gave me help I did not even realize I needed. Without a doubt, this book would not have been started or finished without the investments that a host of people have made in my life and work.

I must first thank Zachary Elkins, who encouraged me to pursue this field of research during my graduate work at the University of Texas at Austin. I am incredibly grateful to him for giving me opportunities and guidance, and for his encouragement and generosity throughout my years in Austin. I am also deeply grateful to a number of other members of the Department of Government at the University of Texas at Austin who supported the research behind much of this book, most notably Daniel Brinks, Gary Jacobsohn, Sanford Levinson, and Christopher Wlezien. Many of my classmates in Texas were important to the early stages of this work, and I especially thank Robert Shaffer, Joseph Amick, Christina Bambrick, Thomas Bell, Joseph Cozza, Jacob Dizard, Connor Ewing, and Kyle Shen for their contributions to my research.

After leaving Texas, I was incredibly lucky to find a new home at the Max Planck Institute for the Study of Religious and Ethnic Diversity in Göttingen, Germany. This wonderful community of scholars has supported my research and challenged me in many ways. In particular I would like to thank Ayelet Shachar and the Department of Ethics, Law, and Politics for their support in ways large and small. Thanks to Elisabeth Badenhoop, Ali Emre Benli, Benjamin Boudou, Derek Denman, Marie-Eve Loiselle, Marieke Riedel, Samuel David Schmid, Martijn van den Brink, and Barbara von Rütte for their comradeship and encouragement.

I am profoundly grateful to Ran Hirschl for all he has done for scholarship in comparative constitutionalism and for me personally. His books were an inspiration to me when I first began to study comparative public law, and it has been my great good fortune to be able to work with him these past two years. He has been an exceptional mentor and a generous friend. Moreover, the scholarly community he created in Göttingen (and now beyond) has been a wonderful resource. Thanks to Anna Fruhstorfer, Berihun Adugna Gebeye, Lisa Harms, Michael Hein, Eugénie Mérieau, and Mariana Velasco Rivera for their many contributions to this book.

The research reported here has also benefited from comments and questions raised during presentations at a number of conferences. Of particular note are panels at "Democracy Beyond Elections," University of Bristol Law School, 2017; Melbourne Institute of Comparative Constitutional Law, University of Melbourne, 2018; "Political Parties, Partisanship, and the Constitution," University of Oxford, 2019; "Political Parties and Deliberative Practices," ECPR Joint Sessions of Workshops, 2019; Political Studies Association Annual Meeting, 2019; Canadian Political Science Association Annual Conference, 2019; and the American Political Science Association Annual Meeting, 2019.

I am grateful to the following journals for permission to reprint material previously published in the following articles: "When Does Public Participation Make a Difference? Evidence From Iceland's Crowdsourced Constitution," *Policy & Internet* 10(2) (2018), 185–217; and "Political Parties and Public Participation in Constitution Making: Legitimation, Distraction, or Real Impact?," *Comparative Politics* 53(3) (2021).

My research in Brazil was supported both morally and financially by my association with the Fundação Getulio Vargas. Thanks especially to Pedro Cantisano, Daniel Chada, Ivar Hartmann, Eduardo Magrani, Greg Michener, Michael Mohallem, Thomaz Perreira, and Diego Werneck for being kind and helpful colleagues, and to Joaquim Falcão and Eduardo Jordão for the opportunity to visit FGV. Relatedly, I thank my research assistants at FGV, Pedro Amaro, João Vítor, and Gabriel Mesquita for making a large dataset useful. Thanks also to Elizete Ignácio dos Santos and Thamires de Lima Silva at Clave de Fá Pesquisa e Projetos for working hard to locate and interview contributors to the SAIC database. In Brasilia, I also thank Carlos Oliveira, who was vital to the collection of data for this project.

My research in South Africa was made possible by institutional support from the University of Cape Town. I am grateful to the Department of Public Law at the University of Cape Town for officially hosting me. I especially wish to thank Elrena van der Spuy, Pierre de Vos, Robert Mattes, and Hugh Corder for their assistance in various ways. I also thank the many kind people at the National Archives of South Africa and Parliament of South Africa for making me feel welcome in their wonderful country, and assisting me with this research.

The field research behind this book was financed by fellowships from the University of Texas at Austin, and the Fundação Getulio Vargas, Escola de Direito do Rio de Janeiro, and also by National Science Foundation through Grant No. SES-1535665. I am grateful to these institutions for their investment in my work.

At Cambridge University Press, I thank editor Matt Gallaway and editorial assistant Cameron Daddis. I am also grateful to the anonymous reviewers for their insights and suggestions.

My family has also supported the writing of this book in their own ways. My children, Isobel, John, and Richard, have had an unconventional and challenging first few years of life with a father who was researching, writing, and toting them around half the world. I thank them for their patience and love and for giving me a reason to keep smiling even on the days when the writing was hard and the data were inscrutable. My wife, Marianna, has put up with a lot and sacrificed a great deal for me to complete this book. Moreover, I am grateful to her for reading and commenting on the manuscript. I could never repay her for all she has done.

1

Introduction

1.1 THE PUBLIC FACE OF CONSTITUTION-MAKING

In the final months of 1995, about one-third of South Africans encountered an interesting full page advertisement in a newspaper or magazine. It was a picture of President Nelson Mandela standing on a pavement outside a building, dressed in a suit, and talking on a cellular phone. The speech bubble above his head read, "Hello, is that the Constitutional Talk-line? I would like to make my submission" (Everatt et al., 1996, 156; Segal and Cort, 2011). This advertisement was part of a large campaign to encourage South Africans to participate in the constitution-making process. The central message was that South Africans of any background, level of education or income could meaningfully contribute to the drafting of the constitution. It intimated that their participation was wanted, and that participation was easy. This message was buttressed by the publication of comic strips that illustrated the constitution-making process and the content of the constitution, and TV and radio programs that brought the development of the constitution into the living rooms, minibuses, and cars of the "rainbow nation." By the time the final constitution was completed in 1996, more than 1.5 million South Africans had participated in some way and cemented the place of South Africa's constitution as a guiding example to the world.

My own interest in citizen participation in constitution-making processes was first piqued when I learned about the Constitutional Loya Jirga that took place in Afghanistan between late 2003 and early 2004. Here, it seemed, was a traditional way in which citizens could participate in deliberations about the content of a constitution. The reality of course was somewhat different. Concerns were raised very early in the process about the extent to which the Loya Jirga could alter a draft that had already been prepared in a way that satisfied both President Karzai and the United States government (International Crisis Group, 2003). The final text of the constitution was a carefully balanced path between the various red lines of the international community, Islamist leaders, and various other power-brokers (Rubin, 2004). Nonetheless, the romantic image of the restoration of a traditional

1

form of democratic participation as a war-torn state moved along the path toward reconstruction is a powerful one.

Participatory constitution-making processes are hardly uncommon, popping up in such unlikely places as the example from Afghanistan described earlier, and having early historical examples in revolutionary France (1793) and in the erstwhile Batavian Republic (1797). Indeed, it is one of the great impulses of the current age to seek to solve thorny problems by consulting the people afresh. And what could be more inspiring for a student of politics and constitutional change than a story about the mass public coming together to deliberate about the fundamental institutions that will govern their community. Normatively, this kind of democratic negotiation of the social contract is highly appealing. For me, though, accounts of public participation in constitution-making processes from Albania to Zimbabwe are for the most party unsatisfying in that they fail to account for the extent to which input from the public is included in the final constitutional text. One of the purposes of this book is to provide an account of three such inspiring cases in which this vital outcome is accounted for.

This heady mixture of hopeful innovation and mass-public mobilization practically writes its own advertising, and the message from Nelson Mandela described earlier is hardly an exception. As we begin to wade into these potentially muddy waters, this public face of participatory constitution-making is worth thinking about for a minute. The broader advertising slogan of the South African Constitutional Assembly was: "You've made your mark, now have your say." Later followed by advertising that seemed to promise that this participation would be effectual, as it read: "You've made your mark. You've had your say. Now we're making sure it counts" (Segal and Cort, 2011, 163). In Brazil, documents produced by the Constituent Assembly in 1987 suggested: "You too are a member of the constituent assembly, participate!"[1] In 2013, Zimbabwe's Constitution Parliamentary Committee (COPAC) promised that its participatory drafting process was "Ensuring a people-driven constitution" (Moyo, 2013). Cuba also included popular consultations in their constitutional revision process in 2018–2019, with the main slogan "My will, my constitution," but also claiming that "The Constitution of a country is the voice of the people" (González, 2019). Each of these slogans and many more besides which I have left out make promises about the constitution-making process. They promise (either implicitly or explicitly) that what is happening in this constitution-making process is a real substantive engagement with the people, in which their views will be taken into account when the drafters put pen to paper. For this social scientist, the last part of the South African slogan in particular seems to raise an empirical challenge, and it is one that I take up with some enthusiasm later in this book.

The title of the book begins to give away its empirical findings and hints at the core thesis. It is of course a reference to Rawls' famous "veil of ignorance"

---

[1] Você também é constituinte, participe!

(Rawls, 1971), but this book does not directly deal with Rawls' contribution to political theory. The way Rawls described reasoning about political arrangements from behind a veil, however, has a resonance with how I describe public participation in constitution-making processes. I argue that public participation in a sense creates a veil that separates the citizens from the elites who do the real work of drafting a constitution. Counterintuitively, citizen-participants do some of the work of erecting a barrier that serves in a perverse way to insulate the constitution from public criticism. They weave the curtain that provides the constitution makers with some privacy themselves. Participation legitimates the constitution, providing it with a democratic covering, perhaps regardless of its substantive content.

This claim may require some further justification, in that one would expect that more participation would create more transparency. Indeed, this may sometimes be the case. But in at least two of the cases that are considered in this book, it seems that public participation also endowed the constitution-making processes with a great deal of popular legitimacy and screened the elite negotiations that really mattered from a clear public view. In the case of South Africa, public participation captures the scholarly (and public) mind to a far greater extent than the "channel" that existed between the key negotiators of the African National Congress and the National Party. Similarly in Brazil, the idea of the "citizens' constitution" seems to have a larger place in the popular imagination than the reality of the power brokering of the parliamentary coalition called the "Centrão." These larger-than-life episodes of mass-public involvement in constitution-making have served in some way to block our view of the realpolitik going on in the halls of power. Whether or not this is part of the intention of designers of constitution-making processes I would not venture at this moment to judge, but I return to the larger implications of these question in the conclusion of the book.

In the chapters that follow, I retell the histories of three noteworthy cases of participatory constitution-making (Brazil, South Africa, and Iceland), seeking to provide a clear answer for this motivating question of how much input from the public really changes the content of the constitution. Moreover, I seek to explain the variation in impact, developing an argument about how political parties engage in constitution-making processes. Taking this exploration of participatory constitution-making even further, I delve into the details of sixteen more cases in lesser depth, and also present some statistical tests of the theory I develop in this book. The research presented here has been my occupation for the better part of a decade, and it has been worth every minute.

1.2 WHY IS A STUDY OF PARTICIPATION IMPORTANT?

There was a time, not so long ago, when scholars were highly optimistic about the possibility that liberal democracy would spread across most of the globe, bringing peace and prosperity with it (Fukuyama, 1989; Huntington, 1993). More recently, events in a number of countries have prompted us to question this hopeful vision and think more deeply about the core vulnerabilities of liberal democracies and what might be done to protect them (Ginsburg and Huq, 2018; Graber et al., 2018). Even before this, a number of scholars brought attention to the surprising weakness of public support for democratic institutions (Norris, 2001; Dalton, 2004). Among the pressing challenges to liberal democracy is a longer-term decline in public trust in political institutions (Hetherington, 2005). Much as the coach of a sports team in the middle of a losing streak might emphasize greater attention to the fundamentals, scholars also advise a renewed focus on the foundations of liberal democracy. Ginsburg and Huq (2018, 3) suggest that "it is only the determined mobilization of citizens, political party elites, and officials committed to the rule of law that can preserve those [democratic] institutions and practices."

In this context, public participation in politics takes on a new urgency. Indeed, the early years of the twenty-first century have witnessed a remarkable spread of innovations in democracy, enabling citizen participation at the local (Baiocchi, 2001), national (Landemore, 2019), and even global level (Dryzek et al., 2011; Global Citizens Assembly, 2019). Public participation in decision-making processes of many kinds seems to have a legitimating effect (Scharpf, 1998; Fung, 2015; Yang, 2016). In particular, increased citizen participation is often seen as having the potential to increase civic virtues and public trust (Grönlund et al., 2010).

Nowhere is public participation seen to be more necessary than in constitution-making processes. Here, the fundamental laws that establish a government are altered or replaced, and a powerful source of legitimation is necessary to ensure public faith in the process and the product. To rationalize the unrestrained power deployed in a constitution-making process, legal scholars appeal to the core concept of constituent power (Kalyvas, 2005; Tushnet, 2015). In modern practice, most significant moves toward constitutional revision or replacement require "legitimation from below" (Oklopcic, 2018, 53), usually through some opportunity for public votes or participation. As Tushnet notes, "at some point in the process of constitution making and implementation, law runs out" (Tushnet, 2015, 641). At this point the "revolutionary road to constitutional legitimacy" must be followed and some form of public participation is often required to legitimate the constitutional change (Tushnet, 2015, 642). In the most romantic version of this legitimating process, citizens are pictured engaging with one another in a wide-ranging debate that gives rise to a "constitutional moment" (Ackerman, 1998, 187).

Indeed, this view of the necessity of public participation in constitution-making processes has a long historical tradition. During the French Revolution, Thomas Paine famously wrote that "The constitution of a country is not the act of its government, but of the people constituting a government" (Paine, 1791, 56). Similarly, von Savigny declared that it is "the spirit of a people [Volksgeist] living and working in common in all the individuals, which gives birth to positive law" (Savigny, 1867, 12).

More recently, in the introduction to a symposium on participatory constitution drafting in the *International Journal of Constitutional Law*, Choudhry and Tushnet (2020, 173) suggest that the currently dominant view is that public participation is "highly desirable" on both normative and pragmatic grounds. The normative claim was given a powerful statement by Hart (2003), who wrote that "How the constitution is made, as well as what it says, matters. Process has become equally as important as the content of the final document for the legitimacy of a new constitution." Pragmatically, public participation in constitution-making has been connected with improved democracy (Eisenstadt et al., 2017a), resolution of conflict (Widner, 2005), expanded rights protection (Elkins et al., 2008; Negretto, 2020), and empowering women (Hart, 2003; Rubio-Marín, 2020).

In pursuit of these normative and pragmatic goals, public participation in constitution-making has taken many forms. Voting is by far the most common means of participation, either through the election of the drafting body or in a ratifying referendum. Between 1789 and 2016, 168 constitutions were ratified through a referendum, and as of 2018, more than a third of in-force constitutions were ratified through a referendum (Elkins and Hudson, 2019). However, it is becoming more common to involve voters earlier in the process through such means as public consultations, petitions, written and oral submissions, and even popular amendments. Landemore (2020b, 180) elegantly summarized this shift toward earlier and more substantive participation, suggesting that

it appears that our understanding of constitution-making has evolved to now mean having direct influence on the content and shape of the constitutional text itself, as opposed to just performatively bringing a ready-made text into existence or shaping it indirectly via elected representatives. The democratic will now is no longer supposed to exercise itself indirectly and at the end of the process but from the start, throughout, and in more direct ways.

Reflecting the view described by Landemore, public participation programs involving early and substantive mechanisms for public input have become a central part of the guidance given by international organizations advising drafting processes (Ghai and Galli, 2006; Hart, 2010; Gluck and Ballou, 2014), making it "inconceivable that a government would attempt to draft a new constitution without at least a nominal commitment to a process in which the public is consulted" (Kirkby and Murray, 2016). The dominant assumption seems to be that a better, more participatory, process may go some way toward overcoming otherwise suboptimal political conditions.

Despite this increasing participation of the public in constitution-making processes, the extent to which public input has influenced constitutional texts has barely been investigated. There are certainly reasons to believe that one purpose of popular involvement is to increase the legitimacy of the constitution. However, many public outreach programs are pitched in terms of giving the public an opportunity to contribute to the constitutional text, and perhaps even to assume the role of coauthor with the members of the drafting body. At this point, we do not have a good sense of the degree to which this actually happens. Is there such a thing as a "constitutional moment" in which the People speak about the constitution and effect change therein (Ackerman, 1991)? If so, what conditions might predict greater or lesser probability for effective public input?

1.3 WHAT THIS BOOK DOES

Inspired by scenarios like the advertisement featuring Mandela, there are two central questions in this book. They work in order, as the first question is descriptive and the second is inferential.

1. To what extent does public participation in constitution-making processes affect the text of the constitution?
2. What explains the variation in this impact?

Beyond these, there are other questions that are considered along the way. Such as, to what extent can drafters use submissions from the public in an effective way – do logistical or cognitive challenges impair their ability to utilize input from the public? Do citizen-participants have the ability to determine the extent to which public input was effective? Does participation increase the legitimacy of the constitution? If so, for how long? And finally, what sort of guidance can we give to designers of constitution-making processes about how best to implement a public participation program.

The theoretical contribution of this book is an application of established understandings of how political parties function to a new setting, and a correction to both the popular mythology of constitution-making and the guidance often given by international organizations. Chapter 2 discusses the theory in some depth and situates it within the literature in political science and law. To briefly state the theory, I propose that the impact of public participation in constitution-making processes varies across cases, and that the variation is determined primarily by the strength of the political parties in the drafting body. Specifically, stronger parties are less likely to include input from the public in the constitutions that they produce, while weak parties are more exposed to public pressure, and thus include more content from the public. In the rare case where a constitution is drafted without the participation of political parties, the impact of public participation is strongest. To be sure, there are many other factors that can influence the degree to which public consultation has an impact. However, this party-mediation thesis suggests that the other variables at work here interact with party strength in such a way that strong parties essentially preclude significant influence from individuals in the constitution-making process and significantly lessen the influence of interest groups in the later stages of the process.

The book also makes a number of empirical contributions to comparative constitutional studies. As detailed later, the empirical chapters feature three main case studies that are based on field research and the collection of new primary source materials relating to the constitution-making processes of Brazil, South Africa, and Iceland. These three chapters provide a concise history of the participatory processes in these precedential cases, using new data to measure the precise effects of participation. This is an area of study where little has yet been done, and these chapters significantly advance our fundamental knowledge in this area. The empirical research in these chapters includes analyses of primary documents generated in the three constitution-making processes under study, such as internal documents from the constituent assemblies, minutes and transcripts of committee meetings, intermediate and final drafts of the constitutions, and written submissions from the public. This documentary evidence is supplemented by sixty-seven semi-structured interviews, most of which were conducted in person in South Africa, Brazil, and Iceland. It follows then that much of the analysis of these three major cases is of a qualitative nature. Where appropriate, computational methods of textual analysis are used. In the chapter on Iceland, an original dataset of submissions from the public is used to create a statistical model predicting the likelihood that these submissions would be included in the final draft of the constitution.

These chapters provide a clear answer to the first question posed earlier, and it is not necessarily an encouraging one. In this first large-scale comparative analysis of the impact of participation on constitutional texts, I show that it is highly unlikely that what citizens submit or propose will be included in the constitutional text. Even in a propitious context in which participation is solicited by leading politicians, many citizens respond, and professional teams of technicians carefully process these inputs and relay them to the drafters, public participation has precious little impact on the constitution. There is some variation between the cases, with Iceland appearing as a relative success, with almost 10 percent of the submissions making an impact. However, it bears repeating that the cases considered in this book were instances where public participation was far more likely to make a difference than in the majority of constitution-making processes. If South Africa's much lauded participation program had such a negligible impact on the constitutional text, we should significantly revise our baseline expectations for other cases. This creates a significant challenge to the conventional wisdom about public participation in constitution-making as described earlier.

Taking the analysis further, the fourth empirical chapter (6) includes sixteen more case studies of highly participatory constitution-making in cases across the globe. These vignettes provide a participation-focused account of a number of cases in which scholars have usually had other concerns. Using a variety of secondary sources, I am able to make connections between political parties and public participation across a wide variety of political contests. Finally, to provide a comprehensive view of this dynamic between political parties and public participation, I also include statistical models that demonstrate the way in which the effects of participation depend on party strength. This statistical analysis includes data on all successful constitution-making processes between 1974 and 2014, testing the party-mediation thesis and the textual effects of participation at scale. While the underlying data in those models is not original, I employ a creative strategy to model the effects of participation that could spark new interest in analysis of participation's effects. Taken as a whole, the empirical chapters significantly advance our understanding of how public participation has performed in the real world.

1.4 OUTLINE OF THE BOOK

The book proceeds by developing a theoretical account of participatory constitution-making, then exploring the facts of constitution-making in both case studies and cross-national statistical analyses, and concludes with a revised assessment of the role of public participation in constitution-making processes.

In Chapter 2, I introduce a theory of party-mediated public impact. As previously described in brief, this book advances a two-part argument, holding that public participation is unlikely to have a significant impact in constitution-making processes, but that this (small) impact varies with the strength of the political parties that are involved in the drafting process. This chapter reviews the state of our knowledge of constitution-making processes, political parties, and political participation through a conceptually oriented discussion. The chapter sets up the empirical work that follows by laying out some theoretical expectations about the interactions between public participation and political parties in constitution-making processes.

The three main case studies allow us to begin to assess the veracity of this theory with reference to the real experience of constitution-making. The case studies are arranged in an order that follows the central argument of this book. The first case study is South Africa, where we find strong parties and low impact from public participation. This is followed by the case of Brazil, where famously weak parties are associated with a middle level of impact. The final case is Iceland, where the constitution was drafted without the involvement of political parties, and the level of impact was high.

The basic intuition behind the selection of the first two cases is a search for most similar systems. Indeed, Brazil and South Africa share most salient features of the constitution-drafting process, facilitating an attempt to control for most institutional aspects of the constitution-making process, while varying the level of the main explanatory variable (party strength). Brazil and South Africa are in some more general terms well paired for a most similar systems comparative analysis, and have been used in that way in previous studies (Lieberman, 2003; Seidman, 1994). Beyond this, the cases are important to consider due to their precedential value as two of the earliest examples of highly participatory constitution-drafting (Galligan, 2013). Yet, there are important differences in terms of the larger historical context that are relevant to the causal claims I make (Simmons and Smith, 2017). Iceland is in many ways less comparable to the other two cases. However, the inclusion of Iceland provides us with a more complete picture of the relationship between public participation and political party strength, as it is one of only a very few cases in which an officially sanctioned constitutional draft was prepared in a process that excluded political parties. In each of the case study chapters, I consider the political features that developed prior to the critical juncture of the drafting moment, identifying critical antecedents that shape the divergence between the cases (Slater and Simmons, 2010). Read together, the cases need not be compared in a direct way, but rather understood as examples of how the two primary explanatory variables (public participation and party strength) interact.

The discussion of South Africa in Chapter 3 includes an introduction to the legal context of the end of apartheid and the transformation of liberation movements into political parties. The chapter also includes a discussion of the 1994 election, including new evidence about the outcome gathered from high-level interviews. Primary sources were vital to the analysis here, including rarely reported internal documents from the Constitutional Assembly. Some of the most compelling support for the theory comes from interviews with drafters, including high-profile figures in the major parties and representatives of the smaller parties. Overall, while the South African constitution-making process was a great success (as is the constitution it produced), the analysis in this chapter demonstrates that the extensive public participation program had a negligible impact on the constitutional text. The constitution was instead the result of difficult negotiations between two strong parties.

Though including comparatively less history than the South African chapter, the discussion of Brazil's constitution-making process in Chapter 4 also takes care to develop a contextually rich account. The analysis in this chapter also relies heavily on primary sources, including a little-studied collection of almost 73,000 submissions from members of the public. These documents reveal patterns of participation, including several campaigns that provided sample text for citizen-participants. Interviews highlighted the differences between Brazil and South Africa, as drafters in Brazil placed much more emphasis on the role of individuals and groups in advocating for changes to the constitution. Brazil's constitution-making process was at times somewhat chaotic, but was characterized by creativity and a high level of participation from both individuals and public-spirited groups. This constitution-making process included a number of innovations, including the use of a computer database to organize submissions from the public and the creation of petitions for amendments during the drafting stage. The constitution that this process produced was influenced in several clear ways by input from the public, demonstrating the space that weak parties leave for effective public engagement.

Iceland's experience of constitution-making in 2011 was ultimately unsuccessful, but both the successes and failures of this case have a great deal to teach us about how public participation works in constitution-making processes. Chapter 5 provides a detailed and carefully researched account of this constitution-making process. As one of the smallest independent states, Iceland's constitution-making can be known much more thoroughly than that of Brazil or South Africa. This chapter again builds on primary documentary sources and interviews, but also includes a statistical analysis of the direct textual impacts of submissions from the public. This chapter demonstrates that, in a case where political parties are excluded from the drafting process, public participation is both more necessary and more effectual. Also 10 percent of the submissions from the public in this case resulted in a change to the constitutional text. The statistical analysis also highlights the fact that the part of the constitution dealing with fundamental rights was the most likely to be changed in response to public participation. This secondary finding is one of the sources of support for the cross-national statistical analysis in Chapter 6. While some might doubt the generalizability of the Icelandic experience, this unique case demonstrates the high level of impact that public participation can have in a constitution-making process that excludes political parties.

Going beyond the focused analysis in the three main case studies, Chapter 6 takes on the task of testing the party-mediation thesis in a robust and expansive way. This chapter begins with a large-N cross-national statistical analysis of the effects of public participation in constitution-making processes in almost all cases between 1974 and 2014. In this fourth empirical chapter, I test whether the findings of the three main case studies are generalizable to a near-comprehensive sample. While the careful measurement of impact that is featured in the case studies is not replicable on this larger scale, this chapter employs a creative strategy to overcome the data problem and quantify the impact of public participation in constitutional texts. The statistical models in this chapter highlight both the overall effects of public participation on the constitution and the role that party strength plays in this process. Specifically, the models show that the effect of public participation is dependent on party strength, with the impact of participation on the constitutional text dramatically declining as party strength increases. To take this finding even further, the chapter also includes sixteen case studies of the most participatory constitution-making processes between 1974 and 2014. These shorter case studies provide additional support for the argument advanced in this book, showing that party strength is a major factor in determining the extent to which input from the public will have an impact on the constitutional text.

The book concludes with a chapter that more explicitly unites the three main case studies and discusses the findings in a synthetic fashion. The concluding chapter also addresses other issues not covered in the previous chapters, including some policy guidance that flows from the central findings of the book. Moreover, this concluding chapter reflects on the implications of the party-mediation thesis for research on constitution-making processes, political parties, and democratic innovations.

Through this wide-ranging study of the relationship between public participation in constitution-making processes, I hope to re-calibrate our expectations and normative aspirations. The evidence presented here shows that we have over the past three decades developed a mythology of the role of "the people" in constitutional change, veiling the hard realities of partisan competition that actually characterize constitution-making processes. I hope the arguments and evidence presented here will push us to think more creatively about how constitutions can be written and the role of the people in politics more generally.

2

Theoretical Foundations of Participatory Drafting

2.1 INTRODUCTION

The narrowest goals of this book are to establish the extent to which public participation in constitution-making processes influences the text of the constitution, and to expound a theory that explains the variation in the level of this influence. However, the research described here has much broader implications, including our understanding of the role of political parties, the ability of average citizens to participate in lawmaking, and the interactions between the mass public and political elites. In this chapter, a theory of party-mediated public participation is described and located within broader debates in political science and law.

The chapter begins with an exposition of the argument advanced in this book, and then moves on to a description of the central concepts that the theory implicates. The discussion of concepts is also used to situate the theory within the existing literature and to show where this book makes its contributions.

2.2 PARTY-MEDIATED POLITICAL PARTICIPATION

The evidence presented in the empirical chapters that follow demonstrates that the impact of public participation on the text of constitutions is minimal in almost all cases – at least in terms of the volume of text that has been added or removed as a result of public input. The cases considered in this book are among the most participatory, but even here, the likelihood that a letter from a concerned citizen will have an impact on the constitutional text is small. This should not be cause for immediate despair among committed advocates of participatory democracy: Even small and unlikely changes can be important both in shaping the institutions of government and in giving citizens an important feeling of attachment and ownership of the constitutional text. Furthermore, I argue that there are systematic ways in which this impact varies.

The central claim in this chapter is that variation in the strength and nature of political parties in the constitution-making process is the most important factor in determining the effectiveness of direct public participation. To wit: in constitution-making bodies that are populated by strong parties, there is very little room for public participation, even when significant resources of time and money are devoted to facilitating public engagement. Conversely, in constitution-making bodies with weak parties (or no parties), there will be a comparatively greater impact from public participation.

This effect is consistent with understandings of political parties as mediating, competing with, or even supplanting other forms of political expression (Richardson, 1995; Webb, 2005; Ceka, 2013). I further argue that the informational challenges of assessing the impact of public participation prevent the majority of participants from estimating the effectiveness of their participation (either as individuals or as members of groups), and that public participation programs are effective in increasing support for a constitution even when drafters do not make any changes to the content of the constitution in response to public input. Stronger and more effective parties might produce better constitutions, but they reduce the impact of public participation.

To be more specific, when the drafting body is dominated by disciplined, programmatic parties, the impact of public participation (to the extent that it exists) will primarily be indirect and work as an element of the agenda-setting process within political parties; when there are direct effects, they will be idiosyncratic, such as in serendipitous meetings between a drafter's existing interests and those of a citizen-participant. This dynamic is exemplified by the South African case. In contrast, in cases in which the parties are comparatively weak, the impact will be of a more direct nature, that is to say creating concrete changes in the text, but in ways that are unsystematic, responding to particular interests. This sort of impact is observed in the Brazilian case. When representatives of political parties are not included in the drafting body, drafters may view public participation quite differently, and respond positively to public input that in their view has merit, regardless of its provenance. The Icelandic case exemplifies this kind of process.

This does not discount the possibility that strong parties facilitate effective political participation within the party organization. Indeed, one of the positive features of strong political parties is their capacity to effectively represent the interests of their members (and broader communities) in the political process (Almond, 1958; Scarrow, 1967; Rosenbluth and Shapiro, 2018). This difference in representational capability actually reinforces the theory described here by enriching or broadening an intuitive claim about how party strength relates to the likelihood that drafters will incorporate input from the public at the drafting stage. I have claimed that weaker parties are more likely to be responsive, but it should also be noted that they are also much more likely to be dependent on such inputs to serve a representational function (Mainwaring, 1999). Strong parties like the African National Congress (ANC) in South Africa may find that the inputs from the public during the drafting process in large part confirm the positions that the party has already taken.[1] Obviously, in cases like Iceland where drafters may have an electoral mandate, but lack a real constituency to represent, they are likely to be highly dependent on these late and direct inputs from the public in order to establish their claim to be democratically drafting a constitution.

A further point of clarification should be added about the level of analysis. The claim made here is related to the political parties themselves, not to the party system. Though there is some obvious overlap between the level of institution-alization in a party system (Mainwaring and Scully, 1995a; Mainwaring, 1999) and the professional qualities of political parties within the system, the theory presented here is concerned with the parties themselves. I make the observation that party systems tend to have parties of similar types, but this is merely epiphe-nomenal for the theory. It is possible that there could be a drafting body that puts a weak party in competition with a strong party, but this would be a rare occurrence.[2]

This argument has left aside, for the moment, the issue of the overall level of democracy. There is some evidence to support the assertion that ostensibly partici-patory means of constitution-making are used in autocratic states just as often as they are in democratic states (Elkins and Hudson, 2019). The dynamic of party-mediated impact is unlikely to be altered much by the level of democracy – at least up to a certain point. The theory could not be easily applied to fully autocratic regimes, but would be well suited to explaining constitution-making processes in cases of "democracy with adjectives" (Collier and Levitsky, 1997).

2.3 CONSTITUTION-MAKING AND POLITICAL PARTIES

This section employs an exploration of the central concepts discussed throughout the book as a vehicle for a discussion of what we already know (or think we know) about how political parties, civil society, and the public engage in constitution-making processes. The various concepts must be considered deliberately, much as an epicure might make their way through the hors d'oeuvres, soup, appetizer, salad, and fish on the way to the main course. The section begins with the (per-haps) overly pedantic step of defining a constitution and moves on to discussions of constitution-making processes and political parties.

---

[1] As was claimed by ANC MP Naledi Pandor who said: "The views put forward in the thousands of submissions received by the Constitutional Assembly attest to the link between the ANC's vision and the will of the people" (G. N. M. Pandor, *Proceedings of the Constitutional Assembly* [April 24, 1996], p. 225).

[2] In the Brazilian case, the Partido dos Trabalhadores (PT) is actually a strong party according to the definition used here, but it was the single exception to the larger pattern of Brazilian parties during the constitution-making period.

2.3.1 *Constitutions and Constitution-Making Processes*

The concept of a constitution perhaps needs no introduction, but it may serve us well to be clear about precisely which aspects of the legal order are dealt with in this book. Following Elkins et al. (2009, 36), this project is solely concerned with the text. In Kelsen's (1945) terms, we are concerned with the formal constitution, not the material constitution. The concept as used here is narrower still, referring only to the official text of the constitution as originally completed by a recognized drafting body. In the cases described here, we are free from concerns about whether the foundational laws of the United Kingdom, New Zealand, or Israel should be considered a constitution. In each of the cases discussed in this book, the participants in the constitution-making process had a clear understanding that what they were doing was constructing "codes of norms which aspire to regulate the allocation of powers, functions and duties among the various agencies and officers of government, and define the relationships between these and the public" (Finer et al., 1995, 1), to quote one classic definition of a constitution. Additionally, since we are concerned with the constitution as it was ratified, we need not trouble ourselves so much with the constitution as it functions or has been amended.

The constitution-making process is a slightly more complicated issue, as it has been realized in a multitude of ways across cases. Again, I adopt a rather narrow definition. We are not concerned with the larger political processes that may – across many decades – create the full body of constitutional law as in the United Kingdom. Nor are we concerned with processes of constitutional revision, either through explicit means (as in formal amendments) or through implicit means (as in Ackerman's [1991] discussion of "higher lawmaking" in the USA). There are many useful applications of such a broad understanding of constitution-making. However, in the cases discussed in this book, there was a clearly delimited time during which a new constitutional text was being drafted.

This narrow focus may concern some readers, so some justification at this point may be helpful. I certainly do not claim that, if public participation has an impact on a constitution-making process, this impact will be limited to the formal constitution, nor will it necessarily be limited in time to the period in which the formal constitution is being drafted. However, as described in Chapter 1, the promises made by political elites in participatory drafting processes are tied to the formal constitution, and not to some longer-term perspective of what the material constitution may become. Thus, it makes sense, at least in the beginning, to limit the scope of inquiry to the formal constitution as it was ratified. The findings here suggest many interesting avenues for further research on the ways in which participatory drafting processes may impact the material constitution in a longer time frame, but those issues are not addressed in any great depth here.

Scholars have long had an interest in how constitutions are made, even in the very narrow sense described earlier. However, foremost among the works of contemporary political scientists have been the writings of Elster. In a seminal article, Elster (1995) described a paucity of scholarly work on constitution-making processes, especially in a systematic and comparative approach. Elster proceeded by laying out the constraints that constitution makers face, their desires and beliefs (interests), and the aggregation of their preferences into a consolidated text. Not wishing to provide a poorer approximation of Elster's broad review, I focus instead on the issue of the actors involved in the constitution-making process, seeking to systematize the variation between constitution-making processes in this regard.

It makes sense to first consider the stages of the process, then the arrangement of actors and institutions. This allows us to be systematic about the constraints and interests that Elster (1995) described. Scholars have divided the stages of the constitution-making process in different ways. The most elaborate division of the process is a five-part scheme devised by Widner (2008, 1522), in which the stages are "negotiation of ground rules; development of interim documents or immutable principles; preparation of an initial text; deliberation and adoption of a final draft; and finally, ratification and promulgation." This categorization of the process describes the South African case quite well, but actually is too specific to be broadly applicable.

Banting and Simeon (1985, 18) propose two different ways of dividing the process. In both cases Banting and Simeon begin much earlier than Widner in their thinking. In a four-stage model, they describe the constitution-making process as proceeding "from mobilisation of interests, through the decision-making stage, to ratification and finally to the legitimation of any change agreed upon." In their simpler division they have three stages, which they call "'idea-generating', agreement reaching and legitimation." By describing upstream and downstream constraints, Elster also implicitly adopts a three-part division of the process. This division is essentially the same as that used by Eisenstadt et al. (2017a), who describe the three stages as being the convening, drafting, and ratifying stages. The three-part scheme is at a level of abstraction that is quite useful for broad comparative work and is the division used throughout this book.[3]

Within the convening stage, a number of events could take place, making it much more difficult in some cases to say when the constitution-making process began than to know when it formally ended. In the South African case we might understand the convening stage to have gone on for at least seven years, and perhaps longer. Leaving aside Banting and Simeon's (1985) idea-generating stage (which has no real beginning point), the beginning of the convening stage of constitution-making in South Africa would be the negotiations between political parties that took place in several stages beginning in 1991. In Brazil, the convening stage might be understood to have begun with the "Diretas Já" protests in 1984, but certainly with the

---

[3] In this chapter both the Elster and Eisenstadt et al. terminology are used where appropriate.

TABLE 2.1 *Institutional arrangements, 1974–2014 (N=254)*

Actors	Number	Percent
Executive only	14	5.51
Referendum only	4	1.58
Constituent assembly only	11	4.33
Constituent legislature only	38	14.96
Constituent legislating assembly only	3	1.18
Executive and referendum	45	17.71
Constituent assembly and executive	12	4.72
Constituent assembly and legislature	1	0.39
Constituent assembly and referendum	17	6.69
Constituent assembly, executive, and legislature	3	1.18
Constituent assembly, executive, and referendum	0	0.00
Constituent assembly, legislature, and referendum	1	0.39
Constituent assembly, executive, legislature, and referendum	1	0.39
Constituent legislating assembly and executive	3	1.18
Constituent legislating assembly and referendum	1	0.39
Constituent legislating assembly, executive, and referendum	0	0.00
Constituent legislature and executive	32	12.60
Constituent legislature and referendum	3	1.18
Constituent legislature, executive, and referendum	13	5.11
Missing	38	14.96

Congressional election in 1986. There is likely more commonality between cases in terms of the events that take place in the later stages, though the actors involved vary quite widely.

Ginsburg et al. (2009) collected data that describe in some detail the various possible arrangements of actors in the constitution-making process. Building on the conceptualization of Elster (2006), their data categorize constitution-making processes into 1 of 23 different possibilities as we move through the stages of the process, with 460 (out of a possible 806) observations between 1789 and 2005. Extending their work in time, I have added new observations to these data, adding coverage through 2014, and simplified the coding into (only) eighteen categories. This date range matches the coverage of data used in some recent influential analyses of constitution-making processes (Eisenstadt et al., 2015, 2017a). Table 2.1 presents the frequency of each of these arrangements of actors in constitution-making processes between 1974 and 2014.[4]

We can see from this table that specially elected constitutional assemblies are very common, but certainly not dominant. There are also two variants of a constitutional assembly proper included in these data. First, in cases in which the sitting legislature took on a secondary function (either by design or by happenstance) as the constitutional assembly, this is coded as a "constituent legislature." In cases in

---

4 There are also many instances of missing data in earlier years.

which a body that was elected as a constituent assembly continued in office as the regular legislature following the completion of its constitution-making work, this is coded as a "constituent legislating assembly" (Ginsburg et al., 2009, 212). In light of recent research in Latin America, it is not surprising to see that both executives and referenda are well REPRESENTED (Elkins, 2017). In fact, both of these are particularly common in less-democratic environments, and when the two are found together concerns about the possibility that the referendum merely rubber stamps an authoritarian move are warranted (Wheatley and Germann, 2013). The main lesson I wish to draw from this perhaps overly complicated table is that there are multifarious institutional arrangements, and that even within the last four decades there has been a great deal of variation in the procedures used to draft and ratify new constitutions.

To be more systematic about the effects of public participation in constitution-making processes, we must take some care to describe the means of participation with which we are concerned. The extent of public participation in the process of constitution-making has been described as having in practice the shape of an hour-glass (Russell, 2004; Elster, 2012). We observe that at the top end of the process (what Elster would refer to as upstream), there is often a great deal of public participation through consultations and other mechanisms of gathering the views of the mass public. The degree of participation becomes more constrained as the process goes on. At the constituent assembly (or other drafting body), there are obviously fewer people involved in determining what will end up in the constitution. Due to the demands of the actual work of drafting, this work is usually completed by just a few people. This can be seen as the narrowest point of the hourglass. It has been a common practice in the modern era to open up the process of ratification to some sort of plebiscitary mechanism, often a binding referendum (Ginsburg et al., 2009). But even when ratification takes place through such indirectly democratic mechanisms as the state conventions that ratified the US constitution, this is a significant widening of the level of participation from the narrow point of drafting. When there is a referendum, we can see this as being an even wider basis of participation than the consultation at the beginning.

Russell was the first to make the comparison to the hourglass, using this metaphor in his discussion of how public participation was incorporated into the Canadian attempt at constitutional revision in 1992. His analysis of the flaws of this attempt at constitutional reform reads as follows:

The top part of the glass was fairly wide, representing the public consultation stage of the process when most of the proposals contained in the Charlottetown Accord were discussed and debated. When these proposals were handed over to political leaders and government officials for negotiation and refinement, the glass narrowed. It came to its narrowest point in the summer of 1992 when the final terms of the Charlottetown Accord were hammered out in a process dominated by first ministers. From that narrow neck the process widened out again in the referendum campaign. This bottom part of the glass, though much shorter, was much wider than the upper half (Russell, 2004, 191).

Other constitution-making processes have had differently shaped hourglasses; however, the idea of a flow of ideas is a helpful way of describing the various forms of public participation that we observe.

Reverting to Elster's preferred metaphor, in the upstream portion of the constitution-making process, public participation has traditionally played a smaller role, but is more likely to generate changes to the constitutional text than any downstream constraint. The most common downstream possibility for public participation is in ratifying referenda. Elkins and Hudson (2019) have shown that such referenda are increasingly common. In the first two decades of the twenty-first century, more than half of new constitutions were approved through a referendum. And as of 2018, more than a third (35.6 percent) of constitutions currently in force were approved through a referendum. Yet, it is unlikely that the possibility of such a downstream check on their power influences drafters' choices to any great degree. In the same project, Elkins and Hudson (2019) find that ratifying referenda have passed 94 percent of the time in the period 1789–2016. This suggests that there is little reason for a constitution maker to worry that their text will be rejected by the voters, and thus little reason to alter the draft in any way to forestall such a rejection. For this reason, among others, the focus of the research in this book is on public participation in the upstream portion of the constitution-making process.

The most important opportunities for public participation then are likely to be in the upstream portion of the drafting process, and to some extent in that restricted middle where the details of the text are decided. Here we can draw upon the work of Eisenstadt et al. (2017a, 2017b), who have created a dataset of constitution-making processes, including 144 cases from 1974 to 2014. Eisenstadt et al. code the level of public participation at the three stages of the constitution-making process as an ordinal variable with three possible values: imposed, mixed, or popular.[5] Of most note for the purposes of the theory advanced here, they classify the convening (or upstream) part of the process as having been "popular" if it included "Systematic civil society input OR strong transparency OR specially-elected drafters 'freely and fairly' elected" (Eisenstadt et al., 2017b). This is a reasonable coding rule for the vast majority of cases, but it is also a very broad condition. One might question whether electing the drafting body actually constitutes public participation in the constitution-making process.

The rarity of a "popular" coding in their data actually confirms the status of the three cases considered in this book as exhibiting a remarkably high level of public

---

[5] Note that Eisenstadt et al. describe the three stages as being the convening stage, drafting stage, and ratifying stage. While this terminology is more substantively meaningful, the idea of a flow as described by Elster and Russell seems more useful in the context of this book.

input. Of the 144 cases they coded, only 18 were coded as having the highest level of public participation at the convening (upstream) stage, whereas 53 included the highest level of public participation at the ratifying (downstream) stage. It should be noted that the kinds of participation considered in the empirical chapters that follow are much more limited than the broadly participatory activities aggregated together in the Eisenstadt et al. data. The research here deals with public participation through the channels created by constituent assemblies as they sought public input during the drafting process. In each case, this primarily involved written submissions from the public, public hearings, and in two of the cases petitions.

Merging the Eisenstadt et al. (2017b) dataset with the Ginsburg et al. (2009) data described earlier can shed some light on the relationship between the actors involved in the constitution-making process and the level of public participation. Keeping only the observations included in the Eisenstadt et al. data drops 108 observations from the combined dataset, as Eisenstadt et al. excluded countries with populations below 500,000. As noted earlier, in the Eisenstadt et al. data, the constitution-making process was broken down into three stages, and the level of participation was coded as either "imposed," "mixed," or "popular." In Table 2.2, these levels are recoded as 1 for imposed, 2 for mixed, and 3 for popular. In the third, fourth, and fifth columns, the mean level of participation in each stage of the constitution-making process is presented for each of the combinations of actors described in the Ginsburg et al. data. While the data are quite sparse, we can see that, among the classes with more than a couple of observations, constitution-making processes that utilized only a constituent assembly had the highest levels of public participation in the convening and drafting stages as coded by Eisenstadt et al. As expected, cases that are coded by Ginsburg et al. as using a referendum for ratification do quite well in the Eisenstadt et al. coding of the level of participation in the ratifying stage.

2.3.2   *Political Parties*

The second major concept dealt with in this book is the political party. The scholarship on political parties is of great importance to the theorizing that this chapter pursues, as it is necessary to describe the kinds of parties that are in place in constitution-making bodies – whether they be sitting legislatures or specially selected bodies – and how the characteristics of these parties affect the level of impact from public participation in the constitution-making process. As described earlier in this chapter, the major distinction of interest for us here is between strong parties and weak parties. The quality of party strength makes some intuitive sense and has long been described as a normative good in political systems (Weiner and LaPalombara, 1966; Cox, 1997). But it is necessary to carefully define how we can distinguish between these two stylized party types. Within any political system, there will be comparatively stronger and weaker parties; however, it tends to be the case

TABLE 2.2 *Institutional arrangements and participation, 1974–2014 (N=146)*

Actors	Number	Participation in convening	Participation in drafting	Participation in ratifying
Executive only	4	1.0	1.3	1.0
Referendum only	2	1.0	2.0	3.0
Constituent assembly only	10	2.5	2.5	1.9
Constituent legislature only	17	1.8	1.8	1.8
Constituent legislating assembly only	2	3.0	2.0	1.5
Executive and referendum	21	1.3	1.4	2.2
Constituent assembly and executive	7	1.4	1.7	1.3
Constituent assembly and legislature	0			
Constituent assembly and referendum	13	1.5	1.7	2.6
Constituent assembly, legislature, and referendum	1	1.0	2.0	3.0
Constituent assembly, executive, and legislature	0			
Constituent assembly, executive, and referendum	0			
Constituent assembly, executive, legislature, and referendum	1	2.0	2.0	3.0
Constituent legislating assembly and executive	2	2.0	2.0	1.5
Constituent legislating assembly and referendum	1	1.0	2.0	3.0
Constituent legislating assembly, executive, and referendum	0			
Constituent legislature and executive	19	1.7	1.9	1.8
Constituent legislature and referendum	5	1.6	2.3	2.6
Constituent legislature, executive, and referendum	7	2.1	2.3	3.0
Missing	29			

that political systems have parties of one type or the other. Thus, there can be general agreement that Brazil has weak parties and South Africa has strong parties. This section will deal with several aspects of political parties, but the end goal is to be able to distinguish with some precision between strong parties and weak parties.

We should begin with a definition of what is meant by a political party. At first glance this may seem unnecessarily pedantic; however, in some cases the distinction between political parties and other important groups in the political system is more complex. For example, in the South African case, the ANC is a political party, but it also includes other groups (potential parties) within its structures, including a major trade union and another political party. The ANC follows the model of other congress parties, forming a coalition of smaller groupings that "take the form of a single, unified party structure" (Diamond and Gunther, 2001, 24). Since long before the first democratic elections, the ANC has included the South African Communist Party (SACP) within its ranks. Thus, some individuals are both members of the SACP politburo and members of the ANC's Executive Committee (EC). The SACP calls itself a political party, but it does not run its own candidates in elections, and its members are not immediately distinguishable from the other members of the ANC when they sit or vote in parliament. For the purposes of our analysis then, we need to be able to say whether the SACP is a political party. This decision has some impact on our assessment of the strength of the ANC as a party within the legislature.

The most influential early works on political parties elided the definitional issue to varying degrees. Duverger's celebrated treatise on political parties neglected (or found it counterproductive) to provide a straightforward definition of the central concept of the inquiry, describing a party as a "collection of communities" (Duverger, 1954, 17). In another classic work, Epstein (1967) was content to allow the common usage of the word to discriminate between what is and what is not a party. Similarly, Key in his study of parties in the USA provides a functional definition, suggesting that "political parties are basic institutions for the translation of mass preferences into public policy" (Key, 1961, 432). Other definitions associate the primary purpose of political parties with placing their members in government, either explicitly through elections (Lasswell and Kaplan, 1965; Riggs, 1970) or inclusive of other means of acquiring power (Janda, 1970). Seeking to formulate the concept in a way that would limit the number of groups that could be usefully considered to be political parties, Sartori (2005, 56) defined the concept as "any political group identified by an official label that presents at elections, and is capable of placing through elections (free or non-free), candidates for public office." The core definitional attributes here are (1) having an official label and (2) presenting candidates for election (under that label). Sartori's careful conceptualization commends it to our attention, and is the definition adopted here. Under this definition, the SACP would not count as a political party since it does not contest elections under its own name. This serves to simplify our analysis of the South African case. Similarly, although a group in the Brazilian Constitutional Assembly called the "Centrão" behaved much like a political party (and certainly exhibited more discipline than many Brazilian parties), it would not be considered a political party because it did not contest elections under that label.

There are certainly also some aspects of the broader party system that are relevant for the inquiry here. Sartori's (2005) agenda-setting work has its greatest impact in terms of describing the number of parties and the degree of polarization in the system. The key connection between the number of parties and the impact of public participation concerns the way in which the number of parties affects the type of negotiation that takes place. On a broad level, the number of parties is an important determinant in the complexity of the negotiations. More specifically, the number of parties determines to some extent the opportunities for direct trades on particular issues, the opportunity for logrolling, or other means by which parties make bargains over policy in more ordinary legislative processes. To this interest in the number of parties and the distance between them, we can add from Mainwaring (1999) the consideration of the level of institutionalization in the party system, who argued that this was particularly important in the third wave of democratization (as exemplified in the case of Brazil).

The central explanatory variable in this book is the strength of the political parties involved in the drafting process. It behooves us at this point to establish the criteria that would enable an analyst to distinguish between strong and weak parties. The idea has some intuitive quality and has been employed to great effect without extensive conceptualization, as in the recent work of Rosenbluth and Shapiro (2018). As the concept is developed here, there are three interrelated qualities of political parties that relate to party strength: (1) centralized leadership, (2) disciplined voting within the legislature (or constitutional assembly), and (3) consistent programmatic commitments. For analytical purposes the first two criteria can be collapsed into the single idea of party cohesion, but in a practical sense these are different issues.

It is helpful also to differentiate this concept of strong parties from others that have been developed in the academic literature. What is meant by strong parties here is different from the electoral sense used in Ginsburg's (2003) work on the development of judicial review, wherein party strength is the difference between the seat shares of the two largest parties in the legislature. Ginsburg's concept of party strength could also be described as dominant/threatened parties. Somewhat in contrast, Huntington (1968, 421) argued that party strength was unrelated to the number of political parties in a system, suggesting instead that "a party, in turn, is strong to the extent that it has institutionalized mass support" (Huntington, 1968, 408). This definition was further developed with the following attributes: (1) the party's ability to survive the departure of a charismatic founder, (2) "organizational complexity and depth," and (3) the desire of political actors to identify with the party, rather than using it as a vehicle (Huntington, 1968, 409–410). Thus, Huntington's concept of strong parties is deeply tied to what we might call today its "brand." This concept then has less to do with the functioning of the party in the legislature (or a constituent assembly).

The concept utilized in this book also differs somewhat from the concept of strong parties used to describe the party system of Venezuela in the mid to late twentieth century (Crisp, 1997). In Coppedge's (1997) book, he describes strong parties as dominating the political system, with deep linkages in civil society. This concept of "partyarchy" describes a political system in which "political parties monopolize the formal political process and politicize the society along party lines" (Coppedge, 1997, 18). There is much overlap between the concept of strong parties as developed in this book, and Coppedge's partyarchy. For example, in a line that seems to presage one of the findings in this book, Coppedge (1997, 39) writes that "In an extreme partyarchy, where political parties monopolize the formal political process, ordinary citizens have few channels for political participation." This dynamic likely holds even in states with something short of partyarchy, as other research suggests that there is a negative correlation between party strength and political trust (Uslaner, 2006; Ceka, 2013). Coppedge's concept of partyarchy also includes high levels of party cohesion and disciplined voting in the legislature as being elements of partyarchy. However, the complete definition seems too strong, as it describes the pathology of strong parties, and not their effective function.

Moving toward a broader concept of strong parties, Gunther and Diamond's (2003) conceptualization of the possible variation in political parties that includes a comprehensive description of the kinds of political parties that exist in almost all political systems. Very helpfully, Gunther and Diamond are clear about the three criteria of difference that feed into their categorization of political parties: (1) formal organization, (2) programmatic commitments, and (3) tolerance/pluralism (Gunther and Diamond, 2003, 171). Their purpose in defining these elements is to create an extensive typology of political parties (with fifteen types). However, the first two criteria seem amenable to the conceptual project in this section. Formal organization is an essential element of party strength, being a necessary condition for both programmatic commitments and for party discipline. Gunther and Diamond suggest that the variation on the second dimension includes parties that:

derive programmatic stands from well-articulated ideologies rooted in political philosophies, religious beliefs or nationalistic sentiments; others are either pragmatic or have no well-defined ideological or programmatic commitments; still others are committed to advance the interests of a particular ethnic, religious or socio-economic group, or geographically defined constituency, in contrast to those that are heterogeneous if not promiscuously eclectic in their electoral appeals to groups in society. (Gunther and Diamond, 2003, 171)

This is the key application of their conceptualization to the present inquiry. Other scholars less carefully conflate the idea of programmatic commitments and strong parties, treating the two words as part of a single concept, as in Hale's (2005) work

on political parties in post-Soviet states. Hale consistently refers to "strong programmatic parties." Similar language is used in Rosenbluth and Shapiro (2018) in their
paean to the virtues of such parties.

The closest analogue to the definition of strong parties I wish to employ here is the
concept developed by Carey and Reynolds (2007) in their work on accountable government in new democracies. Carey and Reynolds' concept has some commonality
with the theorizing of Gunther and Diamond (2003), and is built with two compo-
nents: legislative discipline and programmatic commitments. Carey and Reynolds
argue that the combination of these two qualities is what makes a strong party a
positive contributor to democratic accountability, and that disciplined parties that
lack programmatic commitments are actually harmful to democratic consolidation.
They also note that the tendency in new democracies tends to be that discipline is
easier to establish than programmatic consistency. For the purposes of this book, we
can take these two criteria as being the necessary definitional elements of strong parties, and stipulate that parties lacking one or the other should be classified as weak.
Here, party discipline is evidenced by formal organization as described by Gunther
and Diamond (2003), and even more so by disciplined voting from party members
in plenary sessions of the constitutional assembly. On the programmatic front, we
are primarily interested in whether the political party approaches the constitution-
making process with a clear vision of what the constitution should accomplish or
whether the party is more open to engaging in a quid pro quo with other groups
inside and outside the process over constitutional content. On this basis, it seems
reasonable to assert that South Africa has strong parties and Brazil has weak parties
– though there has been some controversy on this latter judgment (Mainwaring,
1992; Mainwaring and Pérez-Liñán, 1997; Figueiredo and Limongi, 2000).

Moving from a conceptual discussion toward application of the concepts to the
research interests advanced in this book, Schattschneider's (1942) description of the
competition between interest groups and political parties for dominance in the
development of public policy is very helpful. Schattschneider (1942, 193) writes:
"The real choice is between a strong party system on the one hand and a system of
politics in which congressmen are subjected to minority pressures. The assumption
made here is that party government is better than government by irresponsible organized minorities and special interests." This might be extended from the original
context to both an argument to the effect that strong parties produce better constitutions and that strong parties are less likely to include the submissions of content
from the general public in those constitutions. Schattschneider (1942, 196) further
helps us with the theoretical argument advanced in this book, as he describes the
weakness of US political parties as exposing them to influence from pressure groups:

Congressmen succumb to pressure by organized minorities, not because the pressure
groups are strong, but because the congressmen see no reason for fighting at all; the
party neither disciplines them nor supports them. On the one hand, a congressman is

thrown upon his own resources by his party; the party makes no demands on him, does not punish him for desertion, but it also does not fight for him. On the other hand, the pressure group makes a noise like the uprising of a great mass of people, it tries to alarm him and threatens him with defeat. Because the congressman is neither punished nor protected by the party, and because in addition he is in doubt about the power of the pressure group to defeat him for re-election, he decides to play safe. This calculation reverses the normal rules of democratic government completely.

Thus, Schattschneider's argument about pressure groups and the US Congress maps very well onto the argument advanced in this book about the effects of party strength in mediating the impact of public participation in constitution-making processes. Schattschneider's argument presents the negative side of the phenomenon in its focus on the lack of incentives for members of weak parties to hold the party line. They are tempted to defect, and in this case give pressure groups what they want in the constitution. With slightly less power (and perhaps in a more positive sense), the same dynamic applies to input from individuals: in the absence of party discipline and central organization, the members of a drafting body have (1) no disincentive to listen to input from individuals, and (2) no incentive to dismiss what they hear.

The counterpoint to the weak parties described in the quotation from Schattschneider might be the case in which strong parties have already done the good work of interest aggregation and articulation, and that further appeals from the public would be superfluous and distracting. This invokes the functionalist literature on political parties that has for the most part been neglected in this chapter. As most famously described by Almond (1958) and Scarrow (1967), one of the major functions of political parties is to aggregate and articulate the interests of voters. Strong parties are likely to be better equipped to accomplish this task than weak ones. Depending on the electoral system, strong parties may also represent a larger portion of the electorate than weak parties (Rosenbluth and Shapiro, 2018). If that is so, it would accord to some degree with the picture of selectively responsive weak parties that is painted by Schattschneider (1942).

Indeed, Schattschneider's argument has been borne out by more recent concrete examples in US politics, most notably the legislative process that produced the Patient Protection and Affordable Care Act in 2009. Rosenbluth and Shapiro (2018, 96–97) use this example to make the argument that the weak parties in the USA do a poor job of representing the interests of voters. Their account highlights the way in which weak parties allow for powerful interest groups to have their agenda realized in legislation, perhaps to the detriment of more long-term interests in public policy. In this way, weak parties may create more space for input from outside the legislature, but this may not have broadly positive implications for either the quality of democracy or the quality of lawmaking. Rosenbluth and Shapiro conclude their book with a nuanced view of the relative benefits of strong parties, arguing that "Strong parties may not offer what individual voters want at any given time, but they are collective organizations that calculate the costs of policy options against the cost of other options. The resulting offerings may not be as appealing on their surface, but they are more honest and more likely to be viable over time" (Rosenbluth and Shapiro, 2018, 250). In the constitution-making context, it may be the case that strong parties are less likely to give effect to input from the public, but that certainly does not imply that weak parties draft better constitutions.

With respect to the larger theoretical and conceptual goals of this chapter, much of the literature on parties would agree with the assertion I have made here that strong parties are less likely to pay attention to input from the public during the drafting stage of a constitution-making process. On the surface, this seems like a pejorative argument about strong political parties, but it is not necessarily so. This says nothing about the larger issue of how much genuine public input goes into a party's decision on a particular issue or aspect of a constitution. It is highly likely that strong parties include among their qualities a more tangible connection to their base and more agreement between base and elite opinion (Dalton, 1985). The normative question that this dynamic raises is whether it is better in a democratic sense for constitution drafters to pay attention to the objectively unrepresentative people who take the time to actively participate in a constitution-making process, or to the masses of voters who have elected members of the political party to office. This tension is addressed in some of the interviews that are described in the empirical chapters.

Of course, more is said about the political parties in each of the cases in the chapters devoted to them, but we can note here that there is little doubt that Brazil has historically had weak parties (Lamounier and Meneguello, 1985; Mainwaring, 1991, 1992, 1999; Ames, 2002b), while South Africa has strong parties (Gouws and Mitchell, 2005; Lodge, 2004). That said, there is some variation within the party system, at least in the Brazilian case. Notably, during the period of Brazil's Constituent Assembly the parties of the left exhibited much greater discipline than those in the center or right (Mainwaring and Pérez-Liñán, 1997). There are also some indications that Brazil's parties have been moving toward greater discipline within the legislature, though other areas of weakness remain (Figueiredo and Limongi, 2000). The Icelandic case may be unique in the world in that the rules for electing a special assembly to draft the new constitution essentially excluded representatives of political parties from participation (Hudson, 2018a).

2.4 QUESTIONS OF LEGITIMACY AND EFFICACY

This section and the one that follows are organized into considerations of what we might call input legitimacy and output legitimacy (Scharpf, 1997, 1999). Public participation could be motivated (or even required) as a means of legitimating a constitution through inclusive inputs – that is to say, involving the public in some kind of consultation. Alternatively, the constitution could be legitimated through its inclusive or democratic outputs – reflecting the views of the People in the final text.[6] The different theoretical underpinnings of the two pathways of constitutional legitimation are explored here, beginning with the idea that a constitution can be legitimated through public involvement in the drafting process.

2.4.1   *Input Legitimacy*

The theoretical justification for the modern trend toward significant public participation dates back to revolutionary America and France.[7] Many of the current arguments for public participation in constitution-making have their genesis in the writings of Sieyès (1963), later expanded upon by Schmitt (Schmitt, 2008; Stacey, 2011; Loughlin, 2014). Foundational to the discussion of public participation in constitution-making is the concept of constituent power. In the context of participatory constitution-making, we are concerned with original constituent power, as theorized in the French constitutional debates of 1791, and most recently explored by Roznai (2017, 113–117). In Roznai's words, "Original constituent power is exercised in a legal vacuum... It acts outside the forms, procedures, and limits established by the constitution" (Roznai, 2017, 115–116). Exercises of such unconstrained power must, of course, be grounded in some powerful source of legitimation. As many have argued, such legitimation must be tied to some (perhaps) revolutionary act on the part of "the People" (Negri, 1999).

Responding to Kelsen's idea of the *grundnorm* as the source of validity for law (Kelsen, 1978, 8), Schmitt argued that the legitimacy of a constitution comes from the political will that created it. Further, in the midst of a historical argument, Schmitt suggests that *the People* (defined in opposition to other groups of people) possess the constitution-making power (Schmitt, 2008, 125–126). In this sense, the constitution is legitimated by the *input* that it receives from the participation of the People in its creation.

In a more recent book, Colón-Ríos (2012) takes up Sieyès' and Schmitt's ideas about constituent power. Colón-Ríos is particularly concerned with the idea that the democratic legitimacy of a constitution is derived from the process that created it, arguing that "a 'fully' democratically legitimate constitutional regime would have originated in a democratic constitution-making act, one characterized by intense episodes of popular participation and by the absence of any external or internal

---

[6] Some more recent scholarship adds "throughput legitimacy" to this mix (Schmidt, 2013). While there may be good reasons to add this category in many studies, the simple distinction between the ways in which a constitution may be legitimated through some expressive value of providing inputs or through the inclusion of public participation in its outputs is sufficiently differentiated for the theory proposed here.

[7] Although it should be noted that even Sieyès was drawing on earlier ideas about sovereignty (Roznai, 2017, 107).

limits on the content of the new constitution" (Colón-Ríos, 2012, 9). He further argues that "a theory of democratic legitimacy that has constituent power at its centre asks us to look at the actual role that citizens played during the moment of constitution-making" (Colón-Ríos, 2012, 115). In Colón-Ríos' vision, a legitimate constitution must be made in a participatory process and be susceptible to reform through similarly participatory procedures.

A similar concept of public authority in constitution-making is developed in Ackerman's influential theory of dualist-democracy and constitutional moments (Ackerman, 1991). The cases under consideration here provide one of the best possible realizations of a constitutional moment in which advocates for constitutional change work toward "mobilizing their fellow citizens and gaining their repeated support" (Ackerman, 1991, 6–7). Going far beyond the electorally based processes that Ackerman described in the American context, these cases involved the participation of the mass public in direct ways, as potential authors of constitutional text. In the original context of Ackerman's account, "the People" must be involved in constitutional change as a way to legitimate a process of revision that exists outside of the procedures outlined in the text. But the idea of a constitutional moment in which the People and their representatives interact with each other and with constitutional ideas in a new way is compelling. If, as Ackerman claims, the People spoke clearly in the relatively non-participatory constitutional changes that took place in the United States in the nineteenth and twentieth centuries, they speak even more in modern experiments with participatory constitutional change. This participation in itself is likely to have a legitimating effect through this channel of input legitimacy. The question then is whether or not they are heard (as in output legitimacy).

Others have made much more direct and extensible arguments about the legitimating effects of citizen participation. Chambers explained the value of direct participation by linking it to the concept of popular sovereignty. Nothing that the general will of "the People" was always somewhat hypothetical, Chambers develops a new idea of pluralistic popular sovereignty that values the process of consultation, rather than an outcome that encapsulates that imagined general will. Chambers writes:

Process embodies popular sovereignty, first, by giving people voice. We-the-people get to speak, but rather than ("all together now") intoning a shared political catechism, the people speak in many voices which may contradict one another. What is important is that citizens feel that they were heard, that they were part of the process, and that their opinions, interests, concerns, and claims counted for something. (Chambers, 2004, 158)

Under this theory of popular sovereignty, public participation is a necessity, but its impact on the constitutional text is of lesser importance than the inclusive nature of the process. Similar arguments about the inherent value of a deliberative and participatory process (regardless of the content it produces) are made in a recent book by Tekin (2016).

Building on the theoretical and empirical works of the mid to late twentieth century (Almond and Verba, 1963; Pateman, 1970; Dahl, 1971), the literature on public participation has added a great deal of empirical work over the past couple of decades. In contrast with the battle between "classical" and "contemporary" views of participation described by Pateman (1970), the majority of this more recent work has been balanced in its appraisal of the benefits and drawbacks of public participation in policy-making. I find it helpful to divide the relevant literature in this area into three groups. First, there are influential articles in political theory (Mansbridge, 2003, 2014; Pateman, 2012). Second, there is a significant literature in empirical political science that considers political participation both in broad terms (Verba et al., 1993; Brady et al., 1995) and in case studies (Fung, 2006; Wampler, 2007, 2008; Heller, 2012). A third group is situated within the literature on public administration. A number of authors in this third area describe something like an inexorable trend toward greater levels of public participation in policy-making (Cobb and Elder, 1983; Bishop and Davis, 2002; Papadopoulos and Warin, 2007). The majority of this literature has an orientation toward evaluating when public consultation is likely to be successful, particularly from the perspective of the policy maker, and does not go on to consider when public participation is likely to be most influential from the perspective of the citizen-participant. Moving toward the specific research interest in this book, there is also a fourth group of works that should be considered. This book is in part motivated as a response to the prescriptions made in the more practitioner-oriented literature published by think tanks and NGOs like the United States Institute of Peace, and International IDEA (Brandt et al., 2011; Dann et al., 2011; Ebrahim et al., 1999; Gluck and Brandt, 2015; Hart, 2003). While by nature less empirically rigorous, these works are also influential and make bold claims about the value of public participation in constitution making that demand critical evaluation.

Many scholars (particularly in this fourth group) assert that there is a clear trend toward greater public participation in the process of constitution-making and that constitutional processes that neglect this will be inherently less legitimate (Hart, 2003; Benomar, 2004; Banks, 2007). This view is certainly not universally held, and some of the most influential works on the process of constitution-making are much more skeptical about the value of an open or participatory process (Bannon, 2007; Elster, 1997, 2012; Tushnet, 2012). Whatever the normative justifications, there is certainly an observable trend toward greater public participation from the 1990s to the present, perhaps reaching its zenith in the recent constitution-making enterprise in Iceland (Tushnet, 2012; Landemore, 2015; Hudson, 2018a). The experience of Iceland is not substantively different from earlier cases, and could be seen as a more technologically enabled update on previous constitutional processes that sought out public input on the constitution, notably Brazil in 1988, Uganda in 1995, South Africa in 1996, and Kenya in 2010. These examples of participatory constitution-making included public engagement in the constitution-making endeavor through popular consultations, and the opportunity for citizens to submit written proposals of ideas that they would like to see included in the text of the constitution.

Perhaps foundational to this trend is growing awareness of a legal right to participate in constitution-making. Scholars like Hart (2003, 2010), Franck and Thiruvengadam (2010), and Ebrahim et al. (1999) have persuasively argued this point on the basis of statements in the Universal Declaration of Human Rights (UDHR) and the International Covenant on Civil and Political Rights (ICCPR) (especially articles 1 and 25). This right has also been confirmed in international jurisprudence, notably the landmark decision in *Marshall* v. *Canada* (1991), in which the United Nations Committee on Human Rights (UNCHR) applied the provisions about participation in the ICCPR specifically to the area of constitution-making. We might also note, however, that many works in legal theory are silent on issues of constitutional drafting, and the legal rights claimed by the authors above are by no means accepted by all observers (Landau, 2011, 612). Moreover, the right is poorly conceptualized.

The best description of the right to participate comes from Waldron's (1999, 235) political philosophy, in which he describes this claim as "The demand is not merely that there should be a popular element in government, but that the popular element should be decisive. The demand is for democracy, not just the inclusion of a democratic element in a mixed regime." He goes on to say that the specific demand in contemporary political discourse "refers now to the fact that each individual claims the right to play his part, along with the equal part played by all other individuals, in the government of the society" (Waldron, 1999, 236). This sort of underlying claim to "take part in a public affair" now forms the foundation for the involvement of the mass public in constitution-making processes across the world (Hart, 2010). The application of this claim to participate finds particular support from Waldron's (1999) claim that the right to participate in political decisions is especially important in cases in which there is disagreement about the scope of rights that individuals may claim. However, other scholars have suggested that the brief language in the ICCPR that might be seen as touching on constitution-making processes is "probably too vague a principle to be of much good" (Landau, 2011, 621). In any case, the justiciable aspects of such a right could only involve inputs, not outputs.

Much of the literature in this field also advances more normative and nuanced arguments for public participation. One of the most convincing arguments asserts the value of having as many diverse viewpoints as possible represented in the process. This normative claim is made by a number of authors who have been influential in how we think about what a constitution-making process should include. The widely cited 1999 report on constitution-making produced by the

Commonwealth Human Rights Initiative (CHRI) stresses the importance of inclusive participation (Ebrahim et al., 1999). These authors argue that enabling broad participation adds value to the constitutional text and encourages buy-in and support for the constitution from across the population. Hart (2010, 40) also argues this point, stating that even benevolent elites cannot adequately represent the views of disadvantaged and marginalized groups within a society. One could certainly expand on these points with appeals to theories of deliberative democracy (Habermas, 1996; Fishkin, 2009; Landemore, 2012) or new forms of representation (Mansbridge, 2003; Tekin, 2016). However, the actual motivation of constitutional drafters in creating opportunities for public consultation is an empirical question that has yet to be addressed.

2.4.2   Output Legitimacy

The outputs of a constitution-making process are various, but they can be usefully simplified into the categories of systemic and textual outputs, either or both of which could be seen to increase the legitimacy of the constitution. The main systemic output of scholarly interest has been the level of democracy.

At what I have termed the systemic level, there is some disagreement between recently published accounts about whether participation is associated with improved democracy or not. Carey has found that constitution-making processes that were more inclusive led to political systems that were more democratic, had greater constraints on governmental authority, and were more stable over time (Carey, 2009). Similarly, the research of Eisenstadt, LeVan, and Maboudi has shown that more participatory constitution-making processes (particularly when the participation takes place in the early stage of the process) are associated with higher levels of democracy in the years following the ratification of the constitution (Eisenstadt et al., 2015; Eisenstadt et al., 2017a). This is in contrast with research from both Saati (2015) and Wheatley and Germann (2013), who have found that participatory constitution-making processes are associated with lower levels of democracy. The difference may at least in part be attributable to the scope of the studies. Eisenstadt et al. used a large-N analysis based on their original data described earlier, and both Saati and Wheatley and Germann had medium-N samples. However, the tension is worth considering, especially given the long causal chain that exists between the moment of constitution drafting and the level of democracy that may exist in the state a decade later.

It is worth considering the central argument of Eisenstadt et al. (2017a) at greater length, as their work relates closely to the argument advanced here. They summarize their argument as follows: "We claim that participatory constitution-making – which we understand as transparent, substantive, and often direct citizen involvement – has a lasting and systematic effect on subsequent democratization"

(Eisenstadt et al., 2017a, 3). Their statistical analysis establishes a causal link between the level of democracy at several intervals after the ratification of a new constitution and the level of public participation in the constitution-making process, particularly at the upstream (or convening) stage.

Their analysis shows that, while there is a relationship between authoritarianism and imposed constitutions, popular constitution-making processes are equally likely across all levels of democracy. Furthermore, many of the non-democracies that drafted a new constitution in a participatory way saw marked improvements in their levels of democracy. They then use the occurrence of labor unrest as an instrumental variable to control for the potential endogeneity in their causal story, finding that strikes only impact the level of democracy through their relationship with a participatory constitution-making process (Eisenstadt et al., 2017a, 39). Clearly, there are a great many other factors that may determine both the level of participation in the constitution-making process and the level of democracy in the years following ratification. However, Eisenstadt et al. have taken reasonable steps to control for endogeneity and demonstrate a statistically significant effect. Their finding that the convening stage is the most important also buttresses the choice made in this book to focus the analysis on public participation at that stage of the process.

A more nuanced argument advanced by Widner (2005) (also deserving of further empirical analysis) is the suggestion that "Devices to ensure high levels of popular consultation may be more influential in areas without much history of electoral politics and where the legitimacy of delegates may be in question" (Widner, 2005, 507). This claim is echoed in an Interpeace guide to constitution-making, authored by some of the most influential researchers and practitioners in this literature (Brandt et al., 2011, 80). Where there is less of an established tradition of representative democracy, it seems reasonable that citizens may have a lower degree of trust in their elected representatives, and consequently wish to have a more direct role in constitution-making. However, this perspective does not account for the demands for participation made by citizens of mature democracies such as Canada and Iceland. As the experience of Canada shows, even in mature democracies citizens may not trust their elected representatives enough to allow them to negotiate over the constitution while ignoring popular demands (Cairns, 1988). Describing the division among scholars on the merits of participatory processes, Moehler (2008, 27) notes that the group in favor of participation has been much louder than participation critics. Moehler (2008, 31) further asserts that "Faith in the new participatory model is so strong that policymakers and scholars encourage mass participation even where conditions seem prohibitive, such as in Iraq." The conclusion for now seems to be that, even though the majority of the hypotheses about the effects of participation are untested (Moehler, 2008; Ginsburg et al., 2009), this model is very influential and increasingly widely implemented.

Although the relationship between the drafting process and democracy is little studied, there is even less work on the relationship between the drafting process and the content of the formal constitution. At a high level, Negretto's work on constitutional change in Latin America links the institutional features of constitutions to the expectations of the political parties that were involved in the drafting process (Negretto, 2013, 2018). Negretto's work has some insights that are broadly confirmed by the analysis undertaken here, namely that the relative power of political parties within the drafting body is one of the most important determinants of the content of the constitution.

Turning toward research on the text itself, one article with much in common with the type of analysis undertaken here was a study of Egypt's constitution-making process in 2012. There, as in Iceland in 2011, drafts of the constitution were posted online, and citizens were given the opportunity to comment upon, and "like" or "dislike" individual articles through thumbs-up and thumbs-down buttons. The study by Maboudi and Nadi found that draft articles that were given more "likes" on this website were less likely to be changed in later drafts, while those with more "dislikes" were altered at a higher rate (Maboudi and Nadi, 2016). Maboudi and Nadi's work is particularly notable, as it was one of the first attempts to measure the impact of public participation on the development of the constitutional text. My own research on Iceland also focused on the impacts of participation on the constitutional text, finding that, in Iceland's 2011 process, almost 10 percent of the submissions from the public generated a change in the draft constitution (Hudson, 2018a). Another work that addresses the impact of the drafting process on the Icelandic draft constitution is Landemore's recent quasi-experimental study (Landemore, 2017). Landemore used the constitutional proposals drafted by an expert panel and the constitution drafted by the Constitutional Council to set up a quasi-experimental frame for comparing the effects of the process on the text dealing with religious rights. Her finding was that the text drafted by the Constitutional Council was slightly more liberal than the expert draft, and attributed this to the open and inclusive drafting process. Most recently, Saati (2020) has studied the relationship between public participation in the drafting process and the constitutions produced in Fiji in 1997 and 2013. Saati suggests that the constitution-making process was structured in a way that reduced the importance of public participation, and that it is highly unlikely that the content of the constitution responded to public input.

The scarcity of cases where scholars have established an empirical measurement of the effects of public participation on the text of the constitution has to this point limited our ability to say anything about the degree to which social perceptions of constitutional legitimacy are influenced by these outputs. The studies from Maboudi and Nadi (2016) and Hudson (2018a), and this book, go some way toward creating some clarity on this point. This is clearly an area where there is great potential for further research.

2.4.3 *Types of Impact*

In this work, I distinguish between direct and indirect impacts of public participation on the constitutional text.[8] Direct impacts are defined here as concrete changes in the text that respond to input from the public. This impact may range from a change in the wording of an existing provision,[9] to the addition of a completely new right to a constitution.[10] Indirect impacts are defined here as cases in which submissions from the public bring new issues or insights onto the agenda for the constitution drafting body. These indirect impacts are difficult to fully trace as they may occur outside of the formal constitution-making process.

For our purposes here, indirect impact is nearly synonymous with agenda setting, whereas direct impacts are those cases in which there is a clear alteration, addition, or subtraction, to the text of the constitution that comes in response to a submission from the public. Direct impacts become clear where one can chart the evolution of the language of the constitutional text between subsequent drafts. Indirect impact can be observed when submissions from the public raise a new issue or increase the salience of an issue.

To the extent that there are *direct* impacts in constitution-making processes with strong parties, they will be of one of two types. First, there may be direct impacts that follow the more usual pattern of electoral politics, wherein established interest groups may gain the ear of politicians. For example, in the South Africa case, representatives of large corporations central to the national economy were able to make their views known to both parties and to individual drafters, and see that their concerns were reflected in the final text (Author's interviews with "RGBS," April 25, 2016, and "PNTO," May 17, 2016). The sections of the South African constitution that deal with labor relations were to some degree influenced by these discussions between drafters, business groups, and unions. In the second type, we also observe some limited direct impacts in which there is an apparently stochastic occurrence wherein a drafter plucks something they like from among the thousands of pages of submissions from the public (as in the scenario described in footnote 9).

When interviewed for this project, some constitutional drafters provided recollections of a particular instance in which they responded to input from the public in a concrete way, and many could point to a particular word or phrase in the constitution as an example of this. I argue that these instances are, while perhaps not rare, sort of serendipitous. That is to say, these cases in which a drafter inserts language

---

[8] Both direct and indirect impacts are here understood to contribute to output legitimacy.

[9] See, for example, the addition of the word "degradation" in Section 28(1)(d) in the Constitution of the Republic of South Africa (Author's interview with "RGBS," April 25, 2016). This section deals with the rights of children. An NGO advocating for the rights of children asked that "degradation" be added to the existing provision that sought to protect children from "maltreatment, neglect, abuse." In response to this request, a member of the committee drafting that section of the constitution made the requested wording change.

[10] See, for example, the addition of the right to access the Internet in the 2011 draft constitution of Iceland.

in response to a particular input from the public are the result of a special meeting of the interests of the individual drafter and a timely input from the public. The evidence from these interviews seems to suggest that drafters do not consider the balance of public input (or the majority view of the population as determined by opinion polls) to be crucial guidance for what they should put into the constitution. Indeed, comments made during the plenary debates in the South African case in particular support this assessment (Parliament of South Africa, 1995). Instead, politicians filter input from the public through their already formed understanding of what the constitution should do. They selectively choose input from the public that relates to their interests.

This should not be read as a cynical unveiling of the interaction of drafters with public input. Rather, this is a function of a confirmation bias (Ross et al., 1977; Lord et al., 1979; Nickerson, 1998), wherein drafters perceive comments that are in agreement with their own preferences to be representative of a larger consensus in society about the issues in question. Or to express this phenomenon in language that has less of a normative valence, a comment from a member of the public may concretize a previously inchoate preference on the part of a drafter. Beyond this aspect, in some cases drafters assume ownership of particular themes within their designated section of the constitution, and understand their role in part to be one of championing those interests. In this case, they may be more likely to find language they would like to incorporate from the public comments.

Direct impacts in cases with weak parties will be dispersed and disunited, and will correspond much more to the pattern of lobbying impact that we observe in normal law making in these contexts. However, I also argue that there will be many more instances of direct impacts in these cases. In drafting bodies with weak parties, the lack of centralized party control, party discipline, and programmatic commitments creates greater space for policy entrepreneurs to move particular causes into the constitutional text.

2.5 THE THEORY REVISITED

The bulk of this chapter has discussed concepts that are at the center of the phenomena under study, in an effort to both establish clarity about the subjects examined, and to situate the work within the broader scholarly context. The argument advanced in this book can be seen as an attempt to correct the popular mythology of constitution-making and to improve our understanding of the importance of constitution-making processes. The work builds on and also engages with some of the more thematically proximate works described above, in particular the recent research of Eisenstadt et al. (2017a), Maboudi and Nadi (2016), and Saati (2015). While the dependent variables are very different (extent of impact rather than level of democracy), the research presented here should serve to give readers a more skeptical view of how much participation actually goes on in "participatory constitution-making."

The theory presented here also has much in common with other arguments that have been made about the decisions of elites in constitution-making processes and constitutional revolutions. My argument about the reduced impact of public participation in cases with strong parties could be seen as a specific realization of the concept of hegemonic preservation as described by Hirschl (2004). In this application, the political parties act in the constitution-making process to preserve the interests of their constituencies against the possible policy choices of later administrations. Indeed, South Africa was one of the major cases considered by Hirschl in *Towards Juristocracy*. The major point of overlap with Hirschl's work is the interests of the major parties in protecting the economic interests of the most powerful businesses in the country. The process that Hirschl describes negatively impacted the ability of the South African public to influence the constitution-making process by locking in certain aspects of the text – specifically the protection of private property. The aspects of the constitution that deal with group and cultural rights certainly protect the interests of the descendant political group, but are not quite in line with the idea of hegemonic preservation. In Hirschl's interpretation, South Africa's Bill of Rights represented an attempt at legally protecting the privileges of the white minority who knew that their time in power was coming to an end (Hirschl, 2004, 95). This may oversimplify the history to some degree, as the African National Congress (ANC) seems to have decided to support the idea of a bill of rights for both political and principled reasons before beginning negotiations with the National Party (NP). Nevertheless, the story of a limited impact from public participation fits very neatly within the larger argument that Hirschl makes about the entrenchment of rights in constitutions as a means of protecting the material and cultural interests of elites. However, in my account, the lack of popular impact is less about the ability of a powerful elite to protect their interests at the expense of the majority of the population, and more about the way in which the elite-level negotiations between the ANC and the NP forestalled the possibility of effective public input at the drafting stage.

Another theory that bears close relation to that advanced here is the insurance model of constitution-making described by Ginsburg (2003) in his work on *Judicial Review in New Democracies*. In that book, Ginsburg shifted the narrative of justiciable human rights from a demand-side story (wherein citizens demand a legal regime with justiciable rights), to a supply-side story that sought to explain why political elites would consent to having their powers limited by a court with broad power of review. As with Hirschl's work, Ginsburg's theory is most applicable to the South African case, where Ginsburg's description of the way elite political calculus influences the extension of justiciable rights fits the strategy pursued by the South African National Party perfectly: "if they foresee themselves losing in postconstitutional elections, they may seek to entrench judicial review as a form of political insurance" (Ginsburg, 2003, 18). To apply this theoretical insight to the effects of popular participation in constitution-making processes, we might question whether the expansion of justiciable rights in the constitution reflects the impact of public pressure, or the self-interested calculations of political elites. Of even more direct application to the theory advanced in this book, Ginsburg also applies something like the concept of strong and weak parties used here, suggesting that a context of diffuse political power allows for greater powers of judicial review, while strong (dominant) parties are able to constrain this. The application there differs somewhat, however, in that Ginsburg's interest was in effect of diffuse power centers in the political system creating greater uncertainty about who would have power after some future election (Ginsburg, 2003, 25). The effect is the same, in that strong parties essentially preclude strong judicial review, but the causal mechanism is quite different.

Having just seen how the argument advanced here has much in common with other work on the relationships between mass and elite in constitution-making processes, it may be asked, "What does this book argue against?" There are several answers to this, while acknowledging that the book does not challenge much of the recent work on constitutionalism and the ways in which political elites have used constitutions to protect their interests. As noted above, the principal targets of the argument presented here have been the mythology of constitution-making, and the rhetoric that politicians and international organizations deploy to support public participation in constitution-making processes. Specifically, as was described in the first chapter of this book, public participation is encouraged in terms of the vital role of the People as *authors* of the constitution. Not merely as advisers to the drafters, or persons who are represented by the politicians who draft the constitution, but as people who have real power and agency in making a constitution. The research presented here demonstrates that this is not the case, and that it is not likely to be what those who design these programs really intend. And yet the language that is used to sell public participation programs and by deliberate extension to legitimize the constitution creates this picture of popular authorship.

This chapter has advanced an argument about political parties and public participation in constitution-making processes, asserting that where there are strong parties we will find low impact from public input and where there are weak parties we will find comparatively greater impact from public input. The following three chapters assess the impact of public participation in the constitution-making exercises of South Africa, Brazil, and Iceland, before turning to a broader analysis in the fourth empirical chapter. While the case studies cannot present a picture of the full universe of constitution-making processes, they do present the full variation possible in terms of party strength. The three cases demonstrate a causal relationship between the strength of political parties (as defined in this chapter) and the level of impact from the public. The issue is then taken up again in a more holistic way in the concluding chapter.

3

South Africa: Party Domination

3.1 INTRODUCTION

The South African case facilitates an insightful comparison with the Brazilian case described in Chapter 4 on the logic of most similar systems. Both cases involved constitution-making in a context of transition to democracy in which the political party associated with the outgoing nondemocratic regime continued to play a role. As described in Chapter 2, the principal difference of interest is the nature of the political parties and the electoral system. Whereas the Brazilian political system has almost always featured very weak parties, South Africa's political system has featured very strong parties. The two most important parties, the African National Congress (ANC) and the National Party (NP), had clear goals for the constitution-making process and were able to structure the drafting process in such a way as to maintain control over the development of the text. Given the characteristics of the main political parties, my theory would predict that the level of impact from public participation in this case will be low.

It is notable that discussions of the South African constitution (at least among scholars) focus so much on the context of the constitution-making process. While it is not uncommon in many countries to begin constitutional law textbooks with a brief section on the drafting of the constitution, this is much more pronounced in the South African case. At least three of the most widely used constitutional law texts in South African universities begin with a rather involved history of the constitution, in one case going back to the origins of South African constitutional law in precontact indigenous traditional law, and especially focusing on the drafting process in the transitional period of the early 1990s. This approach is justified with reference to an approach to interpreting South African constitutional law that requires a consideration of the political and social context in which the law was written and in which it is applied. In one widely used text, de Vos and Freedman write:

Constitutions are often said to represent a snapshot of the hopes and dreams of a nation at the time of its writing or – more cynically – to represent a snapshot of the relative political power and influence of various political formations involved in the drafting of that constitution. However, constitutions are also living documents that judges have to interpret and apply in an ever-changing political, economic, and social environment. (de Vos and Freedman, 2014, 4)

They go on to detail both the legal and political aspects of the drafting process that unfolded between 1991 and 1996. In another case, the brief history of the drafting process provided in the textbook by de Waal and Currie has been cited as a useful reference to the constitutional history of South Africa by other scholars (van Heerden, 2007; Rapatsa, 2014), and even by a justice of South Africa's constitutional court (Ackerman, 2004). For the purposes of the research conducted here, the important point is that the history of the drafting of the constitution is a matter of some legal and political importance in South Africa today. Understanding the degree to which the public participation process impacted the development of the text is then important both for historical and political research and to the practice of law in South Africa today.

One important example of the significance of the drafting process in terms of both the present status of the constitution and of its broader impacts on politics in South Africa is the move to amend the property clause of the 1996 constitution that dominated South African politics in mid-late 2018. The property clause (Section 25) of the 1996 constitution was one of the most difficult aspects of the text to decide and, as originally drafted, it created a fine balance between the interests of the two major parties. In the intervening two decades, it has come to be seen in some quarters as being a pernicious compromise on the part of the ANC that has set back the possibility of effective reform of land tenure. A party to the ANC's left, the Economic Freedom Fighters (EFF), has pushed the governing ANC to consider changing this clause to more explicitly provide for expropriation without compensation. The ANC launched a process for amending this section of the constitution in early 2018, including a period of public consultation on the proposed change. The difficulties attending a public consultation on such a vital issue (an area in which public input certainly mattered little in 1994–1996) recall the inherent problems in the attempt to give the public a meaningful voice in such a difficult political decision. The level of public input on this change to the constitution was extraordinarily high, easily eclipsing the total number of submissions received in 1995–1996, with 140,000 written submissions sent to the parliamentary committee considering the change (Corrigan, 2018). This episode demonstrates that the participatory constitution-making process of 1994–1996 sets in place both a public expectation for consultation and a practice among politicians of making their decisions without much regard for the content of these consultations.

This chapter seeks to carefully evaluate the level of impact that public participation had on the drafting of the final constitution of South Africa between 1994 and 1996. While the drafting of the interim constitution in 1992 and 1993 is important to the background of this research, it has been very well addressed by a number of prominent works (Waldmeir, 1997; Spitz and Chaskalson, 2000). There are at least two books that present a widely accepted history of the drafting of the final constitution, including one by the director of the Constitutional Assembly (Ebrahim, 1998; Segal and Cort, 2011). This chapter takes a much narrower focus than even these works. The contribution to the historical record made here is in carefully examining the space between the claims made about the role of the public in the drafting process (especially at the time) and the actual impact that public participation had. I begin with a few notes on the relevant history of South Africa and continue with empirical research on this issue of public participation.

3.2 HISTORICAL BACKGROUND

3.2.1 *Apartheid and Constitutional Law*

It is not my purpose here to provide a deep description of how the system of apartheid was created and sustained. However, the history of how this system of racial exclusion was developed and how it ultimately came to an end are vital to understanding the dynamics between the political parties during the constitution-making process in 1994–1996. One of the most important aspects of apartheid with relation to the constitution-making process is the explicitly legal basis of apartheid. In a speech to the International Criminal Court, a senior member of the ANC and former professor of human rights, Kader Asmal, described apartheid as being "underpinned by the legal system – it raised socio-economic pillage based on race to a constitutional principle" (Asmal, 2006, 11). As apartheid was constitutionally enabled, the constitution that destroyed apartheid must be understood within this context of lawless constitutionalism.

Systematic racial discrimination was well established during the period of British colonial rule but became firmly entrenched in law in 1948 when the Nationalists first took power. The NP began to implement grand apartheid with a series of bills during its first term in government. Chief among these were the Group Areas Act (1950), Population Registration Act (1950), Prohibition of Mixed Marriages Act (1949), and the Immorality Act (1950). Though much of the racially based maldistribution of land was accomplished before the NP took power, they furthered this program of racial separation through the creation of ostensibly self-governing territories for indigenous Africans. The creation of these "homelands" served the interests of the apartheid state by giving it a legal excuse to exclude indigenous Africans from any rights of citizenship outside the homelands. This was taken even further through the Bantu Homelands Constitution Act of 1971, which established a legal process through which the homelands (known as Bantustans) could become independent states, thus depriving their inhabitants of South African citizenship (Thompson, 2001, 191).

Facing increasing censure from the international community over its policies of racial exclusion, South Africa left the British Commonwealth and declared itself to be a republic in 1961. As part of this process, South Africa created its first written constitution.[1] The 1961 Constitution advanced apartheid by creating a system of government in which only Whites could hold public office or vote. This constitution entrenched a system of parliamentary supremacy, which in practice meant the supremacy of the cabinet (Devenish, 2012), and included no rights whatsoever. The NP leadership explicitly rejected the idea of including rights in the constitution as this would (they claimed) undermine the principle of parliamentary sovereignty. Under this constitution, apartheid was legally and politically protected in spite of increasingly organized opposition from the Black majority.

As the increasing political and legal weakness of the White minority became clear to the NP government, it took steps to strengthen its position through more institutional engineering in a new constitution in 1983. This new constitution created parallel representative institutions for Indians and Coloureds, while continuing to leave the Black majority without political rights outside the Bantustan governments. This was an extremely strange system of government, and it is hard to believe that the NP thought this would be a solution to its problems. Indeed, this new constitution did not function normally for much of its short life, as the continuing civil unrest led the NP government to proclaim several states of emergency in the 1980s, especially after 1986. However, the amendment procedure established in the 1983 constitution was used in 1993 to ratify the interim (or transitional) constitution that enabled the first democratic elections in South Africa in 1994. Thus, the transformational constitutions of 1993 and 1996 were brought into being without any constitutional interregnum or violation of the existing constitution – a process with ambiguous implications for perceptions of the legitimacy of the new constitutions (Arato, 2000, 144–145). Another lasting legacy of the 1983 constitution that should not be overlooked is that it departed from the Westminster model of parliamentary government and created a much more powerful president. This was a notable change in South Africa's political institutions that survived in the 1993 and 1996 constitutions.

3.2.2   *Constitutional Progress Before the End of Apartheid*

The apartheid state excelled at constitutional engineering – a necessity as it sought to claim some sort of legitimacy even as the minority ruled the majority in an explicitly racist and often authoritarian way. Yet, there were a number of actions taken during the period of apartheid that laid the foundation for both a democratic constitution and a participatory drafting process. The first was the writing of the Freedom Charter in 1955. Responding to increasing levels of repression from the apartheid state, the ANC worked with a number of other organizations

---

[1] The previous constitution was the South Africa Act of 1909, passed by the British parliament.

opposed to apartheid to work toward a peaceful political solution. In a gathering that included representatives from the major ethnic groups in South Africa, the ANC partnered with the South African Coloured People's Organisation, South African Indian Congress, the Congress of Democrats (a predominantly White group), and the South African Congress of Trade Unions to hold a large rally in Kliptown (part of the Soweto township outside Johannesburg; Thompson, 2001, 208). This "Congress of the People" was eventually broken up by the police, but not before the delegates from the various groups had agreed to the basic text of the Freedom Charter.

Had the Freedom Charter been a constitution, it would have been one of the most progressive documents of its time. It included broad protections of classic negative rights, as well as expansive social and economic rights. The Charter also had some rather socialist elements, including a provision that transferred ownership of natural resources, industry, and the banks to the people. It was this provision that was used by the apartheid government to charge 156 of the leaders of the Congress with treason (Southall, 2013, 34). While this Charter was in the first instance a reflection of the views of this broader group, it became the basic constitutional statement of the ANC, and through this channel the Charter influenced the final text of the 1996 Constitution. In its more immediate context, the Congress and the Charter were shortly followed by the banning of the ANC and Pan Africanist Congress (PAC) and a few years later by the ANC's turn to violent resistance through the formation of its armed wing Umkhonto we Sizwe (MK). This period began the divide within the ANC leadership between those who were forced into exile and those who led the resistance from within South Africa.

The ANC in exile spent many years preparing for an eventual role in a constitution-making process in South Africa. The most concrete steps toward a democratic constitution for South Africa were taken in the 1980s as the ANC began to consider in some detail what the constitution of a multiracial South African democracy should look like. To this end, in January 1986, the ANC established a Constitutional Committee, working mainly in exile in Lusaka, Zambia (Brooks, 2015, 137). The committee produced one of the most influential documents of the period in 1989, the "Constitutional Guidelines for a Democratic South Africa," published that year in the *South African Journal on Human Rights* (African National Congress, 1989). This document made a number of important statements about the future of South Africa, most notably a commitment to multiparty democracy and a constitution that would include a Bill of Rights. Neither of these ideas was completely accepted by ANC cadres at the time. A member of this committee, and later justice of the South African Constitutional Court, Albie Sachs, recounts concerns about the advisability of including a Bill of Rights in the constitution that was to come. He describes a committee of Black law students that was formed at the University of Natal-Durban in the 1980s to oppose the idea of a Bill of Rights. Sachs writes:

Their fear was that the Bill of Rights would defend the unjust socio-economic situation created by apartheid, guarantee property rights in terms of which Whites owned 87% of the land and 95% of the productive capital, and impose extreme limits on the capacity of the democratic state to equalize access to wealth. Ultimately the poor would remain poor, albeit formally liberated, and the rich would get richer, though technically not advantaged. (Sachs, 2009, 165)

Sachs argued against this idea at the time, suggesting that a Bill of Rights was necessary to "reassure Whites that they had a protected future in the country" (Sachs, 2009, 165). Sachs was instrumental in the ANC's Constitutional Committee's work in writing a draft Bill of Rights that served to inform the party's positions in the negotiations with the NP for the next decade.

Whether or not the current Bill of Rights has limited socioeconomic transformation is a matter of current debate in South Africa (Sekhotho, 2018). Indeed, the fears expressed by the committee referenced by Sachs echo the criticisms of the judicialization of politics leveled by Hirschl and others. Decrying a form of politics that he titles "juristocracy," Hirschl summarizes the place of the Bill of Rights in South Africa's political system by saying that "the white elite and its parliamentary representatives, faced with the inevitable prospect of an ANC-controlled parliament, endorsed a bill of rights as a means of fencing off certain aspects of their privilege from the reach of majoritarian politics" (Hirschl, 2004, 95). It is possible that Sachs would agree with this assessment, but still argue that it was a necessary price to pay for the support of the NP for the new constitution. Nevertheless, the acceptance of a Bill of Rights on the part of the ANC in exile in 1986 marks an important moment in the party's journey toward a negotiated settlement with the apartheid regime and White South Africa as a whole. The ANC followed up their initial sketch of a Bill of Rights from 1986 with the Constitutional Guidelines mentioned earlier in 1989, and then with a revised Bill of Rights proposal in 1992. As is the case with national constitutions, these proposed Bills of Rights grew more capacious over time. Notably, the right to private property did not show up in ANC drafts until 1992 (Mutua, 1997, 77–78).

Following the unbanning of the ANC in 1990 and the beginning of negotiations between the apartheid regime led by the NP and the ANC, constitution-making began in earnest as a necessary precursor to the first democratic elections. Through a long series of off-and-on negotiations between most of the political parties in South Africa, an interim constitution was agreed to in 1993. This constitution (which provided for a government of national unity that incorporated both the NP and ANC in a power-sharing agreement) was in effect during the 1994 election. The newly elected bicameral parliament also sat as the Constitutional Assembly and worked on the constitution between 1994 and 1996. The text was finally certified by the recently established Constitutional Court in December 1996 and took effect at the beginning of 1997. In the sections that follow, I describe in more detail the historical context that shaped the constitution-making process and the key elements of the drafting process itself.

3.2.3 *Looking toward a Majoritarian Future*

The rapidly approaching end of the system of apartheid became clear to some elements of the NP some time before the leadership endorsed this view. The combination of domestic economic stagnation, international pariahdom, and increasing violence eventually drove the NP leadership to begin negotiations with the ANC leadership, and Nelson Mandela in particular. These negotiations played out in several stages over a period of about eight years – beginning in 1985, while Mandela was still in prison, and continuing through the early months of 1993. These vital negotiations have been well documented by other scholars, particularly in books by Waldmeier (1997) and Spitz and Chaskalson (2000).

Since the focus of this project is on the later constitutional negotiations in parliament between 1994 and 1996, this important part of South Africa's constitutional history is not addressed in much depth here. It should be noted, however, that the negotiations began as a project to bring together all the major political parties in South Africa, including the PAC, Azanian People's Organization (AZAPO), the Inkatha Freedom Party (IFP), the Democratic Party (DP), the Conservative Party (CP), and others. The two major stages of the negotiation process were the Convention for a Democratic South Africa (CODESA), which met from December 1991 until May 1992, and the Multi-party Negotiating Process (MPNP), which met between April and November 1993. The interim constitution was negotiated in the last stages of the MPNP. By the end of the negotiations, it was clear that the only significant action was between the NP and the ANC, particularly through "the channel" between Roelf Meyer (Minister of Constitutional Affairs and Communication) and Cyril Ramaphosa (Secretary General of the ANC).

The negotiating positions of the parties during this time were clearly driven by their assessment of their relative political power in the years to come. There are several aspects of this that bear special mention, though these issues obviously informed a great deal of the negotiation of the constitutional texts (both 1993 and 1996). First, the issue of federalism has had an intensely partisan valence in South Africa. The ANC adamantly opposed federalism in the beginning of the negotiations, preferring a unitary state where its overwhelming advantage in the national popular vote would increase its power (Thompson, 2001, 253). The IFP strongly favored federalism due to its regional base of power in KwaZulu-Natal. The NP also favored federalism, partly for similar reasons to the IFP, but also as part of its broader interest in empowering groups rather than individuals. This leads to a second issue, which is the disagreement between the ANC and NP over group rights. Perhaps partially informed by the work of the apartheid state (and colonial governments before) in dividing Black Africans into legally described groups and empowering traditional leaders as agents of state control, the ANC opposed group rights as a matter of principle. For obvious reasons, the NP and its Afrikaner base wanted to establish group rights to protect their political power and cultural heritage. The ANC's views on this point were long established, dating back to their original constitutional considerations under the leadership of Oliver Tambo in Lusaka, Zambia (Sachs, 2016). This issue of group rights versus individual rights was one of the major factors that led to the breakdown of CODESA in 1992. The resolution of these issues was a compromise in the 1993 constitution, where individual rights are protected (rather than group rights), but seven provinces were created.[2]

A point of commonality between the constitution-making processes in South Africa and Brazil is the legal continuity of the constitutional order. While this was perhaps assumed in Brazil, where the constitution-drafting process was developed by the elected legislature through a period of negotiations within the Congress, this was a more open question in South Africa at least in the beginning of the negotiations. What actually transpired was, at least regarding the legal procedures involved, a smooth and normal process, but one with interesting implications regarding the legitimacy of the constitutions produced. As noted earlier, the interim (or transitional) constitution was drafted by a mix of the elected representative of the White minority (elected in racially exclusionary elections), the leaders of the Bantustans and associated parties, and the leadership of the recently unbanned liberation movements such as the ANC and PAC. In 1993, the ANC had no electorally demonstrated claim to represent the interests of the Black majority, but had through long practice and careful political maneuvering established itself as the preeminent representatives of Black South Africans (at least outside of KwaZulu-Natal where the IFP dominated). Thus, the democratic legitimacy of both the NP and ANC was suspect at this point. However, the constitution negotiated in this process was a vital step between the end of grand apartheid and the holding of democratic elections under a constitution that provided for political and social equality for all South Africans.

Whatever the democratic bona fides of the interim constitution, it was duly passed as the new constitution of South Africa by the legislature as it was then constituted in 1993 (i.e., by the members of the racially based tricameral parliament). The interim constitutional text provided for the procedures through which it was replaced by the new democratically elected legislature in 1996. Thus, while there was a great deal of important political change that occurred, the legal aspects of this constitutional revolution followed exactly the process laid out in each of the constitutions in force at the time. The process of using an authoritarian constitution's amendment process to replace it with a democratic constitution had a recent precedent at that time.

---

[2] South Africans generally prefer to avoid describing this as a federal system of government. One ANC MP described the system as a "unitary system with federal features" (Author's interview with "ZNGC," March 23, 2016).

As Arato's research on the democratic transitions in Eastern Europe demonstrated, there was a great deal to be gained (at least in the short run) from following this overtly legal path to radical constitutional change (Arato, 2000).

A vital issue in the transition process was the timing of the first multiracial elections. The NP appeared to be delaying a decision on this, perhaps as a means of maintaining leverage in the negotiations. However, their hand was forced by the assassination of the prominent activist Chris Hani in April 1993. Tensions had already been very high, as violence in the townships had been increasing, leading to fears of open conflict between the ANC and the PAC.[3] To his credit, President F. W. de Klerk understood that this was a critical moment in the country's history and quickly agreed to an election date of April 27, 1994 (Waldmeir, 1997, 225). This gave the parties a de facto deadline to complete their work on the interim constitution (also called the "transitional constitution" by some participants in the process) and an election to begin campaigning for.

The election of 1994 was celebrated by many around the world, but it was not without its problems. The election had been agreed to take place on April 27, but various logistical problems necessitated a continuation of voting for the next two days as well. The final balance of power between the parties in this election was vital since the new parliament would also sit as the constituent assembly. Most importantly, the new constitution would have to be passed by a supermajority of the members of the lower and upper chambers of the parliament sitting as the Constitutional Assembly.

There have long been rumors in parts of the South African political and academic community that the precise result of the 1994 election was the result of careful negotiation between the NP and the ANC, and not a factual accounting of the ballots. The newly created Independent Election Commission (IEC) faced an extraordinary task in preparing the ballots and polling stations, and in supervising the conduct of the election. As it transpired, there were more than 500 allegations of irregularities in the voting process (Szeftel, 1994). At one point, the computer system at the IEC was hacked, with votes added to the Freedom Front (FF), IFP, and NP, forcing the counting process to begin anew (Harris, 2010).

In the end, the IEC was unable to report vote totals for individual polling places or even regions and resorted to a single number for each party as a national total. According to a contemporary academic account of the election, "The IEC met with party leaders and 'negotiated a result' as one IEC official put it...The IEC declared the election result to be a generally accurate picture of the wishes of the electorate...The alternative would have been to hold another election, probably producing even higher levels of violence than before" (Szeftel, 1994, 469–470). This is perhaps too sanguine an assessment of the election, given the fact that, according

---

3 There has long been speculation that this was part of an intentional campaign on the part of right-wing agitators connected to the NP government.

to this agreed result, the ANC won 62.6 percent of the vote and 63 percent of the seats in the National Assembly. The ANC was thus just short of the two-thirds supermajority required to enact a new constitution.

This issue of a negotiated election result was raised in several interviews conducted during field research for this project. First, in an interview with an individual who was very senior in the ANC at the time of the elections, the respondent stated:

I think essentially Cyril [Ramaphosa] and Roelf [Meyer] and to some degree the IFP kind of came up with a formulation about how the vote should be split in a fair way... I think essentially the ANC agreed that it wouldn't be a good idea for it to have more than a two-thirds majority... But you know it really was a fair reflection of the vote, but I mean it really was not reconstitutable about what the vote should have been, or was. (Author's interview with "TGRU," May 23, 2016)

In a later interview with a very senior member of the NP who would have had direct knowledge of these alleged negotiations, I summarized the claim made in the aforementioned interview and asked this individual to respond to the claim. The respondent stated:

None of us really has an idea as to what the outcome was. It was a little bit speculative... So what I'm saying is that there are a lot of facts that we cannot prove either this way or that way. And certainly not an agreed outcome. There was definitely not an agreed outcome that I'm aware of. I was not part of such negotiations. And neither was Mr. de Klerk. So that is I think an untruth. (Author's interview with "RJFD," May 30, 2016)

Between these two major parties then there is agreement that the actual vote totals of the election were unknown and unknowable. The vote tallies that were printed at the time and continue to be reported in books today are an estimate of what the votes were. The key claim, with immense bearing on the constitution-drafting process – that the ANC and NP negotiated the numbers – was denied by the NP side and by an account written by a senior official in the IEC (Harris, 2010), but upheld by the ANC member referenced earlier and by a contemporary scholarly account (Szeftel, 1994).

The key issue of course is that, if the ANC had achieved greater than two-thirds of the vote, it would have had the power to decide the constitution for itself. Whether the fact that the party fell just short of this is an intriguing act of fate or providence, or the result of some careful calculation or bargaining is unclear at this time. However that number came about, it meant that the ANC was firmly in the driver's seat but would need the support of at least one of the minor parties in the parliament to pass the constitution.

While the election for the lower house of parliament (the National Assembly) received most of the attention then and now, we also need to consider the membership of the reconstituted Senate, since the Constitutional Assembly was composed of the members of the two chambers sitting together.[4] Under the terms of the 1993 constitution, the members of the Senate were to be chosen by the new provincial legislatures.[5] In addition to voting for the members of the National Assembly through a system of closed-list proportional representation, the voters of South Africa chose the members of their provincial legislatures through a similar system of party lists. The provincial legislatures (then and now) were seen as important consolation prizes for parties with strong regional support but which could not compete with the ANC on a national level.[6] The members of the Senate were to be chosen by the provincial legislatures on a partisan basis, with the number of senators from each party being proportional to the number of seats each party held within the provincial legislature. This gave the ANC a solid majority in the Senate but included a strong contingent from the NP. Smaller parties tended to do quite poorly in the Senate.

3.3 DRAFTING THE FINAL CONSTITUTION

3.3.1 *The Constitutional Assembly*

In South Africa as in Brazil, a newly elected representative assembly was given the dual task of ordinary legislation and drafting a new constitution. In the South African case, the hard work of negotiating the details of the process of constitution-making had already been accomplished in the MPNP. Chapter 5 of the interim constitution laid out in some detail the form of the Constitutional Assembly and the procedures it would follow in writing the new constitution. Having learned from their experiences in the earlier negotiations that deadlines had a wonderful power to sharpen minds and encourage compromise (Author's interview with "RJFD," May 30, 2016), the interim constitution required the Constitutional Assembly to complete its work within two years of its first sitting (Section 73(1)). In practice, this meant that the final constitution would have to be completed and approved by the Constitutional Assembly by May 8, 1996. Despite this firm deadline, the constitution-making task began slowly, and the early committee meetings have been memorably described by one party leader as "occupational therapy" for MPs (Leon, 2008, 306). This is perhaps understandable given the fact that many of the principal members of parliament had by that time been involved in several years of intense negotiations, and had recently concluded a tense electoral campaign. Nevertheless, there was a great deal of wasted time in the beginning of the drafting process and a mad rush to finish in late April 1996 (Author's interview with "ZCGI," May 5, 2016).

---

[4] South Africa had a Senate beginning with the Union constitution in 1909. This Senate was abolished in 1981. The interim constitution recreated the Senate as a more federal institution. The upper chamber was renamed the National Council of the Provinces in 1997.

[5] The 1993 constitution also created new provinces and described their boundaries.

[6] The opportunity for the NP to win government in the Western Cape and for the IFP to win in KwaZulu-Natal was an important factor in the peaceful conclusion of the election of 1994.

TABLE 3.1 *Partisan composition of the Constitutional Assembly*

Party	Assembly	Senate	Total	Percentage of Constitutional Assembly
African National Congress	252	60	312	63.7
National Party	82	17	99	20.2
Inkatha Freedom Party	43	5	48	9.8
Freedom Front	9	5	14	2.9
Democratic Party	7	3	10	2.0
Pan Africanist Congress	5	0	5	1.0
African Christian Democratic Party	2	0	2	0.4

The leadership of the Constitutional Assembly reflected the balance of power in the parliament. As mandated in the interim constitution, the Constitutional Assembly elected a chairperson and deputy chairperson at their first meeting. The chairperson was Cyril Ramaphosa of the ANC and the deputy chairperson was Leon

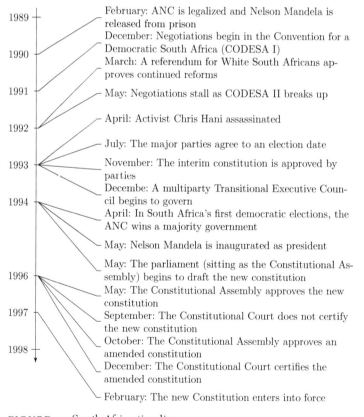

1989 — February: ANC is legalized and Nelson Mandela is released from prison

December: Negotiations begin in the Convention for a Democratic South Africa (CODESA I)

1990 — March: A referendum for White South Africans approves continued reforms

1991 — May: Negotiations stall as CODESA II breaks up

1992 — April: Activist Chris Hani assassinated

July: The major parties agree to an election date

1993 — November: The interim constitution is approved by parties

December: A multiparty Transitional Executive Council begins to govern

1994 — April: In South Africa's first democratic elections, the ANC wins a majority government

May: Nelson Mandela is inaugurated as president

May: The parliament (sitting as the Constitutional Assembly) begins to draft the new constitution

1996 — May: The Constitutional Assembly approves the new constitution

1997 — September: The Constitutional Court does not certify the new constitution

October: The Constitutional Assembly approves an amended constitution

1998 — December: The Constitutional Court certifies the amended constitution

February: The new Constitution enters into force

FIGURE 3.1 South Africa timeline

Wessels of the NP. The other constitutionally mandated body was an Independent Panel of Constitutional Experts (IPCE). The Constitutional Assembly chose seven South African academics to fill this committee and they provided important guidance for the drafters throughout the process. Importantly, the interim constitution gave the IPCE the task of amending the text of the final constitution if it reached majority support but fell short of the supermajority required for ratification (Section 73(3)).

The organization of the various committees is important for our analysis, as the strict hierarchy allowed leaders of the ANC and NP to continue to negotiate at an elite level on the language of the constitution, while involving junior MPs in the somewhat academic work of discussing potential provisions and dealing with the demands from citizens through public meetings and written submissions. The large number of Committees creates a rather frustrating layer cake of bureaucracy, but the hierarchies demonstrate how the process was run.[7]

The largest real negotiating body was the Constitutional Committee, which was composed of forty-four members of the Constitutional Assembly, again in proportion to their overall number of seats. It was discovered that this group was too large to actually decide the finer points of controversy and was eventually functionally replaced by a subcommittee of twenty members of the full Constitutional Committee. The subcommittee was not empowered to make final decisions, but rather reported its decisions to the full Constitutional Committee for a vote. The members of the subcommittee varied according to the issues being dealt with, further adding to its efficiency (Ebrahim, 1998, 181). Alongside the Constitutional Committee sat a management committee made up of a dozen members of the Constitutional Assembly, which dealt with procedural and logistical rather than substantive issues.

Much of the work of roughing out the substance of the various chapters of the constitution was to be done by six Theme Committees. The Theme Committees were the main point of contact for members of the public and representatives of interest groups who wished to deliver a written submission or presentation. The original intention for the Theme Committees was to process the information thus received and then send reports up to the Constitutional Committee for the actual drafting of the text (Constitution Committee, 1994). In the end, the Theme Committees did more than this and provided drafts of their assigned chapters to the Constitutional Committee. The subject matter for these committees was divided as follows: (1) Character of the democratic state, (2) structure of government, (3) relationships between levels of government, (4) fundamental rights, (5) judicial and legal issues, and (6) specialized structure of government (such as public administration and security services). Much of the work of the Theme Committees was

---

7 While it might be appealing for reasons of space and the stamina of the reader to abbreviate these committee names, that would also likely create additional confusion about which committee was being spoken of. For that reason, the committee names are written out in full in this chapter.

actually undertaken by a Core Group of each Committee. These Core Groups were agreed to have representatives of the major parties, though at this level proportionality was not possible. Thus, each Core Group had two members from the ANC and one each from the NP, DP, PAC, and IFP (Constitution Committee, 1994). In both the Theme Committees and Core Groups, MPs from the smaller parties were assigned to multiple Committees and were in some cases unable to attend meetings due to scheduling difficulties (Author's interview with "GQOL," May 26, 2016).

The Theme Committees were each assisted in their work by a Technical Committee made up of a number of academics with expertise in the area of law that the Theme Committee was dealing with. There was some concern among the members of the Constitutional Committee that the Technical Committees should not unduly influence the work of the Theme Committees (Constitutional Committee, 1994). However, in at least some Theme Committees, the actual work of putting constitutional language together fell to these Technical Committees (Constitutional Committee, 1995). In interviews, a number of members of both the Constitutional Assembly and the Technical Committees asserted that the experts had a great deal of impact on the development of the text.

3.3.2   *Party Discipline in the Constitutional Assembly*

The key explanatory variable in this analysis of public participation is the nature of the political parties. In the Brazilian case, we can draw upon decades of empirical research that conclusively demonstrates the weakness of the political parties. Of particular interest for this research project is the analysis of voting in Brazil's National Constituent Assembly that was undertaken by Mainwaring and Pérez-Liñán (1997). However, in the case of South Africa, the literature is not as well developed, and we are further limited by the unavailability of the equivalent of roll-call vote data that could be used to construct a measure of party unity in the Constitutional Assembly. There is some research on party discipline in the broader context of South Africa's parliamentary system. Taking a long view of the development of political parties in South Africa, Thiel and Mattes (1998) argued that the centralized and disciplined nature of the parties could be attributed (at least in some cases) to their genesis as hierarchical and quasi-Leninist liberation movements. Other parties were created in the Westminster tradition, and thus have strong discipline as part of their identity.

The tallies in the votes to ratify the 1996 constitution are not particularly instructive, as they were overwhelmingly in favor, nor were there a multitude of votes in the plenary sessions of Constitutional Assembly on amendments of procedural issues. In the first ratification vote on May 8, 1996, only the African Christian Democratic Party (ACDP) voted against the Constitution, while the IFP and Freedom Front (FF) abstained or were absent. This is a picture of complete party-line voting, but it does not tell us much. In the second ratification vote (after the text was amended to meet with the Constitutional Court's approval), the party lines were essentially the same, with continued opposition from the ACDP, and boycotts and abstentions from the IFP and FF. No member of the Constitutional Assembly voted against their party.

Party discipline was in fact supported by the text of the interim constitution, with a section that was carried over into the final constitution. In the section of the 1993 constitution that deals with the vacation of seats (Section 43(b)), a member of the National Assembly is required to vacate their seat if they cease "to be a member of the party which nominated him or her as a member of the National Assembly." This is not an indefensible provision in a constitution that establishes an electoral system of closed-list proportional representation. However, it serves to increase the power of the political party at the expense of the individual member of parliament. So, during the drafting of the final constitution between 1994 and 1996, members of the Constitutional Assembly depended on the good graces of their party leadership for the normal hierarchical appointments in parliament, appointment to their preferred Theme Committees and higher Committees, and for the continuance of their seat in parliament more generally. Such strong party discipline was in fact ANC party policy. The 1994 Code of Conduct for ANC MPs required members to be subject to the authority of the party leadership and forbade them from using parliamentary procedures to undermine that leadership (Lodge, 2004; Boraine, 2014). This is certainly not an institutional context that would encourage anything other than fealty to the party. Although most of the focus in researching parties in South Africa has been on the ANC, some research has suggested that the "ethos of strong party discipline" pertains "across the political spectrum" (Steytler, 2005). The ANC's united front demands a similar approach from its opponents in parliament.

There is also evidence to suggest that party discipline was paramount in the negotiations in the Theme Committees. The documentary record focuses on the submissions from the parties, which seem to have been the main points of discussion as documented in the minutes of meetings. In many of the interviews conducted for this project, respondents indicated that the party's position on a particular issue was the most important factor – certainly above input from the public. One respondent described the situation within the ANC as follows: "So, once a decision has been taken at a conference, whether you are comfortable or not with that decision, when it has to be discussed in a public forum, like in parliament, or in portfolio committees, or in these Theme Committees in the course of the formulation of the constitution, then you have to abide by the position of the party" (Author's interview with "DLSR," March 15, 2016). This statement certainly includes the idea of voting with the party, but even more than that a requirement that, in the negotiations in the Theme Committees, party members would follow the party line even if they did not share the party's decision. Other accounts bear this out, suggesting, for example, that, although the ANC's official position in the constitutional negotiations was to include a prohibition on discrimination on the basis of sexual orientation in the constitution, this was not the view held by the majority of the party members (Oswin, 2007; Thoreson, 2008). In the post-constitution-making era, the ANC has continued to rely on party discipline to carry through policies that are unpopular among its membership and even its MPs (Davis, 1996; Beall et al., 2005).

3.3.3   *Genesis and Scope of the Popular Participation Program*

In contrast with what we will see in the Brazilian case, where the opportunities for public input (the popular amendments in particular) were the results of demand from the public and civil society groups, the formal public participation program in South Africa came about through the decisions of the Constitutional Assembly, and not in response to demands from the public. Although the opportunities for participation were extended from the top down, there was a significant volume of public input at both stages of the constitution-making process. The leadership of CODESA had extended an invitation to members of the public to contribute to the negotiating process by sending letters with what they would like to see in the new constitution. In response, there was a grassroots movement to send letters to CODESA and later to the MPNP; however, these received relatively scant attention from the negotiators representing the political parties. Included in the National Archives of South Africa are hundreds of letters to the parties at CODESA, including letters from schoolchildren (who in some cases seem to have been directed to write by their teachers), racist postcards, and letters from civil society groups and concerned citizens.

It is difficult to say whether or not the majority of the writers of these letters had a sense of how much attention their submissions received, or whether they had an impact on the interim constitution. However, there is one interesting series of letters in the archive from a concerned citizen who wrote five letters to the negotiators at CODESA and the MPNP. This person's third letter includes a line of the sort that might be expected from someone in his position:

My letter of 30th March 1992 was written in response to an invitation for the members of the public to address Codesa on issues relation to the Constitution and Bill of Rights. Unfortunately, whilst I asked that copies of my letter be circulated to all the delegations, I never received confirmation that this was, in fact, done. If it was done, then I was studiously ignored by all the delegations... I trust that the man on the street is not going to be ignored when deliberations on these issues recommence... (McLoughlin, 1993)

His last dogged letter states: "I enclose herewith copies of my letters of the 30th March 1992, 16th October 1992, 26th March 1993, and 20th April 1993 to which I have not yet had a reply. Kindly let me hear from you by return" (McLoughlin, 1993). Clearly, this was an individual who was paying attention, participating, and not seeing the fruit of his labors. It is likely that this person's assiduous campaign was unique, but these quotations reflect the broader disaffection that a participating citizen might feel if they were following events closely enough to determine whether or not their submissions had an effect on the text produced by the negotiators.

The experiences of drafters, civil society groups, and members of the public at CODESA and the MPNP informed their approach to popular participation in the drafting of the final constitution several years later. One of the striking aspects of the genesis of the public participation program for the final constitution-making process is that it does not seem to have been a contentious decision or the result of much careful thinking. On the contrary, according to an individual who was in the leadership of the Constitutional Assembly, the public participation program was created because of public statements made by members of the Assembly to the effect that there would be public consultations about the content of the constitution (Author's interview with "GQOL," May 26, 2016). The executive director of the Constitutional Assembly, Hassen Ebrahim, described the situation following the meeting as: "Essentially the task that we had was to ensure that we had a constitution drafted by more than 40 million people" (Segal and Cort, 2011, 146). This sort of appeal to the public was in line with the ANC's practice of politics (Brooks, 2018). However, the public participation process was not a partisan project. According to one member of the Management Committee, there were no objections to starting this large program of public consultation (Author's interview with "ULTY," May 5, 2016).

Even if the project was essentially non-partisan, the utility of a centrally managed system for public participation is a matter that should receive more debate. The parties certainly differed in the size and diversity of their constituency and thus in their ability to represent the interests of South Africans in general. The ANC in particular made claims that suggest it relied far more on other sources of information about the views of the people than on those created by the Constitutional Assembly. In one interview, an ANC member of the Constitutional Assembly described a dialogic process through which the leaders of the ANC shaped the views of the people about the constitution, but also sought their input (Author's interview with "CEQW," March 10, 2016). The ANC's own party structures were seen as key to understanding the views of the people. Even leaders of other parties were willing to concede that the ANC had a "significant tradition of popular participation" (Author's interview with "PNTO," March 10, 2016). However, responding to a question about the impact of participation, an ANC member stated that, "The heart of what we wanted to achieve was to make sure that every South African is able to follow the constitutional process and be able to be part of that process. So we did everything to facilitate them getting involved in that process" (Author's interview with "CEQW," March 10, 2016). This sounds less like direct impact and more like a process designed to increase perceptions of legitimacy and ownership, but also reflects an interest in moving beyond those party structures to be as inclusive as possible. Another ANC member asserted that the party had always wanted a large participatory process (Author's interview with "JJVA," May 3, 2016). On balance, then, it seems that, while the public participation process was most in line with the traditions and desires of the ANC, it was not in practice a partisan project.

As the staff of the Constitutional Assembly planned the public participation process, they had very little to work with. There was no budget for public consultations, a media campaign, or for the processing of letters from the public. Additionally, those planning this process were unaware of any previous examples of public participation in constitution-making, thus depriving them of the opportunity to learn from how the process was implemented in Brazil a decade earlier for example. In the end, the staff of the Constitutional Assembly developed an ambitious plan to hold public consultations in many locations around the country, create broadcast and print media campaigns, and solicit written comments from members of the public. This effort was financed with donations from foreign governments, particularly those in Scandinavia (Author's interview with "GQOL," May 26, 2016). The Public Participation Programme launched with a large public meeting near Cape Town in February 1995 and continued until about February 1996 (Salazar, 2002, 69). Given the rather haphazard nature of the beginning of the process, its eventual scope and accomplishments are all the more impressive.

It is important to make a correction at this point concerning the volume of public participation in the South African constitution-making process. The number of submissions from the public is often described as being slightly over or under two million (de Vos and Freedman, 2014, 24). One well-researched book on the constitution-making process provides the number of submissions from the public as 1,753,424 (Segal and Cort, 2011, 148). However, this number actually includes both signatures on petitions and substantive written submissions. The number of written submissions from individuals and civil society groups (which were not usually separated by the technical staff) actually stands at 15,292 (Gloppen, 1997, 257–261). Of these, 8,409 were made available for public viewing on the Constitutional Assembly's website (described later) and are now accessible to researchers through the University of Cape Town's library.

The public outreach aspects of this program eventually involved a website where documents demonstrating the progress of the Constitutional Assembly were regularly posted. This was quite a groundbreaking attempt at transparency for its time. Additionally, the Constitutional Assembly accepted submissions from the public via email to an easily remembered address at submit@constitution.org.za. Few South Africans would have been able to use either the website or the email, but those who did were quite pleased with it. One submission begins with "First of all, let me congratulate you on this wonderful method of communicating with our government!" (de Klerk, 1995). Members of the public could also contribute through a phone call to the Constitutional Assembly's "Talk-line." All of these channels for public input were advertised in the popular press (Segal and Cort, 2011, 155–156).

One of the great things about this initially ad hoc process of public consultation in South Africa is that the management of the Constitutional Assembly hired a research firm to conduct an empirical analysis of the effectiveness of the program in two waves in 1995 and 1996. The agency hired to undertake this research, Community Agency for Social Enquiry (CASE), then hired another firm (Research Surveys Pty) to conduct face-to-face interviews with an astonishing representative sample of 3,801 South Africans. The results of this research were then presented to the Management Committee in the form of a thirty-eight-page report. The results of that study do not cover the primary interest in the present project – whether or not the public participation program impacted the text – but do give us some excellent information about how effective the Constitutional Assembly had been in reaching the South African public.

In terms of basic knowledge of the constitution-making process, the survey researchers found that approximately two-thirds of South Africans had heard of the Constitutional Assembly, and of these three-fifths knew that its role was to draft a constitution or make law (Everatt et al., 1996, 5). At the time that the second survey was conducted, the public draft of the constitution had been in circulation for about three months. At this point, 8 percent of respondents had seen the draft and 5 percent had read at least part of it, though 84 percent expressed a desire to read the constitution once it was ratified (Everatt et al., 1996, 23–24). The best opportunity for personal contact with the constitution-making process was through local meetings with members of the Constitutional Assembly. CASE found that, in 1995, 18 percent of respondents had heard of such meetings, and of these 62 percent had attended one. In 1996, only 13 percent of respondents had heard about a meeting and of those only 11 percent had attended. Of those who attended, almost half reported that they participated by asking a question or making a comment (Everatt et al., 1996, 15–16).

Of especial interest considering the data analyzed later in this chapter is the fact that 29 percent of respondents knew that the Constitutional Assembly was accepting written comments from the public. Among those who knew this was possible, 10 percent said that they had written to the Constitutional Assembly. Looking at the full survey sample, only 1 percent said that they had contacted the Constitutional Assembly (Everatt et al., 1996, 18–19). Feelings of ownership are thought to be important in building the legitimacy of a new constitution (Hart, 2003; Chambers, 2004), and in this survey it was found that 48 percent of respondents felt that they had been a part of the constitution-making process. Around the same number reported that they thought that the Constitutional Assembly genuinely desired the participation of the public (Everatt et al., 1996, 19–22). An optimistic 41 percent of respondents reported that they thought the Constitutional Assembly would give their input serious consideration (Everatt et al., 1996, 22). On the related question of whether the final text of the constitution would reflect their views, 35 percent responded in the affirmative (Everatt et al., 1996, 27). Even those who had not heard that it was possible to contribute to the constitution-making process believed that it was important for the Constitutional Assembly to consult

the public (83 percent of respondents). The authors of the CASE report summarized the situation this way: "In short, regardless of whether individuals feel that
their own submissions would be treated seriously if they sent them in or not, the
overwhelming majority believe that the Assembly is right in consulting the public"
(Everatt et al., 1996, 23).

Despite the statistics on the reach of the public participation program collected
by the CASE researchers, some members of the Constitutional Assembly remained
unconvinced. One ANC member stated that "the ordinary people have never really
been represented in these interactions with parliament" (Author's interview with
"DLSR," March 15, 2016). This respondent lamented the fact that the public consultations took place in towns in the countryside, but not in small villages. This is true,
but the Constitutional Assembly did go to great lengths to hold public meetings in
very remote parts of South Africa, including the sparsely inhabited Northern Cape.
The transcripts of the public meetings describe well-planned and orderly engagements between members of the public and members of the Theme Committees.
Even if some members of the Constitutional Assembly describe these meetings as
having had no effect on the text (Author's interviews with "DLSR," March 15, 2016;
"RGBS," April 25, 2016), they did produce interesting engagements between the
people and their representatives.

At one meeting at the National Assembly in August 1995, Hassen Ebrahim
(Executive Director of the Constitutional Assembly) responded to some criticism
of the deals being made in the constitution-making process with the following
impassioned (and somewhat humorous) statement:

Chairperson, Mr. Vincent from NADEL [National Association of Democratic Lawyers],
perhaps gave me the most important opening when he dealt with the question of anxiety
of civil society and the question of smoke filled rooms where the horse trading is suppos-
edly taking place... Chairperson, we are now moving towards the end of our first phase
of Constitution making. During this phase we have invited all of society to present their
views on what they felt the Constitution should contain. In this regard, we have identified three particular role players. The first role player would be those political parties
represented in the Constitutional Assembly and those political representatives who were
elected in April precisely to draft the Constitution. But the second role player is that of
civil society. I wish to explain a bit of civil society as well. But thirdly, the third role player
is perhaps the most important role player, and that is the ordinary individual on the street
who has also a voice... I can also confirm that we have had more than 300 attendances
from politicians in these 25 constitutional public meetings throughout the country in
very, very difficult areas which are not even listed on the maps... What happens to your
submissions and your views and are they compromised in smoke filled rooms?... In fact
if you talk of real horse trading, then horse trading took place this week. It took place on
Monday in the very committee you referred to. It took place in full view of the public
and the media. It did not take place in smoke filled rooms. In fact, smoking is banned
in our meetings. (Constitution Assembly, 1995)

3.4 ANALYSIS OF THE DRAFTING PROCESS

3.4.1 *Process of Textual Development*

Tracking the development of the text of the constitution over time and between persons is a key interest in this research project, but it is at this point somewhat limited by the availability of the documentary evidence. The National Archives of South Africa contain many documents relating to the constitution-making process, but some of the specific items mentioned in the minutes of meetings of the various committees do not seem to have been kept. Preliminary drafts prepared by the Technical Committees and in most cases the Theme Committees are among the missing items. A senior member of the Management Committee expressed some frustration at how these documents were handled at the end of the constitution-making process (Author's interview with "GQOL," May 26, 2016). In correspondence with the author, a member of the technical staff suggested that documents not created for publication had been carelessly dumped into the National Archive, and not cataloged. This makes retrieval by researchers next to impossible.

Nevertheless, we can sketch out the general progress of the text based on other sources. Obviously, there were a number of documents created prior to the 1994–1996 drafting process that had important influences on the final constitution. Several of these have been described already, including the Freedom Charter, the ANC's draft Bill of Rights, and Constitutional Guidelines for a Democratic South Africa. The constitutions of 1909, 1961, and 1983 also have some influence on the style of constitution-writing and the form of some of the major institutions. Much more important is the 1993 interim constitution, which not only established thirty-four binding Constitutional Principles, but also contributed a great deal of language to the final Bill of Rights and to the sections on the parliament, cabinet, and provincial governments. The extent of shared language between the final text of the constitution and these antecedent documents is reported in Table 3.2.

Beyond these various historical antecedents, the development of the text began in the Theme Committees. Here, the various political parties presented submissions with both proposed language and arguments about that language. The committee meetings featured debate between the parties over the text in specific and general terms. Most importantly for the purposes of this research project, it was also in the Theme Committees that the submissions from the public were supposed to be given attention.

The actual process of how those submissions came to have any bearing on the text of the constitution depended very heavily on the work of both the broader panel of experts and the Technical Committees that assisted the Theme Committees. The technical staff received the often handwritten submissions from the public and made them consumable by the drafters. This involved transcribing the submissions and translating them into English. The processed submissions were

TABLE 3.2 *Shared text with the 1996 constitution*

Document	Shared words	Percentage of 1996 text
1909 Constitution	140	0
1961 Constitution	473	0
1983 Constitution	1,031	2
1993 Constitution	6,866	15
November 1995 draft	9,840	22
May 1996 draft	38,050	86

compiled in a number of large volumes that were printed at regular intervals as more submissions were ready for the drafters. These phone-book-like collections of submissions included (in most cases) a summary of content at the beginning that listed how many submissions had been received on various topics, but were less specific than the Brazilian database that will be described later, and as no demographic data were associated with the letters that had been received, this could not be passed on to the drafters. As we will see later, the amount of attention that these volumes received varied between drafters, but was in general not a systematic analysis.

Having considered the positions of the various parties, the views of the public, and representations from industry and civil society groups, the Theme Committees sent their reports to the Constitutional Committee. It was the role of the Constitutional Committee to negotiate the finer points of the text and to consolidate the work of the various Committees into one final constitution. As in the earlier MPNP, the channel between the leaderships of the ANC and the NP was vital to seeing the project to its completion. In this way, there were important elements of both publicity (as in the Theme Committee meetings and plenary sessions of the Constitutional Assembly) and secrecy in the private meetings between leaders.

At the end of the process, the panel of experts integrated the drafts from the various committees into one final text. After this, Philip Knight – a Canadian legal scholar who was an advocate for "plain language" in the drafting of legal statutes – revised the language of the constitution to make sure it was understandable to laymen. One of the Technical Committee members described him as the "principal drafter," and the "owner of the draft" (Author's interview with "ZCGI," May 30, 2016). But this role (and the goal of using plain language more generally) was certainly not without some controversy. One prominent South African lawyer described this final cleansing of the language of the constitution as the "Canadian Laundromat," while a member of the Constitutional Assembly referred to this process as the "plain language laundromat" (James, 1997; Murray, 2001). However, that member of the Technical Committee noted that there has been no confusion over the interpretation of the 1996 constitution, so the plain language program must have been successful (Author's interview with "ZCGI," May 30, 2016).

3.4.2   *Copied Text from Submissions from the Public*

Despite this cleansing of the language, looking for matches between the text of the submissions and the text of the constitution is a reasonable place to start in establishing the extent to which public participation affected the text of the constitution. To that end, I used pattern-matching software (WCopyfind) to search for similar strings of text[8] between the submissions from the public and the constitution. In the South African documents, there are 189 instances in which there is shared text between the constitution and the submissions. In most of these cases, the submissions quote from the interim constitution or the highly publicized draft constitution of November 1995 (on which comment was requested), using language that was carried over into the final constitution. Many of these submissions go through a section of the constitution line-by-line, noting areas where changes could be made. Some of these submissions made very clear marks (e.g., with bold or underlined type) denoting what the author thought should be added or removed from the draft published in November 1995. Despite this careful work on the part of the authors of these submissions, there does not appear to be any impact on the final text from these interventions. It is relatively straightforward to look for edits in the final text of the constitution that respond to this type of feedback, and there is no evidence that these submissions had an impact. This is rather surprising, given that this kind of detailed and clear comment on the language of the constitution would seem to be of the most use to drafters – at least if we understand the constitution drafters as authors who have asked for feedback on their work. It is perhaps naive to think that there would be any instance where the words of a submission from the public were taken verbatim and added to the constitutional text. Nevertheless, after a thorough investigation, we can conclude that this type of impact is completely absent in the South African case.

It is particularly notable that the very detailed submissions of this type from organizations such as the South African Agricultural Union (representing the majority of commercial farmers in the country) and the Chamber of Mines do not appear to have generated any concrete changes in the constitutional text. Even where there is no impact on the final text, these submissions are substantively interesting in that they show that many South Africans were sufficiently engaged in the constitution-making process to thoughtfully consider the published draft and suggest revisions. In comparison with the Brazilian case considered in Chapter 4, this seems to be a step forward.

There are, however, a few cases where the final constitutional text lines up with the requested change. Perhaps most notably, a number of the social and economic rights proposed in a letter from Archbishop Desmond Tutu (writing to report on a meeting with a group of lawyers in the Western Cape) were added to the draft

---

[8] Strings with a length of six words, allowing for one imperfection within the string.

constitution within a couple of months of his letter. One member of the technical staff mused in an interview that there may have been some impact from submissions in the area of socioeconomic rights, but they then reversed themselves saying that socioeconomic rights were going to be included in the constitution regardless of what the public had to say on the issue (Author's interview with "EAKX," April 25, 2016).

Among the South African written submissions, there are many submissions that share text with other submissions – though to a far lesser extent than we will observe in Brazil. The most notable campaigns appear to have been organized by Christian groups. The largest campaign, with at least sixty-one submissions that appear to have originated from the same basic text, is an objection to the legalization of pornography. This group of texts claims to speak for the "silent majority" of South Africans. The second-most numerous set of submissions (with twenty-two copies) objects to the legalization of homosexuality, and demands that the words "sexual orientation" be struck from the clause on equal protection in the interim constitution. In this second case, the language about sexual orientation is often included in a larger discussion surrounding issues of concern for conservative Christians. The third-most copied group of texts (only eleven) makes essentially the same demand as the second group, but the wording is very different. Going down the list we find very few copies in each group, suggesting that the majority of the submissions in the South African case were not organized, but rather the work of individuals, or at most small groups of people. Organized groups were involved in making in-person presentations to the Theme Committees, however. It is likely that they had some agenda-setting impact through that channel (Author's interview with "ZCGI," April 25, 2016), but none of the writing campaigns described here was successful.

3.4.3 Topic Models

Topic models are something of a blunt instrument for this type of analysis, so the discussion here will be fairly brief. Topic models are particularly useful for determining what documents are about, as a corpus of documents, and as individual members of that corpus. I have applied an unsupervised form of topic modeling (latent dirichlet allocation) to each of the corpora of submissions from the public in the three cases studied in this book.[9] This allows us to do several things: (1) Understand broadly what topics were covered in the submissions, (2) determine which topics were more popular in the submissions, (3) see how closely the topics are related to each other, and most importantly (4) determine how many of these topics are included in the final draft of the constitution.

The method of latent dirichlet allocation (LDA) applies Bayesian statistics to the problem of uncovering the relationships between words and between documents.

[9] This was implemented with the "lda" package in R.

LDA assumes that each document in the corpus contains a mixture of latent topics and uses an iterative process of "walking" through the documents to update both the topics and the probability that a given document contains each topic (Blei et al., 2003). The analysis begins with random assignments of words to a specified number of topics (in this case fifty),[10] and then proceeds by updating the words in each topic and the probable mixture of topics that each document contains. This is repeated many times to achieve stability in the assignments, and thus certainty in the model. Each topic then is a list of words that are regularly found together in the documents that make up the corpus. It is up to the analyst to carefully consider each list of words and determine whether or not the list can be understood to represent a coherent and substantively meaningful topic. If the analysis does not produce a list that could be recognized as a coherent topic, various parameters can be adjusted, most importantly the number of topics to be identified. A common way to consume these topics is by reading the top twenty or fifty words that are the most common indicators that a document contains the topic.

This method uncovers coherent topics within the corpus, including many that are highly specific. Examples include topics relating to elections, federalism, the environment, transportation, gender, pornography, abortion, animal protection, national symbols, languages, recognition of God, gay rights, and family law. While there is some noise, the topics identified this way are clear areas of interest for the South Africans who participated in the process. The topic model also uncovers the way in which issues were bundled for many participants, as, for example, one topic groups together submissions that dealt with abortion and prostitution and another includes land, property, and industry. Agreeing with the analysis in the previous section, the topic model of the submissions shows that conservative interests appear to be overrepresented. The topic model on its own does not indicate the positive or negative meaning attached to words like "abortion," but reading through the full texts of the submissions provides a clear understanding that most participants held conservative views on the issues in controversy.

Comparing the final text of the South African constitution with the broader distribution of topics, I find that the constitution (as a document within this corpus) is a mixture of only eight of the fifty topics from the submissions. Most of the content of the constitution (47.6 percent) is captured by just one topic that contains words we would associate with the division of powers in both vertical and horizontal ways.[11] The seven other topics from the written submissions that are found in the

---

[10] There is no clear rule about how many topics should be included in an LDA topic model. One approach to this problem is to re-run the model a number of times with different numbers of topics and see which number returns the most coherent and differentiated topics. I took this approach with these corpora and found that specifying fifty topics returned the most sensible lists of words for each topic.

[11] The top twenty words in this topic are (stemmed): govern, nation, provinci, local, province, legisl, power, shall, function, section, execut, commiss, constitut, council, parliament, legislatur, presid, level, provis, and principl.

constitution address religion, the justice system, the rights of children and families, community development, national symbols, law and order, and fundamental rights. Notable topics in the submissions that were left out of the constitution (at least as measured with this method) include Islam, animal welfare, pornography, cannabis, agriculture, the death penalty, an Afrikaner volkstaat, and the military.

The substantive meaning of this rather low topical correspondence between what the writers of the submissions were talking about and the content of the constitution requires some careful interpretation. For one thing, as noted earlier, the context in which a matter was raised is not clear from a topic model and must be interpreted through a careful reading of the full text. Additionally, even when there is agreement, it is not clear whether the draft constitution that was published during the process influenced the content of the submissions[12] or if the submissions influenced the draft. Since the constitution in this case only includes eight of the fifty topics, these matters may not affect the key lesson from the analysis. At the very least, this low number of shared topics suggests a significant disconnect between the content of the constitution and the content of the submissions. It may not be reasonable to expect that the majority of the topics will be included in the constitution, but this is a strikingly low proportion. As a point of comparison, the Brazilian constitution contains a mixture of thirteen of the fifty topics from the corpus of submissions. These are spread much more evenly than the South African case. In the sparser data of the Icelandic case, nine of fifteen topics are found in the final draft of the constitution. In Chapter 4, this line of inquiry in the Brazilian case will be considered further.

3.4.4 *Polls and Petitions*

Direct submissions to the Constitutional Assembly were certainly not the only source of information about public opinion available to the drafters of the constitution. South Africa's polling firms were founded relatively later than those in many countries, but had gained a great deal of experience in the last years of the apartheid regime. During the negotiations that ended apartheid and brought about the first fully democratic elections, polling data were used by the major parties to make calculations about how the deals being reached would affect their chances to hold onto, or gain, power. One scholar of South African politics invoked Rawls (1971) to describe the impact of polling on the negotiations over the constitution, stating that "the widespread availability of survey data shredded the 'veil of ignorance', radically reducing the amount of uncertainty about the present and future interests, and thus enabled what Rawls called 'present position', that is, self-interested bargaining which ultimately helped to produce a constitutional agreement that was largely in the interests of the strongest political parties" (Mattes, 2012, 179). In more contemporary South African politics, there are few incentives for politicians to pay much

---

[12] The date of writing is not available for many of the submissions.

attention to polls, as the party line is the only thing that matters in deciding how to vote in parliament (Mattes, 2012, 193). Reports on polling data from this period in South Africa are less available than in the Brazilian case, but there could have been no doubt among South African political elites about what the people wanted the constitution to say in several key areas – and the constitution did not deliver.

Although it is certainly much different from polling random samples of voters, the South African process included millions of signatures on petitions that were sent to the constituent assembly. As with the written submissions from individuals discussed earlier, conservative interests dominated this area of participation. Summing up the impact of public opinion on a few controversial parts of the constitution (in particular through petitions), one participant in the process said:

The three or four biggest petitions were not given effect… There was a massive petition in favor of continuing to privilege Afrikaans as an official language. That was not heard. There was a massive petition to ensure that the death penalty remained. That was not heard… There was a big petition about the right to bear arms. It had hundreds of thousands of signatures. I think that was just a non-starter from the start. (Author's interview with "EAKX," March 23, 2016)

Even where the demand articulated in a petition was achieved, there is no especially strong reason to think that the petition was decisive.

Nonetheless, signing a petition was by far the most popular way to participate in the constitution-making process. Of the approximately two million written interactions between members of the public and the drafters of the constitution, less than 1 percent were substantive submissions described in the previous sections (Murray, 2001, 817). Almost everyone who participated in the constitution-making process did so through signing a petition. The fact that these petitions had so little effect and were given so little notice by the drafters calls the larger participation program into question in a significant way.

3.5 IN THE WORDS OF THE DRAFTERS

3.5.1 *Evidence from Interviews*

An important place to turn in seeking to understand how these popular inputs influenced the constitutional text is the drafters themselves. I spent the first four months of 2016 in South Africa, combing through archives and conducting interviews. I was able to complete twenty interviews with members of the Constitutional Assembly. These were semi-structured interviews conducted in person either in the home of the respondent or in their office. The respondents include people who were at the highest levels of the ANC and NP at the time and some who remain in government. I also had interviews with members of the other parties represented in the Constitutional Assembly. Given the sensitive nature of some of these issues in

South African politics today, all respondents were guaranteed anonymity, and they are identified here by a randomly generated four-letter label.[13] In general, the South African politicians I interviewed were remarkably straightforward and candid about their experiences in drafting the constitution.

In interviews with the author, drafters of the South African constitution all but denied the possibility that the submissions from the public significantly impacted the text of the constitution. Indeed, many of the drafters who were interviewed for this project provided rather negative assessments of the impact of public participation on their work. One individual who played a very important role in organizing the campaign for public participation even suggested that impact on the text was not the point of the process for public engagement (Author's interview with "GQOL," May 26, 2016). Rather, the process for public engagement was designed to create a sense of attachment between the people and the constitution.

In another interview, a negotiator for the ANC suggested that the process was a "party-driven negotiation," and that what mattered was the substance of the constitution, not its source (Author's interview with "CEQW," March 10, 2016). In a statement that closely aligns with the theory described in this paper, another ANC member asserted that decisions on the content of the constitution were made at the party conference and that members would abide by the party position. To the extent that comments from the public were heard, this respondent argued that they confirmed the ANC's positions (Author's interview with "DLSR," March 15, 2016). One opposition MP referred to the whole process of public consultation as a "sham" (Author's interview with "LCWS," March 24, 2016). Another member of the Constitutional Assembly described the impact of public submissions on the constitutional text as "close to zero" and "mere window dressing" (Author's interview with "HTWP," April 26, 2016).

Even in their published works, some of the members of the Constitutional Assembly are rather dismissive of the impact of public participation. For example, Tony Leon (then leader of the DP) wrote in his memoirs that "Whether a single clause or section was altered as a consequence of public input or pressure is doubtful" (Leon, 2008, 306). On the same page, Leon writes that "The [Theme] Committees had no mandate to conclude agreements; and I quickly realized that they were little more than a form of political occupational therapy"(Leon, 2008, 306).

On the related issue of whether the views of individual citizens are valuable to drafters, a similar negativity reigned. One member of an opposition party suggested:

You do get a lot of single-issue lunatics…The brutal truth is you know, short of being some major figure in the world, or in this country, so if Desmond Tutu said something that would have got a lot of attention…It's unfair this, but it's the way of the world. You did not give much attention to what one individual said, because in the nature of things

---

[13] This same anonymizing procedure is followed in each of the case studies.

it would then have been an endless process... So you did tend to pay more attention to organized inputs... It's very hard for an individual (however meritorious or serious minded) to influence a process like that. But I think that a reflection of reality, not an anti-individual bias. (Author's interview with "PNTO," May 17, 2016)

Reflecting the views of many of the interview respondents in a rather colorful description, another opposition member of the Constitutional Assembly stated:

If random Mr. X says something, how do you begin to process it? How much weight do you attach to it? It's, you know, like Stalin said of the Pope: 'How many battalions does the Pope command?'... The views of, in a sense, organized public, chambers of commerce, traditional leadership, the Volkstaat Council, organized agriculture, were far more seriously taken than random comments by random individuals. I think it served a completely different purpose, and the purpose was legitimating the constitution... The South African public felt like they'd been part of the process, and therefore made the end product more legitimate, (Author's interview with "LCWS," March 24, 2016)

However, this view was not universally held, one ANC member suggested:

I don't think what we do is to be guided more by the numbers than by the cogency of the reasoning behind a particular submission... We know that the majority is not necessarily correct at all times... So, there could be one individual who could come and convince a committee of parliament on a particular issue, while hundreds and thousands of others say something different, I mean see it differently. So, as leaders, as representatives of the people, we are required to use something like a strainer, to see which can go through and which need not go through. (Author's interview with "DLSR," March 15, 2016)

Across party lines, the South African drafters were broadly appreciative of the public participation process as a means of building public confidence in the legitimacy of the constitution, but were quite certain that there had been very little impact on the text from these public inputs.

3.5.2 *Evidence from Transcripts*

The plenary sessions of South Africa's Constitutional Assembly were recorded in the South African parliament's Hansard transcripts. This provides us with a complete record of the way in which submissions from the public were considered at this highest level of debate. However, the real forum for negotiations over constitutional content was the committees. The Constitutional Committee was the most important forum for high-level interparty negotiation, but most of the work relating to the submissions from the public was undertaken in the Theme Committees. There are minutes for each committee meeting, but these do not contain much detail. Audio recordings and transcriptions were made for a few meetings of Theme Committee 4 (which dealt with the Bill of Rights), but the rest appear to be unrecorded, or at least any record made at the time was not included in the National Archive. In this section, I first deal with the records of the plenary sessions of the Constitutional Assembly, and then describe what we can glean from the comparatively sparser record from the Theme Committees.

The plenary sessions of the Constitutional Assembly (in which the members of the National Assembly and the Senate sat in joint sessions) were occasions for the leaders of the parties to not only record some hits on their primary political opponents but also to address an audience outside the chamber. In these plenary debates (a record spanning some 1,188 pages), fifty-three speeches make explicit references to the submissions from the public and their bearing on the drafting process. Some of these are merely reports from the chairs of Theme Committees that detail how many submissions the committee has received, and provide some statement of how the report that they have forwarded to the Constitutional Committee takes these into account. The majority of the speeches that mention submissions from the public do so in a more substantively interesting way. These mentions of submissions from the public could be grouped into three categories: (1) exhortations for the Constitutional Assembly to learn from past examples and take public input seriously, (2) self-congratulation for how well the Constitutional Assembly has involved the public in the drafting process, and (3) criticisms that the Constitutional Assembly has not done enough to address the input from the public. I will describe each of these themes in turn.

While the public participation program in South Africa arose without significant planning, it found widespread support among members of the Constitutional Assembly, across party lines. Many of the senior members of the Constitutional Assembly had been participants in the negotiations over the interim constitution, and thus had experience with how submissions from the public could be mishandled in the midst of an intense interparty negotiation over critical choices in crafting the institutions of government. This experience led many to caution their colleagues in the early days of the process of drafting the final constitution that care would need to be taken to ensure that public participation was meaningful. For example, at the first meeting of the Constitutional Assembly, Janet Love (ANC) highlighted both the need to learn from past experience and the difficulty of reconciling expertise and public input.[14] Salie Manie (ANC) raised similar points, stating that:

People are talking about the miracle we have achieved, and I want to support that, but I think we also need to recognise that the previous process was also accompanied by shortcomings...We must admit that there was very little grassroots involvement in the process...We need to ask where the people on the ground and where the people in the Chamber fit into the process, and then develop a structure that ensures that all the people understand where and how they fit into that process.[15]

---

[14] J. Y. Love, Proceedings of the Constitutional Assembly (August 15, 1994), p. 46.
[15] M. S. Manie, Proceedings of the Constitutional Assembly (August 15, 1994), p. 57.

In a more pointed call to action in a later debate, Brigitte Mabandla of the ANC argued:

However, effective participation implies more than the establishment of consultative mechanisms. It also means that the concerns of our people should be taken seriously. Accordingly, people should not only be heard, but we must deliberate seriously on the needs and concerns articulated by our people.[16]

This suggestion that inputs from the people must be taken seriously was echoed by others, including Mohammed Valli Moosa (also from the ANC), who put this into even more powerful terms:

The legitimacy of a constitution is in no small way influenced by the legitimacy of the process which produces it. The proposals before the assembly today provides for extensive measures, in order to secure the involvement of the public. No stone will be left unturned in ensuring the involvement of all South Africans in the process. In doing this, merely calling on the public to make submissions, as we have done in the past, is simply not good enough. Only those with the means, the knowledge and the confidence to make submissions will do so. In other words, we will be flooded with submissions from those privileged sections of our community only. We need to take steps to ensure that the views of the disempowered majority in this country are also received in this House.[17]

Moosa's commentary presages a claim made in the practitioner literature of the early 2000s that was described in Chapter 2: That perceptions of the legitimacy of a constitution will be tied to the process through which it was written (Hart, 2003). Moreover, Moosa perceptively highlights the difficulty of effectively engaging with less-privileged South Africans, who would have less access to news about the proceedings, and perhaps also fewer opportunities to contribute their thoughts. This was of course borne out in the process, as many of the written submissions appear to have come from wealthier individuals with more conservative views. Clarence Makwetu (an ANC MP) echoed Moosa's comments, arguing that:

This exercise will be only worthwhile if it does not end up being another forum for academics, rich people, persons living in urban areas and elites only. The constitution-making process should earnestly endeavour to hear the views of the ordinary person in the street and those who live in the remotest parts of our country. Those people should feel part of this process and, at the end of the day, they should be able to claim this constitution as their own.[18]

[16] B. S. Mabandla, Proceedings of the Constitutional Assembly (September 5, 1994), p. 136.
[17] M. V. Moosa, Proceedings of the Constitutional Assembly (October 31, 1994), p. 221.
[18] C. M. Makwetu, Proceedings of the Constitutional Assembly (October 31, 1994), p. 239.

Other speakers also made reference to the legitimating effects of participation, most notably Roelf Meyer, who had been the chief negotiator for the NP during the process for drafting the interim constitution.[19]

The preliminary comments on the role of public input in the constitution-making process were brought to a close with some instructions from Cyril Ramaphosa, the chair of the Constitutional Assembly, who opined that: "We would like to believe that all information is not just going to be washed down the drain, but that it will be dealt with by the Theme Committee members who will, at a technical level and at a secretarial level, also be assisted by staff."[20] Even this final statement belies some doubt that the public participation process will actually have its intended effects on the development of the constitutional text. A year and a half later, Roelf Meyer appealed for the same thing, saying to his colleagues in the Constitutional Assembly that: "all of us should assume the responsibility of applying our minds to working through those submissions again, ensuring that in the process we are satisfied that all relevant submissions have been considered and attended to in such a way that we can give a response to those that took the trouble to make the submissions to the Constitutional Assembly."[21] In a reprise of the theme of the commentary in 1994, Patricia de Lille of the PAC stated that "I am just concerned that the constitution-making process will be reduced to the horse-trading that we saw at the World Trade Centre[22] in Kempton Park."[23]

As the drafting process unfolded, there were more mentions of submissions from the public as the chairs of the Theme Committees gave speeches updating the plenary group on the progress made in their committees. However, there is not much of substance here. The next significant mentions of the participation program for the most part take the form of self-congratulation, as at the end of the process many speeches thanked members of the public for their role in the drafting process. In April 1996, as the legally mandated date for completion of the final constitution approached, Cyril Ramaphosa congratulated all involved saying:

Participation in this process by interested parties, role-players, experts and, above all, the people of our country, has been facilitated, witnessed and encouraged. In order to bring the views of the South African public directly into the process, we launched what we can today call one of the country's biggest exercises in participatory democracy in the form of the public participation programme. Over two million people responded to the call by the Constitutional Assembly to participate in the constitution-making process. People participated by attending meetings arranged by the Constitutional Assembly. They participated by writing letters, by making submissions and even by making phone

---

[19] R. P. Meyer, Proceedings of the Constitutional Assembly (October 31, 1994), pp. 244–245.
[20] M. C. Ramaphosa, Proceedings of the Constitutional Assembly (October 31, 1994), p. 266.
[21] R. P. Meyer, Proceedings of the Constitutional Assembly (March 29, 1996), p. 13.
[22] Site of the negotiations that produced the interim constitution.
[23] P. de Lille, Proceedings of the Constitutional Assembly (March 29, 1996), p. 16.

calls to the Constitutional Assembly...We have made all efforts to respond to every submission.[24]

The next day his ANC colleague M. J. Mahlangu similarly praised the participatory process, noting its emotional impact on the members of the Constitutional Assembly:

Those were exciting moments for all of the CA members who participated in those discussions – to listen to the variety of the people of our community saying, for the first time in the history of South Africa, to the legislators of this country: This is how we want the constitution to be drafted, this is how we want our lives to be.[25]

Naledi Pandor of the ANC sounded a distinctly partisan note in her praise of the public participation process as she said: "The views put forward in the thousands of submissions received by the Constitutional Assembly attest to the link between the ANC's vision and the will of the people."[26]

The opposition parties were much less positive in their assessment of how public participation had influenced the drafting of the constitution. While the NP had very little to say about public participation (either in support or criticism), some of the minor parties did not hold back. Colin Eglin of the DP sounded a much more pessimistic note as he reflected on the way that the reality of the process had not quite lived up to its hopeful beginnings:

I must say a few words about this process. It started with public participation *in extenso*, the analysis and the collating work done by the six theme committees, the drafting, the redrafting and yet more redrafting in tandem with discussions of the Constitutional Committee and the subcommittees of the Constitutional Committee, and then, towards the end, multilateral and bilateral discussions. During this period the process has undergone certain changes of character from time to time, from tremendous transparency and inclusiveness at the early stages to a certain amount of opaqueness and exclusiveness with regard to the party-political bilaterals in recent weeks. As the process has taken place, its character has changed.[27]

The harshest critic of the way in which public participation had been bypassed in the constitution-making process was Kenneth Meshoe of the ACDP. In a number of speeches, he made specific references to aspects of the constitution where he claimed that public input had been ignored. These primarily related to religious issues, including the form of the reference to God in the preamble, and the failure of the constitution to regulate areas of concern for conservative Christians, such as pornography and abortion. Meshoe's comments on this theme highlight the same

---

[24] M. C. Ramaphosa, Proceedings of the Constitutional Assembly (April 23, 1996), p. 82.
[25] M. J. Mahlangu, Proceedings of the Constitutional Assembly (April 24, 1996), p. 180.
[26] G. N. M. Pandor, Proceedings of the Constitutional Assembly (April 24, 1996), p. 225
[27] C. W. Eglin, Proceedings of the Constitutional Assembly (April 23, 1996), p. 102.

dynamic described by Eglin, as the appearance of participatory constitution-making was undone by the reality of secretive negotiations. One of Meshoe's specific charges concerned the preamble, as he argued:

Thousands of ordinary Christians and citizens made submissions to the Constitutional Assembly about the preamble, in the hope that they would be considered. Now it appears that those concerns and submissions have been swept under the carpet. How can only two people from two political parties, namely Dr Boy Geldenhuys of the NP and Dr Blade Nzimande of the ANC, make a decision against millions of South Africans who voiced their desire by requesting the inclusion of "in humble submission to Almighty God" as the introduction to our preamble? This was done early in the morning in a committee consisting of two people, and we were not informed about that when the promise was made.[28]

Meshoe capped his criticisms of the way that the drafting process had (in his view) disregarded input from the people by demanding that some articles of the constitution be subjected to popular ratification. Laying down the gauntlet in perhaps unparliamentary language, Meshoe said: "Do honourable members[29] have the guts to let the public approve or dismiss the work done over the past months?"[30]

A middle path that in some ways explains the difference of opinion between the ANC and the minor opposition parties about how the public participation process was managed is found in Ohm Collins Chabane's response to Meshoe's complaint. Chabane described the ANC's approach to the submissions from the public as being part of a holistic process of considering many inputs about the constitution. He claimed that the ANC did in fact take submissions from the public into account, but not in the mechanistic way that Meshoe seemed to describe. Chabane argued:

We did not think that consideration of submissions meant that each and every issue raised on paper, in a telephone call or in a public meeting would need to find its way into the constitution. We thought that it meant we had to consider all the views, weigh their value with regard to other issues which were being raised by others, and take final decisions on various matters. That is how we have approached the issue, and that is why we, as the ANC, are sure that we did consider the various submissions which came from the public, political parties, public forums and all forums which we decided to approach people to participate in.[31]

We might note that Chabane's description of the process followed by the ANC says nothing about how much of the input from the public actually made it into the constitution. His comment is focused on the idea that the ANC took public

---

[28] K. R. Meshoe, *Proceedings of the Constitutional Assembly* (April 23, 1996), pp. 112–113.
[29] This is the usual way to refer to members of parliament.
[30] K. R. Meshoe, *Proceedings of the Constitutional Assembly* (April 24, 1996), p. 326.
[31] O. C. Chabane, *Proceedings of the Constitutional Assembly* (April 23, 1996), pp. 130–131.

inputs into account alongside the other sources of information that they thought were important.

Another member of the ANC from a different Theme Committee also defended another area of discrepancy between the submissions from the public and the content of the constitution, this time on more substantive grounds. Robert Davies argued that some of the submission from the public made proposals that were not appropriate for the new political dispensation in South Africa:

In preparing this Bill, we have had to confront a number of submissions and proposals... Several of these appeared to derive from notions that majority rule would inevitably lead to financial mismanagement and there was therefore a need to tie down future governments in the constitution in ways that the previous minority regime was not, and which did not apply to any other governments in the world. Some such proposals were based, frankly, on thinly disguised attempts to protect vested interests of the old order. To have acceded to them would have amounted to tying future governments down to arrangements which, at best, might seem to be reasonable now, and, at worst, reflected some fad in vogue in Newt Gingrich's Washington, but which may not necessarily be appropriate several decades from now when, we hope, this constitution will still be in force.[32]

What is obviously missing in all these references to submissions from the public, consultations, and hearings is any real attempt to engage in debate about the content of the constitution and its relationship to the input from the public. The exchanges between Kenneth Meshoe and various members of the ANC appeared to show a difference of opinion about how submissions from the public should be treated. However, it is clear that partisan dynamics are at work in these exchanges. Meshoe's ACDP was one of the smallest parties in the Constitutional Assembly and had not been successful in arguing its admittedly parochial interests with the larger parties. On certain issues, the ACDP might have been arguing a position held by the majority of South Africa's population. But this argumentative strategy was not necessarily a principled stand for greater democracy – it is a classic appeal to higher authority from a party on the losing side of a negotiation. On the whole, the plenary debates do not contain very much actual negotiation. Debates about the ways in which public submissions should be brought into the constitution should have happened in the Theme Committees and debates about constitutional language would have happened in the Constitutional Committee and its working groups. Thus, all that was left for the plenary meetings was broader rhetorical interventions. Nonetheless, these references to public participation in the larger debates help to fill in the picture of how political elites in South Africa treated input from the public in the constitution-making process.

---

[32] R. H. Davies, Proceedings of the Constitutional Assembly (April 24, 1996), p. 208.

Despite the relative scarcity of documentary records from the Theme Committees, there are two passages from the transcripts from Theme Committee 4 that illustrate both a problem with submissions from the public and their possible usefulness for drafters. During one of the first meetings of Theme Committee 4, the leader of the DP (Tony Leon) reminded the committee of the difficulties of incorporating the submissions from the public in the interim constitution that had been completed at Kempton Park in 1993. Discussing the need for an advertising campaign to encourage participation, Mr. Leon said that it should be:

Not Kempton Park style where you had Humanity for Hens[33] and everyone else who wrote in – just their stuff arrived and straight into the dustbin because of the problems of time... I mean the other factor we've got to ask ourselves political parties here represent the voters, the citizens of South Africa, all of them. How do you weigh up I mean you know we get a representation from an interest group or whatever it is, Humanity for Hens is the one that sticks in my mind for example. I mean you know what weight do we give it, I mean because the point is, it's very necessary but we are going to be festooned with paper. I mean when people start you know writing in they write in and the people who don't write in, who gets submissions from another way, it – we also got to take them seriously. But we also got to take ourself [sic] seriously as political representatives and it's also going to be an evaluation exercise perhaps we sort of just have to feel our way. (Hon. Anthony Leon, November 7, 1994, Theme Committee 4, Constitutional Assembly, Cape Town)

Mr. Leon's comments shed light on three key themes: (1) the vast amount of time required to give reasonable attention to submissions from the public, (2) the question of how representative the submissions are, and (3) the tension between representing the voters who placed these representatives in parliament and giving effect to the perhaps contradictory demands in the submissions.

The issue did not really come up again in the transcripts from the Theme Committee until almost a year later, when the lead negotiator from the NP (Sheila Camerer) attempted to prevent the committee from submitting a report to the main coordinating committee that went against the NP's position on the right to life and the death penalty. Camerer argued:

Isn't it a little premature perhaps to sort of finalise this report to the CC [Constitutional Committee] before we've actually had an opportunity here in this committee to discuss the public submissions... Because if you read the papers, there is an – you can be in no doubt as to what a lot of members of the public think about the right to life and limitations on that right and the way it should be qualified perhaps in relation to a possible death sentence... in my two previous experiences of Constitution – Constitutional negotiations... The public always came aboard and sent in a lot of submissions which were never really taken into account properly... but I mean anybody looking at those

---

[33] An NGO concerned about the treatment of fowl, particularly advocating for keeping laying hens in a free-range environment.

submissions, would be left with a clearer impression that the public is very concerned about certain issues in this Bill of Rights. (Hon. Sheila Camerer, August 7, 1995, Theme Committee 4, Constitutional Assembly, Cape Town)

The members of the ANC and DP on the committee quickly pointed out that Camerer only brought the submissions up as a way to support her party's position, and that there had been ample time up to that point for all concerned to deal with the content of the submissions – perhaps most appropriately by including this input in their party submission to the committee. Further, one of the ANC members questioned whether the NP would be willing to accept the majority view on other topics – the unstated rhetorical answer being a clear no. Here, one of the main possibilities for parties to make use of the submissions – as support for their position – was quickly shut down by the other parties. These two vignettes from the South African case amply illustrate the primacy of party in the constitutional negotiations and the difficulty drafters had in bringing the submissions from the public into the discussions in a meaningful way. The transcripts more broadly certainly do not lend any support for the idea that the submissions from the public had an impact on the constitutional text.

What emerges from the transcripts from both the plenary meetings of the Constitutional Assembly and the few transcripts from Theme Committee 4 is a picture of submissions from the public being used opportunistically, rather than examined systematically. South African politicians were very much aware of the need to legitimate the constitution through a large program of public consultation. The action of going to the people and listening was clearly important to many. However, apart from a few comments from Patricia de Lille,[34] and Roelf Meyer's injunction to act in such a way that one could "give a response to those that took the trouble to make the submissions to the Constitutional Assembly,"[35] the idea of accountability for the way that submissions were included in the draft seems to be missing. We also observe very few instances where submissions from the public are directly brought to bear in negotiations over text. Part of this is due, of course, to the sites for which we have transcripts. However, it is notable that the few times that attempts were made to use the authority of the people were the last resort of parties that had already lost the battle.

3.6 THE CONSTITUTIONAL PRINCIPLES AS A LIMITING FACTOR

As discussed earlier, the 1993 constitution was the product of negotiations between a non-democratic government and the as-yet unelected leadership of the ANC. While

---

[34] P. de Lille, Proceedings of the Constitutional Assembly (March 29, 1996), p. 16.
[35] R. P. Meyer, Proceedings of the Constitutional Assembly (March 29, 1996), p. 13.

winning a free and fair election is certainly not the only way that a political party can establish legitimate claims to political power, it is still important to note that the two major players in the negotiations over the 1993 constitution lacked this credential. It is of further note that, while much of the negotiation over the 1993 constitution and other issues discussed at CODESA and the MPNP took place in the open, it was well known then and now that a great deal was decided in private, and often just between Meyer and Ramaphosa. All of this matters because the constitution that was written by the elected representatives of the people between 1994 and 1996 was limited in its possible content by the Constitutional Principles contained in the 1993 constitution. Mutua (1997, 81) describes the Constitutional Principles as an "iron box" for the ANC and a "shield" for the White minority. Presenting a view that undermines the legitimacy of the 1996 constitution, Mutua (1997, 81) goes on to suggest that "In a sense, the validity of the 1996 Constitution rests on the all-white Parliament that approved the Interim Constitution, and the Constitutional Court, which is an appointed body. The Constitutional Assembly, the body actually representing the will of all South Africans, essentially rubber-stamped prior political choices, despite projecting the perception that it was making a new constitution." In this argument, Mutua contests the legitimacy of a process that sought to ensure the continuity of constitutional law, rather than establish a break with the apartheid past.

Other scholars have focused more on the problems inherent in the two-stage process. Summarizing arguments against the democratic bona fides of the 1996 constitution (which is not his own argument), South African legal scholar Botha (2010) writes:

One line of argument might interrogate the manner in which the sovereignty of the people, in whose name the Constitution was adopted, was systematically weakened by a two-stage process that bound the people's elected representatives to prior agreements between political elites. As a result, it might be argued, the voice of 'the people' was drowned out by the buzz of elite bargaining, the noisy arguments of lawyers and the pronouncements of judges. Sovereignty was splintered by a political deal which fragmented the constitution-making process and turned it into the preserve of lawyers, judges and technocrats. Constituent power was effectively reduced to constituted power, which had to comply not only with the procedural requirements entrenched in the interim Constitution, but also had to heed the 'solemn pact' represented in the Constitutional Principles.

Botha goes on to present his own argument, which holds that the two-stage process was both the best that could have been done and an idea that came from the ANC, and so was not problematic as the abovementioned quotation would suggest.

However, it is a vitally important critique of the process from the perspective of the research questions advanced in this project. The analysis discussed earlier has shown that public participation had very little impact on the text of the constitution, either in broad terms of agenda setting or in the specific words that are found in the completed text. This lack of impact has been argued to have been a result of the fiercely partisan nature of the negotiations, but this low-impact outcome was to some degree foreordained by the fact that the 1996 constitution would have to be in compliance with the Constitutional Principles. On this basis, even if the whole of the population of South Africa had demonstrated their steadfast opposition to federalism, the drafters of the constitution would still have been required to create an essentially federal vertical separation of powers (see Constitutional Principles XVII–XXVII). The interim constitution was even less open to popular input than the final constitution, having been negotiated in a much less transparent way and with a constant threat of violence hanging over the proceedings. We should not forget that, in the early 1990s, South Africa's townships were wracked by violence, the right-wing extremist Afrikaner Weerstandsbeweging (AWB) actually launched a violent assault on the CODESA proceedings, and fears of a military coup were also very real. In this context, there was not much room for public input on the interim constitution. By the time the drafters arrived at the negotiations over the final text, they were significantly bound by the Constitutional Principles and by deeply entrenched party positions.

3.7 CONCLUSION

The South African case allows us to examine the impact of public participation in a political system with strong parties. The constitution-making process was dominated, to a large extent, by the key conflict between the NP and the ANC over a number of issues, including group rights and economic concerns. As described earlier, the conflict in this case was between two strong parties with very different electoral bases. Added to this was the very real possibility of the outbreak of large-scale violence if the process had not been properly managed. The NP entered into this process with the knowledge that they could not win control of parliament (and thus the presidency) for the foreseeable future and needed to protect their interests against future actions of the ANC through the constitutional text wherever possible. Beyond these immediate and very pressing concerns for economic stability and preventing bloodshed, both parties had been considering how the constitution would have to change to accommodate multiracial democracy for many years – decades in the case of the ANC. The practical import of these various factors was that in the constitutional negotiations (which unfolded over a period of six years in various forms and stages) the positions of these two main parties were in many areas very clear and firmly entrenched. Both parties understood their prerogatives and the necessity of getting to a text that would, to the greatest extent possible, protect the interests of their constituencies.

In this context, it was never likely that public participation could have a real impact on the text. And, in stark contrast with the views and recollections of the Brazilian and Icelandic drafters that are discussed in later chapters, the South African drafters were on the whole very pessimistic in their assessment of the impact of public participation on the development of the constitutional text. The South African public participation program may not have been quite as efficiently managed as the Brazilian process, but it did reach a broad swath of the population. The failure of this process to influence the text demonstrates that a willing public and a well-financed program are insufficient supports for effective public participation. Even the best arguments and suggestions from citizen-participants are unlikely to have an impact when the text of the constitution is a battleground between well-prepared and highly disciplined political parties.

Yet, there is reason to believe that the public participation process was successful in generating legitimacy for the constitution and the process that created it. The survey research conducted by CASE that was described earlier in the chapter certainly lends credence to the idea that the members of the South African public both overestimated the effectiveness of their participation and that their participation increased their feelings of ownership of the constitution. Summarizing the participatory process from the perspective of rhetorical analysis, Salazar writes: "The [Constitutional] Assembly establishes its own legitimacy by stimulating the existence of popular 'collective wisdom' and by projecting the fiction that the Constitutional Assembly, beyond its legislative frame, realizes – makes real – the voices of that collective will. The operation is neither fully credible nor fully completed nor entirely successful" (Salazar, 2002, 74). This connection between a fiction of participatory constitution-making as a realization of the collective will and the legitimacy of the constitution is important in all the cases considered in this book, but perhaps most important in South Africa. The public participation program was a success insofar as it enhanced the legitimacy of the constitution. However, this advantage may be based on a false assessment of the effectiveness of popular involvement.

4

Brazil: Citizen Entrepreneurs

4.1 INTRODUCTION

The popular mythology of the Brazilian constitution-making process gives pride of place to the role of citizens in shaping the text. Indeed, the constitution of 1988 is often referred to as the "constituição cidadã" (citizens' constitution), using the evocative title given to the constitution by the president of the constitutional assembly, Ulysses Guimarães, in his speech promulgating the new constitution.[1] In the same speech, Guimarães claimed that the constitution was created by the "breath of people, of the street, of the square, of the favela, of the factory, of workers, cooks, underprivileged people, indigenous people, squatters, businessmen, retirees, civil servants and military personnel, testifying to the contemporaneity and social authenticity of the text that now comes into force."[2] The members of the Constituent Assembly whom I interviewed in 2015 were effusive in their description of the role and influence of the citizens of Brazil in the making of the constitution. As one respondent stated: "What we had during the constitutional assembly was a nearly permanent dialogue with society, many meetings and hearings to make the constitution compatible with what Brazilians hoped for in that new political moment" (Interview with "AOTK," November 20, 2015).[3] Public statements by Brazilian politicians consistently give the impression that the public participation in the drafting process was vital and effective.

This chapter interrogates this popular mythology, seeking to empirically test the claim that this was the citizens' constitution. There could be a range of meanings behind the label of the citizens' constitution. This could be a claim that, in

---

[1] Ulysses Guimarães, October 5, 1988, Ata da 341a. Sessão, Assembleia Nacional Constituinte, Brasília.
[2] "Há, portanto, representativo e oxigenado sopro de gente, de rua, de praça, de favela, de fábrica, de trabalhadores, de cozinheiros, de menores carentes, de índios, de posseiros, de empresários, de estudantes, de aposentados, de servidores civis e militares, atestando a contemporaneidade e autenticidade social do texto que ora passa a vigorar."
[3] "Mas o que tivemos durante a constituinte foi um diálogo quase que permanente com a sociedade, muitas reuniões e audiências para compatibilizar o que os brasileiros esperavam daquele novo momento político."

contradistinction to the constitution under the military regime, this new constitution was drafted to serve the interests of the people. It could also imply a sense that the people of Brazil had moved for this constitution in some meaningful way. However, the approach that is taken in this research is to suggest that, if the opportunity for public participation is pitched in terms such as "you too are a member of the constituent assembly" (as the public participation process was advertised in Brazil), then it would follow that the text of the constitution should show some impact from public participation. If, as Guimarães claimed, the constitution was infused with or born from the breath of the people, then we should see evidence throughout the text that this popular participation had an impact.

The constitution-making process in Brazil began thirty years ago, and is not well known to scholars who do not specialize in Latin American politics. A few sentences to briefly justify the decision to make Brazil's experience of constitution-making one of the primary foci of this book are therefore helpful at this point. Beyond the analytical advantages of the most similar systems' comparison between Brazil and South Africa, Brazil on its own presents an important case for the research questions tackled in this book for several reasons. First, Brazil was one of the first countries to draft a constitution in a process that included significant levels of direct public participation. Second, the various means of popular participation in Brazil were highly innovative and featured the best technology then available. Third, some of these avenues for public input were created by government offices without apparent popular (or necessarily elite) demand, while others were demanded by social groups. Fourth, the political context in Brazil, featuring a democratic transition amid a chaotic party system, pushed drafters to think about the immediate political implications of decisions on constitutional content and raised the stakes of these decisions for many actors. These factors make the Brazilian case an excellent source of empirical data on the impact of public participation, and a good case to explore in the interests of learning what might be successful in other cases.

The Brazilian constitution as ratified in 1988 ended up being a very long, unwieldy, and perhaps unworkable document. Then President José Sarney was blunt in his judgment of the penultimate draft in a famous televised speech on July 26, 1988, saying that the constitution would make the country ungovernable. He further argued that the constitution also posed risks to businesses, labor relations, families, and Brazilian society itself (Folha de São Paulo, 1988). When I interviewed him in 2015, Sarney was perhaps more positive in his outlook, but repeated his skepticism about the text as it was initially ratified in 1988, suggesting that many amendments to the initial text were required to achieve governability (Interview with the author, November 19, 2015). Sarney lost the argument in 1988, as his televised address was followed by a speech in the same format a day later in which Guimarães responded with a forceful endorsement of the constitution. Guimarães argued that the draft would be the constitution of the people and would be the guardian of governability (Bonavides and de Andrade, 1989, 495).[4] The Congress sitting as the Constituent Assembly sided with Guimarães and overwhelmingly approved the draft.

Certainly, the comparative rate of amendments to the Brazilian constitution suggests the unfinished or perhaps problematic nature of the constitutional text. Brazil's constitution stands out in a comparative analysis, averaging more than three amendments per year since 1988. The threshold to pass a constitutional amendment in Brazil is not especially low, but this does not seem to matter much in this case. In President Sarney's view, it is in practice easier to pass a constitutional amendment than regular legislation (Interview with the author, November 19, 2015).[5] Passing a constitutional amendment is a relatively unremarkable occurrence in contemporary Brazilian political life. The chief of staff of a prominent senator suggested to me that the constitution remains somewhat dysfunctional and requires constant amendment to get things done in government – even necessities like making minor alterations to the tax code (Author's interview with "MHKR", November 18, 2015). However, the core principles of the 1988 constitution have remained unchanged by these myriad amendments (Zaiden Benvindo, 2016).

This lengthy, complex, and perhaps yet unfinished constitution is a product of a lengthy, complex, and participatory process. The Brazilian case is the anchor for this comparative study, with South Africa and Iceland providing us with cases that feature variation on the key independent variable: the strength of the political parties. In this chapter, we will consider the various elements of the drafting process that contributed to the constitution of Brazil, with particular emphasis on the political parties and the various mechanisms for public participation.

4.2 HISTORICAL BACKGROUND

In each of the cases considered in this book, I argue that the political context is one of the keys to understanding how public participation was or was not effective in producing changes to the text of the constitution. Brazil's process of transition from a civil-military authoritarian regime to democracy in the 1980s has been thoroughly examined by political scientists, including the influential works by Stepan (1989), Mainwaring (1999), and Ames (2002a). The elements of that transition that are most important for our present inquiry are the enduring weakness of the political

---

4 "A Constituição, com as correcções que faremos, será a guardiã de governabilidade... Esta Constituição, o povo brasileiro me autoriza a proclamá-la, não ficará como bela estátua inacabada, mutilada ou profanada. O povo nos mandou aqui para fazê-la, não para ter medo." Quoted in Bonavides and de Andrade (1989, 495).
5 Constitutional amendments require a 3/5 majority in both chambers of the Congress (rather than the simple majority required for ordinary legislation), but do not offer the president the opportunity for approval or veto.

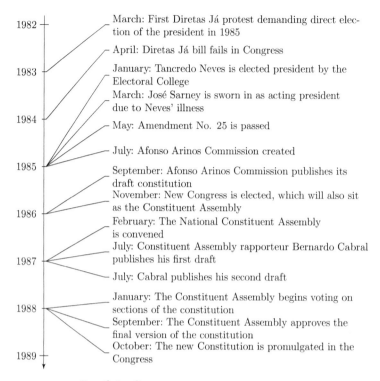

1982 — March: First Diretas Já protest demanding direct election of the president in 1985

April: Diretas Já bill fails in Congress

1983 — January: Tancredo Neves is elected president by the Electoral College
March: José Sarney is sworn in as acting president due to Neves' illness

1984 — May: Amendment No. 25 is passed

July: Afonso Arinos Commission created

1985 — September: Afonso Arinos Commission publishes its draft constitution
November: New Congress is elected, which will also sit as the Constituent Assembly

1986 — February: The National Constituent Assembly is convened
July: Constituent Assembly rapporteur Bernardo Cabral publishes his first draft

1987 — July: Cabral publishes his second draft

January: The Constituent Assembly begins voting on sections of the constitution

1988 — September: The Constituent Assembly approves the final version of the constitution
October: The new Constitution is promulgated in the Congress

1989

FIGURE 4.1 Brazil timeline

parties, the continued strong role for the president, the active participation of interest groups at various levels of politics, and the repertoires of political action that were learned during the protest movement for direct election of the president (known as Diretas Já).

Brazil experienced elements of a liberal political system late in the Imperial period, but did not achieve full democracy until the end of Getulio Vargas' "Estado Novo" dictatorship in 1945. That first period of democracy was marked by political instability and a post-war economic decline. This democratic interlude ended with a military coup in 1964. The military regime ruled Brazil under a system of limited political competition until liberalization began in the early 1980s. Many of the political parties and social movements that contributed to the 1988 constitution had their roots in the opposition to this military regime. The ratification of the new constitution in 1988 signaled the completion of the formal aspects of the return to democracy. More than this, many Brazilians associated the return to procedural democracy with improvements in social and economic conditions. These broader hopes for what the return to democracy would accomplish are the reason that the constitution of 1988 became such a long and all-encompassing text.

The importance of the Diretas Já movement to the return of democracy in Brazil and to the drafting of the constitution should not be underestimated. By the mid-1980s, Brazil had been ruled by a military dictatorship for two decades, and things were beginning to come apart. In particular, the economy was in a severe state of disarray, with high levels of inflation and unemployment (Parkin, 1991; Cardoso and Urani, 1995). As early as 1982, there began to be encouraging signs that a democratic opening was possible. The elections held that year were the first since the coup that allowed direct election of state governors, and opposition party candidates won executive office in the key states of São Paulo, Rio de Janeiro, and Minas Gerais. Perhaps more importantly, the revamped party of the dictatorship (Partido Democrático Social, PDS) lost its majority in the Chamber of Deputies (Skidmore, 1988, 234).

Fundamentally, Diretas Já was about the election of the president (the name itself referencing the key demand of "direct elections now"), but the movement was larger. For years, smaller groups of Brazilians had been campaigning for various political causes, but they began to work together more in the early 1980s. As Hochstetler (2000, 170) describes it, "The crowning moment of this strategy was indeed the campaign, which pulled literally millions of people into the streets for festive rallies for direct elections of the president in 1985." A number of notable rallies took place in the early months of 1984 (including one that exceeded one million participants in Rio de Janeiro in April), forcing media coverage and a response from the military regime (Bertoncelo, 2009, 185). In the end, the Diretas Já movement was unsuccessful in its primary goal, and the electoral college selected a new president in 1985. Yet, Diretas Já achieved a notable success in laying the groundwork for popular mobilization in the constitution-making process that began two years later. Despite the indirect election of the president in 1985, the 1982 elections had given the opposition parties enough seats in the electoral college to make an important step toward democratization. The electoral college rejected the military regime's candidate and selected Tancredo Neves to be the new president. Neves was a strong supporter of a new constitution, and although he died before taking office, his election was an important event in the larger constitution-making process.

Within this broader political context, it is vital to note the effects of the choice of drafting body. Perhaps as a compromise with the still-powerful military leadership, the choice was made to have the Congress that was elected in 1986 both exercise its normal powers and also sit as a constituent assembly (Martínez-Lara, 1996, 57). This decision invoked both concerns about self-dealing on the part of the legislature (Elster, 1995; Ginsburg et al., 2009) and brought the problems created by weak and clientelistic political parties directly into the constitution-making process. It was also an early defeat for the popular movements that had formed to support public involvement in the drafting process (including many who had participated in the Diretas Já protests), and demanded a separately elected constituent assembly (Michiles et al., 1989, 45).

TABLE 4.1 *The constitutional drafts*

Draft	Date	Words	Articles	Similarity to final (%)
1967 Constitution	Jan 1967	21,808	189	22
Afonso Arinos	Sept 1986	38,545	436	27
Preliminary draft	Jun 1987	56,770	501	37
Cabral I	Jul 1987	52,310	496	37
Cabral II	Sept 1987	42,234	264	54
Draft A	Nov 1987	43,558	271	59
Draft B	Jun 1988	46,362	245	84
Draft C	Sept 1988	47,486	244	88
Draft D	Sept 1988	46,924	245	90
Final draft	Oct 1988	39,903	245	–
Constitution in 2020	Aug 2020	54,373	250	63

4.3   THE NATIONAL CONSTITUENT ASSEMBLY

Following agreement on the broad outlines of the drafting process, the Assembleia Nacional Constituinte (National Constituent Assembly) began its work on February 1, 1987. The 559 members of the Constituent Assembly were divided into eight committees, each tasked with a specific area of the constitution to debate. The committees' work included holding between five and eight hearings where they were to listen to presentations from members of the public and representatives of interest groups with a stake in that part of the constitution. Though some have criticized this aspect of the process as a distraction (Rosenn, 1990), contemporary accounts suggested that these hearings were not well attended by members of the Constituent Assembly (Jornal da Tarde, 1987). The text was drafted in eight mostly distinct stages. The development of the constitutional text was as tortuous as one might expect in a process that involved such a large and undisciplined drafting body. To aid the reader in understanding the order of the drafts and how much the text changed between them, those data are summarized in Table 4.1. The most infamous of these various drafts was Draft A, compiled by the powerful Systematization Commission in November 1987. This draft sought to bring together the disparate sections prepared by many authors into one document. Its failure in this pursuit was immortalized with the nickname of "Frankenstein" (Gomes, 2006). The move from Draft D to the final text involved individual votes on each of the 245 articles – requiring majority approval in both of two rounds of voting. Finally, the text was lightly edited for style.

During the period when the constitution was drafted, the chronically unstable Brazilian party system was in a period of greater than normal flux. As Mainwaring (1999) argues in his book on the Brazilian party system, various aspects of Brazil's political history had prevented the natural emergence of an institutionalized party system. Beyond this, the party system had been purposefully re-engineered by the

Brazilian government twice during the twentieth century: First by the authoritarian Getulio Vargas in 1945 and then by the military regime in 1979. The renovation post 1979 was particularly important in its effect of splintering the opposition to the slowly retrenching military regime into numerous political parties. Between the coup in 1964 and the new law governing political parties in 1979, there were only two parties: Aliança Renovadora Nacional (ARENA), which represented the military regime in the Congress, and the sanctioned opposition party, the Movimento Democrático Brasileiro (MDB). The "reform" of 1979 was designed to weaken the ability of the MDB to be successful in the election of 1982 by creating an environment in which the MDB was likely to split into a number of new parties. Thus, when the Congress (also sitting as the Constituent Assembly) was elected in 1986, the political parties were still either new or recently renamed.

The members of the Congress were an interesting mix of individuals who had supported the military regime as members of ARENA, others who had been members of Congress under the MDB or one of the new parties, and a large number of people with minimal experience in the federal Congress. One group within the Constituent Assembly also deserves special notice. Because the terms of senators under the 1967 Constitution were eight years in duration, there were twenty-three senators in the Congress that was seated in 1986 who were holdovers from the electoral system as it existed under the military dictatorship. This led to an under-representation of more liberal interests in the Constituent Assembly (Rosenn, 1990).

After the election of 1986, ten parties were represented in the Congress (and thus the Constituent Assembly.[6] The immediate successor to the MDB, the Partido do Movimento Democrático Brasileiro (PMDB), fared even better than expected in

TABLE 4.2 *Parties in the Brazilian Constituent Assembly (Feb 1987)*

Party	Number	Percent
Party of the Brazilian Democratic Movement (PMDB)	303	54.2
Liberal Front Party (PFL)	135	24.2
Democratic Social Party (PDS)	38	6.8
Democratic Labour Party (PDT)	26	4.7
Brazilian Labour Party (PTB)	18	3.2
Workers' Party (PT)	16	2.9
Liberator Party (PL)	7	1.3
Christian Democratic Party (PDC)	6	1.1
Brazilian Communist Party (PCB)	3	0.5
Communist Party of Brazil (PCdoB)	3	0.5
Brazilian Socialist Party (PSB)	2	0.4
Social Christian Party (PSC)	1	0.2
Party of the Brazilian Women (PMB)	1	0.2
Total	559	

[6] This was the first election after the return to civilian rule, and also the first election in which illiterate citizens had the right to vote.

the 1986 election, capturing more than 50 percent of the seats in both the Chamber of Deputies and the Senate. With this commanding position in the Constituent Assembly, the PMDB had enough votes to implement its agenda for the constitution without support from any other party. This did not happen for two reasons. First, like almost all of the Brazilian political parties, the PMDB was almost entirely lacking in party discipline. Second, with the exception of the Partido dos Trabalhadores (PT), none of the political parties had published proposals for the constitution either during the 1986 election or even during the main portion of the constitution-drafting process.

Mainwaring and Pérez-Liñán (1997) have shown that these parties were remarkably undisciplined in their voting behavior during the constitution-making process. The combination of low ideological identity within the parties, legacies of clientelistic behavior, and low party discipline created both a very fluid party system within the Constituent Assembly and a context in which individuals and groups outside the legislature could have influence. The lack of party unity was so severe that the PMDB actually split late in the constitution-making process as the left wing of the party departed to form the new Partido da Social Democracia Brasileira (PSDB) in June 1988.

Later in the constitution-making process, it became apparent that some sort of discipline would be necessary to carry the project to completion. In this context, a coalition of members of various parties formed, called the Centrão. The Centrão was able to form a united front to pass changes to the procedural rules of the Constituent Assembly and eventually to pass a final draft of the constitution. The Centrão is thus an example of the difference between parties in the electorate and parties in the legislature. This dynamic echoes in Brazil's contemporary political system, as there is evidence to suggest that the parties are now more disciplined in their voting, but the individualistic nature of the electoral campaigns remains (Figueiredo and Limongi, 2000).

There is also debate about whether the Centrão was a procedural coalition solely or whether there was a more significant ideological aspect to the coalition. In an interview, one prominent member of the Centrão described his view of the group as a necessary coalition to stop the leftists in the Constituent Assembly (Author's interview with "KPUE", Brasília, November 19, 2015). In Ames's (2002a) account, it was both. The Centrão was created to make it easier to amend the draft constitution that was published by the central committee that had integrated the drafts from the thematic committees (Commissão de Sistematização). But, the motivation for altering this draft was an objection to its content, which was seen by members of the Centrão as being far too progressive and perhaps even socialist.

Crucially for the argument advanced in this book, the lack of party discipline (and overall systemic weakness) provided a space for effective public participation. In fact, activists for various constitutional causes paid more attention to constitutional issues over a longer period of time than any of the parties. The noted historian of the Brazilian constitution-making process, Martínez-Lara (1996, 196–197), writes:

The weakness of political parties had its counterpart in the aggressive role played by organized interest groups in shaping the decisions of Congress. The process of constitutional renewal displayed the enormous strength and complexity of Brazil's civil society. A wide range of organized interest groups and professional lobbies of all imaginable variations mobilized to press the Constituent Congress. Among these, [was] the movement for popular participation which managed to persuade Congress to provide direct access to the constitutional deliberations, through the popular amendments, as well as the incorporation of some direct forms of participation in the constitutional text itself. In their attempts to influence the decision-making, these groups showed a high level of organizational sophistication, using all types of available methods: direct influence in the selection of candidates responsive to their demands, the use of all forms of media communication, as well as more direct methods, such as rallies and demonstrations.

As Martínez-Lara describes, many civil society organizations (CSOs) were better organized than the political parties. The weakness of the parties and their lack of an agenda for constitutional reform allowed outsize influence for these groups. To be sure, there were areas where the agenda of CSOs was blocked, most notably in the removal of a provision on land tenure reform late in the drafting process. However, there were a number of victories for groups outside the Constituent Assembly. In the balance of the chapter, we will examine in more detail the various forms of public participation that were used by individuals and groups and assess the impact that these public interventions had on the development of the constitutional text.

4.4 POPULAR PARTICIPATION – INDIVIDUALS

Popular participation in the constitution-making process in Brazil took place in several ways, principally through (1) written submissions, (2) public hearings, (3) direct lobbying of Constituent Assembly members, and (4) public demonstrations. Both the state government of São Paulo and the federal Senate organized opportunities for citizens to make written submissions to the Constituent Assembly. These are dealt with in separate sections later.

In addition to the more formal systems for citizen participation described in the following sections, many Brazilian citizens participated in the constitution-making process by sending letters and telegrams to their elected representatives. Most of these are lost, or preserved only in the personal records of the representatives. The staff at the Congressional archive report that there is no single, centralized repository of the correspondence received by members of Congress. However, one large collection of letters was preserved in the archives of the Museum of the Republic and was the subject of a book and a museum exhibit that coincided with the twentieth anniversary of the ratification of the constitution (Santana, 2009). The letters (numbering 5,245 in this collection) were recognized as a historical resource when they began to arrive in the 1980s, and have since been professionally curated and digitized.

The letters were also well studied in a doctoral dissertation written by a Brazilian historian, Maria Helena Versiani. The collection that Versiani (2013) analyzed includes a large number of letters related to a campaign that began in 1985 for a participatory constituent assembly. That demand was ultimately refused, but the campaign led to the creation of more opportunities for citizen engagement than might otherwise have existed.7 The letters also include a large number of requests for constitutional provisions that would make a difference in the day-to-day lives of Brazilians. One early group of these letters was sent to a commission of legal scholars and politicians (the Afonso Arinos Commission) who wrote a draft constitution in 1985 that was intended to be a basis for the later drafting process in the Congress (this draft is discussed further at the end of the chapter). The majority of the letters were written during the time that the Constituent Assembly was elected and installed, in 1986 and 1987. Explaining the very few letters that arrived in 1988 (the year the constitution was promulgated), Versiani suggests that by that time more letters were irrelevant to the drafting process (Versiani, 2013, 147). Broadly, Versiani argues that these letters were an important form of political participation and focuses on the letters in relation to their authors. She does not advance an argument about how these letters impacted the text of the constitution.

A large number of the letters (1,308 or 30 percent) were written by groups, but the vast majority are from individuals. In addition to various idiosyncratic personal requests, many of the letters conformed to scripts created by the social movements that sprang up during the transition to democracy, especially in the Diretas Já movement. Also, many of the letters communicate a concrete and pressing physical need. These authors describe situations of hunger and deprivation and direct their requests to the president or other political leaders (Versiani, 2013, 154–155). While the letters came from almost all states of Brazil, the vast majority were sent by residents of the more economically developed cities of the south and south-east (Versiani, 2013, 161). Versiani makes an effort to describe the various economic situations represented in the letters, but it is notable that more than half of the letters were typed on a word processor and most of the remainder were composed on a typewriter, suggesting that the majority of the authors were educated and relatively prosperous (Versiani, 2013, 164), or were assisted by people who were. It is also notable that the majority of these letter writers were men.

One of the earliest government-organized systems to facilitate citizen participation in the constitution-making process came from the state government of São Paulo. The newly formed Secretariat for Decentralization and Participation set up a system in 1986 that allowed citizens to contribute to the dialogue about the new constitution by calling a phone line or by sending in a letter (de Mendonça, 1987). These contributions were then put together in a book that was presented to the Constituent Assembly by the governor of the state of São Paulo, Franco Montoro, in May

---

7 I discuss this issue more in the section on popular amendments.

1987. A summary of each of the nearly 5,000 suggestions in this book, along with the name, address, and occupation of the person who called or wrote, was published in the journal of the Constituent Assembly (Assembleia Nacional Constituinte, 1987, 408–498).

The content of the book, entitled *As Sugestões do Povo de São Paulo à Assembleia Nacional Constituinte* (Suggestions of São Paulo People to the National Constituent Assembly), was covered lightly by the press at the time. The observations of the journalists are interesting both for their vaguely elitist interpretation of what the people had to say and their correspondence with what we find in the other principal source of written suggestions (covered later).

For example, one newspaper article notes that one of the subjects of concern for those who participated in this program was a suggestion that the selection of the manager (técnico/treinador) of the national soccer team should be the subject of a nationwide plebiscite (Christiano, 1987). To most scholars, this would not seem like an important issue for the constitution to cover – and this was certainly the judgment of the journalist. A search of the larger set of suggestions collected by the federal senate (SAIC – detailed in the following section) shows that this individual was not unique. In the 72,719 suggestions in that database, "futebol" (soccer) is mentioned 506 times, while the national team (a seleção brasileira) is mentioned 30 times. At least five individuals proposed that the manager of the national team should be elected in some fashion.[8] This particular issue is not surprising in the context of Brazil's obsession with soccer, but it serves to illustrate the fact that citizens were in some cases more eager to participate than informed about what a constitution normally accomplishes.

Nevertheless, the majority of the suggestions in this volume addressed topics that were germane to the political discussions going on in the Constituent Assembly.

4.4.1 *SAIC: A Cutting-Edge 1980s Database*

One of the most fascinating pieces of documentary evidence from the constitution-making process in Brazil comes from an initiative to collect the views of Brazilian citizens via postcards. For some months in 1987, Brazilians could pick up a preprinted card at a post office, fill in some information about themselves in the spaces provided (such as age, sex, education, occupation, income, and place of residence), and write some suggestions for the constitution in a box that covered about half of this card (the full card being about half the size of an A4 page). The initiative was managed by the federal Senate's information technology office, known as Prodasen (Processamento de Dados do Senado Federal). The data included in the

---

[8] For example: "Sugiro que o treinador da seleção brasileira seja eleito (por prazo determinado) mediante todos os prefeitos municipais do Brasil. Sendo as grandes capitais poderia se dar um 'peso' maior de voto. Por exemplo, o prefeito de São Paulo ou do Rio de Janeiro, teria um peso de três votos Creio que uma escolha assim não deixaria motivo para queixas a ninguém, porque, afinal, o treinador da seleção brasileira de futebol seria eleito pelos mais legítimos representantes do povo" (suggestion no. 43488, SAIC).

returned cards (72,719 were sent back to Prodasen) were then entered into an electronic database called the "Sistema de Apoio Informático à Constituinte" (SAIC),[9] and the information made available to the drafters of the new constitution.[10] The suggestions thus collected were manually coded according to subject (for example, "pro-presidentialism"). The Prodasen staff then created a massive book with tables detailing the levels of support and opposition for various possible constitutional provisions, often broken down by demographic and geographic categories (Monclaire et al., 1991). Beyond this postcard-based set of submissions, the Prodasen office was very active throughout the drafting process in preparing submissions from the public for the use of the members of the Constituent Assembly. A number of tables describing aspects of the SAIC database are found in the Appendix to this chapter.

The submissions included in the SAIC data show interesting patterns, especially patterns of text repetition. There appear to have been both large- and small-scale campaigns to send in specific text, or a specific submission to the Constituent Assembly. In some cases, it looks like a small group of neighbors got together to write the same suggestion on several cards, in others it appears that an individual or organization organized a small campaign for a particular provision. In addition to these small-scale attempts to influence the Constituent Assembly, there are some instances where a particular submission was copied many hundreds of times. I provide examples and details of some large and small campaigns later in this section.

To fully capture the patterns of text repetition, we can look for matching pairs of texts. The idea of a pair of submissions matching in their content has a fairly intuitive meaning, but there are myriad ways in which this analysis could be conducted. In the analysis conducted here (using WCopyfind 4.1.5), a matching pair is found when two submissions contained identical strings of text of a length of at least six words (allowing for one imperfection per string), and the total number of matching words between the two texts was thirty or more. Altering any of these parameters would change the number of matching pairs that are found. Among the 72,719 suggestions, there are 845,040 matching pairs. To put this number in some kind of perspective, if all of the 72,719 texts were essentially identical, this method of finding repeated text would return 2,643,990,121 matching pairs.[11] So, while the number of submissions that were part of a scheme of submitting identical submissions is very large, they did not completely dominate the database.

Interestingly, only six of the submissions have enough matching text with the 1988 constitution to show up as a match with these parameters. None of these

---

[9] System of Computer Support to the Constituent Assembly.
[10] However, in my interviews (albeit twenty-eight years later), the respondents were unable to specifically recall this database.
[11] 72,719(72,7219-1)/2.

TABLE 4.3 *Degrees of pattern matching*

Percentage of shared text	Number of pairs
Greater than 25%	838,239
Greater than 50%	750,844
Greater than 75%	378,632
Greater than 90%	194,038
Greater than 95%	143,386
Greater than 99%	89,476

TABLE 4.4 *Degree of shared text*

Min.	0
1st Quartile	60
Median	73
Mean	73
3rd Qu.	90
Max.	100

six instances indicates that the constitution drafters directly incorporated the suggested text. Rather, the authors of those submissions quoted parts of either the 1967 constitution or public drafts of the new constitution to help illustrate their ideas.

I would not put too much importance on the specific numbers of repetitions of text here, but rather emphasize the broader point that, even in this most accessible form of public participation (at least for those who were literate and within walking distance of a post office), there was not a great deal of spontaneous participation. Rather, we can see that this means of participation was utilized by organized groups who sought to push forward very specific proposals. This strategy is particularly interesting given the fact that members of the Constituent Assembly were most likely to consume these submissions as summary tables from the Prodasen database rather than as pieces of text. Thus, the drafters would be unlikely to know that the information in the tables did not represent the work of isolated individuals, but instead represented verbatim copying of a prepared text.

When discussing something like constitutional reform, it is entirely possible for two texts to randomly share thirty words found in a number of six-word strings, meeting the matching threshold. There are far too many matching pairs to examine them all manually, but my extensive investigation of these texts shows that matching pairs sharing a low overall percentage of matched text (let us say below 30 percent) are almost always about the same issue, but not actually copied from a single source. In cases where the overall percentage of matching text exceeds 50 percent it seems much more likely that the texts have a single motivating source. Obviously, as we go up to levels of matching text approaching 100 percent, we have certainty that the pairs of texts were part of a well-organized campaign. Table 4.3 shows the numbers of matching texts at various levels of overall percentage of matched text contained in the recipient text. Table 4.4 lists some descriptive statistics that highlight the variation in the percentage of copied text within those submissions found to have been part of a matching pair using the method described earlier.

Among the subset of matching pairs in which the recipient text shares greater than 50 percent of its text with the source text, the most shared text has 889 copies. The subject of this submission is quite peculiar. It dealt with the professional prestige of private detectives. Here is the text in full:

1- For private detectives to be a participant as an auxiliary to the national security of the country. 2- That the services of private investigation and information may be unhindered for all purposes of social public interest. 3- We want autonomy for civil associations and their free or independent members to be considered as scientific-technicians and unhindered, self-employed professionals of the middle level. (SAIC Submission no. 69992)[12]

This particular version of the submission is not likely to be the real genesis of the text, but it was the one that had the most in common with all the possible examples of this pattern. Yet, it is still interesting to note that the postcard I have transcribed earlier was sent in by an urban resident of the city of Fortaleza (a state capital in the North-East region of Brazil), who had very little education (first grade), was married, in his thirties, and earned about minimum wage. This individual is typical of those who submitted this text, most of whom appear to be residents of Fortaleza or Salvador, with low levels of education and income, and mostly males. It seems very unlikely that the people who submitted these postcards had any personal stake in the issue and must have been motivated to participate in some other way.

The second most copied text in the SAIC database concerns religious education. The following text was copied at least 433 times: "Religious education is maintained in the new Brazilian constitution, guaranteed by the state, in all schools as part of the education system, respecting the religious plurality of the Brazilian people" (SAIC Submission no. 68196).[13] As with the first example, what is in some sense the most "perfect" text is probably not the source of the others, but this text was submitted by an unemployed, unmarried, poorly educated woman in her mid-twenties, from the city of Paranavai (located in the southern state of Paraná). Based on key word searches related to this submission, I estimate the actual number of submissions

---

[12] 1- Para que o detetive particular seja um ser participante como auxiliar para a segurança nacional do País. 2-Que sejam livres os serviços de investigações particulares e informações para todos os fins de interesse público social. 3-Queremos autonomia para as associações civis e seus filiados liberais ou autônomos que seja considerado como técnicos-científicos e liberais, os profissionais autônomos de nível médio.

[13] A educação religiosa seja mantida na nova constituição brasileira, garantida pelo Estado, em todas as escolas, como parte integrante do sistema de ensino, respeitando a pluralidade religiosa do povo brasileiro.

related to this campaign to be closer to 1,000.[14] Most of these submissions came from residents of three municipalities in the prosperous north-western part of the state of Paraná.

The third most copied set of submissions is different from the first two. In this case, it appears that a survey made its way into the dataset, with at least 250 copies transcribed. Without examining the original cards, it is difficult to say whether these survey responses were written on the usual cards, or whether they arrived on their own preprinted form. Whatever the manner of writing, the transcriptionists very nicely included all the marks to show how the senders responded to the questions. The fourth most copied submission, with at least 161 participants, was a request for the international language Esperanto to be taught in schools (SAIC Submission no. 51007).

There are also smaller-scale patterns of copied text that are of interest. For example, in one case, a group of three neighbors got together to submit the same proposal, in this case a short request for public servants to have their salaries increased quarterly (SAIC Submission no. 2). In another case, a single individual submitted the same proposal ten times, with ten different members of the Constituent Assembly named as the intended recipient (SAIC Submission no. 12325). We could go on, but these examples serve to demonstrate that both individuals and organized groups worked on the belief that higher numbers of submissions would be more likely to produce a change in the constitutional text.

One of the remarkable features of the SAIC database is the demographic information about the authors of the submissions that it includes. At the time of the drafting, this would have been useful if any member of the Constituent Assembly had been interested in breaking down the submissions by gender, location, occupation, or any other category of difference for which there was data. However, it is also useful for scholars today, allowing us to establish how representative of the broader population the participants in the drafting process were. The Appendix to this chapter includes a number of tables that describe these demographic characteristics in some detail.

In broad terms, the participants included people from all walks of life and all regions of the country, but were not descriptively representative of the population. Despite the fact that more than 14,000 of the authors of these submissions reported being without income, the middle class was overrepresented. Similarly, despite the impressive number of illiterate people who found a way to participate (686), the participants were in general much more educated than the average. For example, 16 percent of the participants had completed tertiary education, compared with less than 5 percent of the broader population (World Bank, 2020). The disparity in participation in gender was particularly notable: 66 percent of the participants were

---

[14] This discrepancy is most likely a result of one of the parameters of the text-matching search, which required that the minimum shared content must exceed thirty words. This submission is quite short, and many of the copies probably dropped below that threshold.

male and 44 percent were female. This demographic disparity between the participants in the process and the population of Brazil is not especially surprising. Many
practical reasons would lead to the expectation that richer and more educated people would be more likely to participate. Yet, it is somewhat discouraging that the
disparities were so high.

4.4.2 Following Up with the SAIC Participants

Another interesting aspect of these postcards is the inclusion of the writers'
addresses, which could make it possible to track down some of the people who
sent in suggestions, and interview them about their recollections of the constitution-
making process in 1987–1988 and their opinions about the constitution as it stood in
2015–2016. I hired a research firm in Rio de Janeiro (Clave de Fá Pesquisas e Projetos) to locate and interview a random sample of twenty-five of these individuals
who resided (then and now) within the Rio de Janeiro metropolitan area. We narrowed the sample to a randomly sorted list of 1,850 names on the basis of geography
and age. In practice, locating these individuals some thirty years after they sent in
their proposals was quite difficult. The research firm was able to locate and contact
a large number of them (238), but most did not respond to messages or calls, many
did not recall sending in the postcard or were not willing to talk to researchers. By
the time our resources were exhausted, they were able to complete twelve interviews
with individuals who contributed to the SAIC database. These were semi-structured
interviews conducted in person (though one respondent chose to respond to questions via email). The local researchers then sent audio recordings of these interviews
to me.

TABLE 4.5 *Profiles of SAIC follow-up respondents*

Age	Gender	Education	Income	Occupation	CSO	Party
30–39	Male	2nd complete	3–5 MS	Communication	Yes	Yes
20–24	Male	3rd complete	0	Agriculture	No	No
20–24	Male	3rd incomplete	1–3 MS	Student	No	No
30–39	Male	3rd complete	10–20 MS	Manufacturing		
30–39	Male	Post-graduate	>20 MS	Service	Yes	No
30–39	Male	3rd complete	>20 MS	Public admin.	No	No
25–29	Male	3rd complete	3–5 MS	Communication	Yes	Yes
40–49	Female	Post-graduate	10–20 MS	Service	No	No
30–39	Male	3rd complete	5–10 MS	Service	Yes	Yes
15–19	Male	2nd incomplete	0	Student	Yes	No
15–19	Female	1st complete	<1 MS	Service	No	No
30–39	Male	3rd complete	5–10 MS	Education	Yes	Yes

We cannot claim too much on the basis of twelve interviews, especially since these individuals are not descriptively representative of the participants as a whole. The individuals who could be located, and who would agree to an interview, have today achieved a higher than average level of education and income. However, there are some common themes in the interviews that can help us understand what happened in the public participation campaigns in 1985–1988. Some characteristics of these individuals are related to how easy they were to locate three decades later. The majority were young men who went on to work in professional capacities within the city of Rio de Janeiro. With one exception, the individuals we were able to locate expressed ties to parties of the left, even if they had never joined a party. Six of them directed their suggestion to Jamil Haddad, one of the founders of the Socialist Party of Brazil (PSB), who was at that time a Senator. Several of these respondents recalled that they had received some sort of advertising from an individual politician requesting submissions, and one was able to name Haddad as the sender of these advertisements. Surprisingly, given the patterns found in the copied texts described earlier, none of them contributed their suggestions as part of a larger campaign. Several had been part of the student movements, while others were members of trade unions.

There was variation between these respondents with regard to both their expectations of impact when they submitted the suggestions and their assessment of how much their participation actually impacted the constitutional text. Interestingly, there was near-unanimity on the point that, even if there was no impact, public consultations are a valuable and important part of the constitution-making process.

Their responses to questions about their current political beliefs and behavior were heavily colored by the political crisis that gripped Brazil during the period in which the interviews were conducted (2016–2017). Even so, the fact that they almost universally expressed distrust of politicians, and disappointment in the way that the constitution has functioned, is in line with the "distrusting democrats" that Moehler (2008) found among the participants in the constitution-making process in Uganda. When asked whether his political views were more on the left or the right, one respondent simply replied "disappointed." While voting is mandatory in Brazil, it is possible to vote with a blank ballot as a form of political protest. Two of the respondents reported that they vote with a blank ballot because they do not trust the electronic voting machines used in Brazilian elections, indicating significant disenchantment with the political system.

4.4.3 *Analysis of Individual Impact*

Ultimately, what we want to know is whether all of this public input resulted in changes in the text of the constitution. There are several layers to this question or levels at which we could be satisfied that there was some impact from public participation. The analysis here will be very similar to the study of South Africa in the previous chapter. First, there could be a general correspondence between the topics covered in the submissions from the public and the content of the constitution. Second, there could be pieces of text, phrases, or even whole paragraphs that are copied from the submissions from the public into the final draft of the constitution. Third, there could be cases where the drafters publicly discuss a submission and decide whether or not it should be included in the constitution. I address these approaches in turn in the following paragraphs.

We can apply the same method of topic modeling that was used in the chapter on South Africa to the submissions from the public that are found in the SAIC database. With the large number of submissions, we can fit a fifty-topic model with some confidence. When comparing the larger topic model to the text of the Brazilian constitution, I find that it contains a mixture of thirteen of the fifty topics from the corpus of submissions. The topic that accounts for the greatest proportion of the constitutional text (0.326) deals with the vertical distribution of power.[15] The second most common topic in the constitution by this measure actually contains language associated with the organization of the constitutional text. The other topics from the submissions that are included in the constitution deal with: policing and security, crime and punishment, the justice system, the public service, inequality, agrarian reform, international relations, wages and benefits, and workers' rights. In a developing country with high levels of both material inequality and violence, it is hardly surprising that these issues were well represented in the popular submissions. The fact that these are also included in the constitutional text is more interesting. Some of the notable topics in the submissions that were not included in the constitutional text (at least as measured in this manner) included: poverty, Christianity, medical treatment, soccer, regulation of broadcast media, regulation of the price of food, access to tertiary education, language education, and religious education.

As in the South African case, it is difficult to establish any causal link between the topics covered in the submissions and what we find in the constitution. The same concerns about the direction of influence discussed in the previous chapter apply here. However, the higher level of correspondence between the topics in the submissions and the constitution is notable. (Recall that, in the South African case, only eight of the fifty topics were found in the constitution, whereas we find thirteen here.) For one thing, these topics bear a remarkable similarity to the matters dealt with in the popular amendments that I discuss later. The close relationship between the content of the individual's submissions and the larger campaigns further suggests the influence of CSOs and other groups in motivating people to participate by writing individual submissions. It also makes it more difficult to distinguish between the extent to which individuals might have made a difference through these written

---

[15] The top twenty words in this topic are: "States, national, state, counties, unity, given, resources, social, district, entities, through, activities, territory, development, competence, taxes, additional, will be, tax, regime."

contributions and the effects of group participation. Given the demonstrable causal effects of the popular amendments as described later, I find it more likely that the correspondence between the text and the submissions is due to that form of participation. However, these themes are the core of Brazilian politics then and now, and it would be more surprising if these topics were not addressed in a constitution as long and detailed as the one produced by the Constituent Assembly.

One might hope to find a passage in the constitution that was directly copied from a submission from a member of public. While further investigation would be required to make sure that a piece of text was genuinely novel in the submission, it could be a strong piece of evidence for the impact of public participation on the text of the constitution. However, with regard to the texts from the SAIC database and the final draft of the 1988 constitution of Brazil, there are no instances where text from the submissions from the public was included in the Constitution with a. Even with fairly generous search terms (looking for a phrase of only six words, allowing for one imperfection within that phrase), I was unable to find any copied phrases that were original to the author of the submission. We cannot draw firm conclusions from this, but I would argue that it at least suggests that drafters did not have the suggestions in front of them while they were writing the articles of the constitution. If they did, they did not consider them to be sources of text.

This analysis of the submissions of individuals to the Constituent Assembly reveals interesting patterns of engagement, but does not show significant impact on the text of the constitution. Most remarkably, drafters almost never mentioned submissions from the public during their deliberations (I revisit this issue later in the chapter). Additionally, although the interviews reported here took place long after the constitution-making process was completed, none of the interview subjects could specifically recall the SAIC database, suggesting that this was not a particularly impactful resource for them. The more likely path for effective input from outside the Constituent Assembly is through interest group lobbying and civil society activism. We turn our attention there in the rest of the chapter.

4.5 POPULAR PARTICIPATION – GROUPS

Probably the most important form of popular participation in the constitution-making process in Brazil was interest group activism. This took several forms, including the campaigns we see in the SAIC data, lobbying of individual members of the Constituent Assembly, large rallies in Brasília, São Paulo, and Rio de Janeiro, and campaigns to support popular amendments. Among the interest groups were business organizations, trade unions, CSOs, and nongovernmental organizations (NGOs). Important sectors represented in this process included urban trade unions, unions of agricultural workers, and organizations representing rural landowners. We should expect that the demands of organized groups with large numbers of members will be more influential than comments from individuals – however interesting or informative those submissions may be. Interest groups of course have resources unavailable to individuals. Additionally, they are often repeat players in the legislative process and may have existing connections in the Congress to individual members and to parties. In some cases, interest groups also have expert knowledge of particular subject areas and may be seen by legislators as providing more valuable information than the average citizen.

There are two elements of Brazil's political history that are important frames for this discussion. First, Brazil has a long history of corporatism, dating back to Getulio Vargas, first period of power in the 1930s (French, 1991). Second, CSOs became increasingly important in the later years of the military dictatorship and acquired a great deal of valuable experience in the Diretas Já protest movement in the mid-1980s. By the time of the constitution-making process in 1987–1988, CSOs and unions had well-developed and extensive repertoires of collective action (Tilly, 1978), including large-scale strikes, large demonstrations, petition campaigns, and lobbying members of Congress – many of which we see repeated in the constitution-making period.

Since the focus of the analysis here is on the constitutional text, rather than contentious politics, I use data collected by Brandão (2011) to connect the demands made in demonstrations and protests associated with the constituent process with changes in the text of the constitution. Brandão's dataset includes 250 events, including protests, strikes, meetings between CSOs and politicians, television advertisements, and even an art exhibition. Here, we are most interested in the identification of demonstrations, formal presentations of demands, and related activities that were designed to support changes in the text of the constitution, and is therefore limited to the period between January 1987 and October 1988. Most of these events were covered in the press at the time.

There were in fact fewer large demonstrations than some of the accounts of the process would imply. Throughout the entire country during the drafting period, Brandão (2011, 83–84) identifies only forty protests or demonstrations, and many of these were directed at the quasi-constitutional end of having a direct election for the presidency in 1988. Many groups were repeat players, holding in-person demonstrations in Brasília several times during the drafting process. The geography of Brazil created an interesting context for protest. Since the capital is in the interior, protesters (either from the industrial south or the less-developed north) had to travel long distances in order to present their claims in person. This led to the development of a form of political action know in Portuguese as a "caravana" (convoy). In a number of cases, a CSO (such as a labor organization or a rural workers association) hired a number of buses to transport hundreds or thousands of protesters to Brasília. In the most impressive case, the União Democrática Ruralista (UDR) hired 250 buses to transport 30,000 of its supporters from all over the country to the capital to lobby against the redistribution of agricultural land (Jornal do Brasil, 1987b). There they camped for three days. The group on the other side of that issue,

Confederação Nacional dos Trabalhadores na Agricultura (CONTAG), engaged in a similar protest some months later, in which 7,000 of its supporters (along with members of other labor organizations) camped in a park in the capital in an attempt to pressure the Constituent Assembly to include language in the constitution that would facilitate the redistribution of agricultural land.

Other groups that staged protests in Brasília included associations representing the interests of labor, students, teachers, and indigenous peoples. In fact, the largest number of protests (10) in Brasília involved indigenous groups. Indigenous leaders lobbied members of the Constituent Assembly both in large rallies and in personal meetings (Brandão, 2011, 110–111).

Especially in the last months of the constitution-making process, the large protests had very specific aims, tying this form of participation to the other means of public input in an interesting way. One innovative aspect of the constitution-making process that has remained unique to Brazil is the ability of the public to submit what were known as popular amendments (emendas populares) to the Constituent Assembly. The popular amendments were concrete proposals for changes (additions or deletions) to the constitutional text that were supported by signatures from thousands of Brazilian voters. This form of participation is discussed in some depth in the section that follows, but we should note here that several of the demonstrations were associated with individual popular amendments. In those cases, CSOs invested time in a process that involved (1) drafting a concrete proposal for a change in the draft constitution, (2) collecting at least 30,000 signatures, (3) presenting the petition to the Constituent Assembly, and (4) holding a large rally to make sure that the Constituent Assembly paid attention to their concerns.

4.5.1 *Popular Amendments*

The history of how the popular amendments came to be part of the constitution-making process in Brazil also reveals the way in which the organizers of the campaign for public participation understood the best means of making an impact. As noted earlier, the original demand from the organizations pushing for a more democratic constitution-making process was for the Constituent Assembly to be a separate body from the Congress. When this demand was unmet, some of the most influential of these organizations began to turn their attention to educating the public about the constitution-making process, and to demand an opportunity for the public to submit amendments to the Constituent Assembly. They were successful on both fronts – producing pamphlets on how to participate in impressive quantities and making successful lobbying visits to Brasília, convincing the Congress to change the rules of procedure for the Constituent Assembly to include the popular amendment process (Michiles et al., 1989, 58–59). This avenue for public participation was approved by the Constituent Assembly within the first month of its work and received support from several political parties, especially those on the left (Backes and de Azevedo, 2008, 35).

It is interesting that the energies of these participation planning groups (Plenários pro Participação) were not directed toward capturing the postcard-writing campaigns described earlier in the section on SAIC. Rather, these activists in particular thought that the best way to create popular impact was to collect signatures on petitions for additions or amendments to the text. Many established CSOs also directed their efforts to this part of the process, especially groups representing urban and rural labor, agricultural workers, and religious groups.

The legislation governing the process for the popular amendments limited each Brazilian citizen to signing only three popular amendments. Each amendment would need to receive at least 30,000 signatures from individuals, as well as formal endorsements from at least three recognized civil society groups or state and municipal governments in order to be added to the agenda of the Constituent Assembly. While the collection of signatures was on one level more simple than the campaigns to submit identical text that we see in the SAIC data, it was likely more involved. Activists went door to door, especially in cities like São Paulo and Rio de Janeiro, asking people to sign the petitions (Author's interview with "JWBS," December 10, 2015). The plenários also developed more creative means to collect signatures, including setting up booths on sidewalks to collect signatures from people walking by. In one classically Brazilian move, the plenários in Rio de Janeiro staged a giant parade assisted by the Samba schools, in which they celebrated the opportunity to contribute to the constitution and collected more than 30,000 signatures on various popular amendments (Agência Estado, Rio, 1987).

In practice, neither the activists collecting signatures nor the bureaucrats who processed them were able to check how many amendments an individual had signed. The volume of paperwork created in this process was astounding. By July 1987, an entire wall of the offices of the Systemization Commission (where the popular amendments were received and verified) was lined with stacks of boxes filled with pages of signatures (Jornal do Brasil, 1987a). A month later, as the Conferência Nacional dos Bispos do Brasil (CNBB) completed a campaign, they delivered their popular amendments to the Constituent Assembly in eight cars carrying a total of 400 kilograms of paperwork (Veja, 1987). And yet, one of the chief organizers of these campaigns noted that citizens who were genuinely excited about this opportunity to participate in the process worried about signing their third petition, concerned that something even better would come up later and they would not be able to sign it (Author's interview with "JWBS," December 10, 2015).

In all, 12,265,854 signatures accompanied the 122 popular amendments that were sent to the Constituent Assembly (Michiles et al., 1989, 104). Of these, eighty-two were determined by the Constituent Assembly to have followed the required procedures (especially the number of signatures) and were added to the agenda for the Constituent Assembly to consider. Given the rules described earlier, no fewer than

4 million Brazilians must have participated in this process, and the number is likely to be higher. With a voting-age population of 82,074,718 at the time, at least 5 percent of Brazilian voters must have signed a petition for a popular amendment to the constitution. The organizers of the campaign for popular amendments estimated the rate of participation (using the number of registered voters in the 1986 election) at between 6 and 18 percent of registered voters (Michiles et al., 1989, 104). That is a truly extraordinary level of public engagement in a constitution-making process. Granted, placing one's signature on a petition for an amendment to a draft constitution is not the most intensive of political acts in either time or attention, but it is still a significant achievement on the part of the activists who envisioned and executed the campaign.

Of the eighty-two that were found to be procedurally valid, only nineteen were accepted by the Systematization Commission, and thus recommended to be included in the final draft of the constitution (Mendes Cardoso, 2010, 75). In the course of research for a thesis in law, a Brazilian researcher (Rodrigo Mendes Cardoso) discovered a research note completed by a member of the legislative staff at the Chamber of Deputies (Ana Luiza Backes) in response to a query from one of the Deputies (Paulo Abi-Ackel). In that research note (reproduced in Mendes Cardoso's thesis appendix), Backes analyzed the popular amendments and identified which had been included in the final text of the constitution in whole or in part, although she also noted that, while these were approved, the same subjects were covered in other forms of popular participation, and she could not say with certainty that the popular amendments were the sole cause.

Taking Backes' list of successful amendments, I compared the text of these popular amendments with the text of the constitution to identify precisely what the changes were. The successful amendments were in many cases those that had been supported by the largest and most well-organized CSOs, such as the CNBB, CONTAG, or the Central Única dos Trabalhadores (CUT). There does not seem to be any relationship between the number of signatures on the amendment and its probability of success. The successful amendments run the gamut, from one which technically failed to reach the required number of signatures (only 14,717) to one of the largest with 418,052. The average number of signatures on these successful popular amendments was 114,402.

These successful popular amendments are quite easily assigned to the broad category of rights and more specifically to one of two themes: family issues and labor issues. None of these amendments dealt with concerns about the electoral system or the powers of the president for example. There is only one that deals with an institutional issue (powers and divisions of municipalities). In general, they deal with the government's duty to support families and to ensure that urban workers and landless agricultural workers would see an improvement in their quality of life. Looking at the final text of the constitution, Articles 5 (fundamental rights),

7 (workers' rights), 182 (urban development), 184 (agricultural reform), 220 (freedom of expression), 226 (family rights), 227 (duties of and toward families), and 231 (indigenous rights) respond at least in part to the popular amendments. In the clearest case, Article 18 §4 is a verbatim copy of the language of popular amendment number PE00029-6. Only one of the successful amendments asked for the removal of language. In response to PE00110-1, what was Article 13 §XXV (paid labor mediation) in the July 1987 draft (Cabral I) was removed from the final constitution.

One of the more controversial issues in the constitution that can be connected to these popular amendments is that the right to property is limited by the proviso that property must fulfill its social function. This is a common concept in Latin American constitutions and was not new to Brazil (being found in the 1967 constitution). However, in the 1988 constitution, the social function of property was explicitly applied to the expropriation of agricultural land in Article 184. This addition to the text is a response to popular amendment number PE00013-0, which was sponsored by the CNBB. Other issues, such as the demand that religious marriages be recognized as having civil effects (PE00007-5, found in Article 226) were unlikely to be subjects of great controversy, but were important to some CSOs.

In all, I count sixty-two individual demands from these nineteen popular amendments that are reflected in the final constitution. This constitutes a significant degree of impact from public participation in the constitution-making process. The unique procedure through which this impact was achieved complicates the comparative analysis to some degree, but also produces an opportunity to reflect on how popular amendments might be useful in other constitution-making processes. While I argue that the political context and, in particular, the weakness of the political parties created a space for effective public participation, the combination of a specific textual proposal, clear support from thousands of signatories, and public protests is a powerful demonstration of popular will that would be difficult for any politician to ignore.

It is important to note that the entire process for popular amendments (from its initial approval as a change to the rules of procedure to the eventual success of some amendments) was highly dependent on support from members of the Constituent Assembly. To begin with, unlike the informal petitions that have been part of many constitution-making processes (including South Africa), the popular amendment process was an official and regulated part of the Constituent Assembly process in Brazil. The opportunity to submit popular amendments was added to the internal rules of the Constituent Assembly after members of the popular organizing committees made a journey to Brasília to lobby in person. According to one of the organizers of the campaign in São Paulo, the chief supporters of the popular amendments within the Constituent Assembly were Plínio Sampaio (deputy leader of the PT), Mario Covas (a founder of the PMDB), and José Carlos Brandão Monteiro (a founder of the PDT) (Author's interview with "JWBS," December 10, 2015). This demonstrates once again the relative unimportance of political parties in these

decisions. While there are good reasons to associate the campaign for popular participation with the political left, the initiative received vital support from the leadership
of at least three parties.

4.6 POLLING DATA

Although polls are not a form of public participation, they do merit some attention
as we seek to determine the extent to which these constitutions reflect the demands
of the people. The Brazilian media made extensive use of public opinion polling
before and during the constitution-making process. Beginning in 1985, prior to the
election of the Congress that simultaneously sat as the Constituent Assembly, the
press commissioned surveys about popular perceptions of the process. A number
of the polls and surveys in this period revealed a significant lack of understanding of the process among average citizens. Eighteen months before the November
1986 election, only 9 percent of residents of Rio de Janeiro could correctly describe
what the Constituent Assembly would be tasked with doing (Jornal do Brasil, 1985).
Another poll taken in early 1987 demonstrated a high level of misinformation about
the constitution-making process. This survey also revealed a familiar trend concerning what many people hope new constitutions can achieve for them: better
economic conditions. Forty-eight percent of those surveyed said that their greatest
hope for the new constitution was the control of inflation (Chiaretti, 1987). At the
same time, other polls also noted a very high level of interest in participating in the
constitution-making process. A Gallup poll taken shortly after the election of the
Constituent Assembly showed that the majority of Brazilians with a superior level of
education wanted to participate in the constitution-making process and that three-
quarters of all Brazilians wanted the constitution to be submitted to the people for
approval (Globo, 1987a).

   Perhaps most useful for the present research was a series of surveys conducted by
Gallup Brasil in 1987. In the middle of the drafting process, Gallup partnered with
the largest media conglomerate in Brazil (Globo) to produce a fairly comprehensive
survey about the constitution, which *O Globo* published in a series of newspaper
articles. This survey included a sample of 1,349 voters, randomly selected within
specified geographic areas (within the cities of Rio de Janeiro and São Paulo) and
designed to be representative in terms of age, sex, and class, and collected the data
with in-person interviews. This series provides us with some good data for comparing
what the majority of the population (at least those living in urban areas) wanted the
constitution to say and what the drafters actually produced. Additionally, these data
provide a point of comparison for the database of letters described earlier, allowing
us to see if the levels of support for various provisions are the same between the
self-selected participants and the random sample.

   One of the most important issues in the Brazilian constitution-making process
was the choice between a parliamentary or a presidential system. This Gallup poll

showed that only 21 percent of respondents could correctly describe the difference between these two systems, but that, among those who could, presidentialism was favored by 50 percent, with parliamentarism supported by 39 percent. This topic was coded slightly differently in the database of submissions from the public to the Constituent Assembly, but if we combine those against presidentialism with those for parliamentarism, and vice versa, we find that 80 percent (512) supported parliamentarism and 20 percent (129) favored presidentialism. Although the outcome was unclear for the majority of the drafting period, presidentialism eventually won the day. Given President Sarney's activity to ensure that presidentialism would be continued in the new constitution, it is unlikely that either the poll or the letters in SAIC were influential on this point, but it is worth noting that both polls and newspaper editorial pages favored the presidential option (Martínez-Lara, 1996, 139–146). This is, however, an interesting insight into both how the Brazilian public understood the issue and the difference of opinion between the self-selected participants and the poll sample.

In another article on the survey, O *Globo* reported that 56 percent of those polled supported the inclusion of the right to strike in the constitution (Globo, 1987c). The constitution does provide for this right. The same report showed that 75 percent of the sample thought that trade unions should be free of government control. The constitution does regulate trade unions to some degree, but probably not in ways that the poll respondents would object to. The poll also showed that the majority of respondents (59 percent) wanted an end to obligatory union contributions from workers' pay. The constitution does allow for obligatory contributions from professional workers, but makes union membership voluntary.

The Gallup data continued to receive feature reporting in O *Globo* for several weeks, covering a number of issues of importance in the constitution-making process and Brazilian politics more generally. Of particular interest were mandatory voting (71 percent against), voting rights for illiterate people (71 percent in favor), an internal security role for the military (75 percent in favor), conscription (62 percent in favor), constitutionalization of a forty-hour work week (57 percent against), compulsory education until the age of 16 (72 percent in favor), some form of religious education in schools (76 percent in favor), retirement benefits for homemakers (91 percent in favor), equal pay for men and women (95 percent in favor), allowing the government to keep files on citizens' activities (63 percent in favor) but allowing citizens to access their file (58 percent in favor), and that the government should limit the number of political parties (71 percent in favor).[16] Many of the relevant provisions in the constitution are broadly in line with the desires of the populace as captured in this survey. Also notable for the present research project was the feeling among the vast majority of respondents that the individual characteristics of their

[16] (Globo, 1987d, b, b, h, f, g, e)

elected representatives were much more important than the party and their support for electoral systems that would make the party less important (Globo, 1987d).

4.7 IN THE WORDS OF THE DRAFTERS

To fully establish the linkages between public participation and the text of the constitution, we must ask the drafters themselves – either through interviews with them now or in the records of what they had to say at the time. This section of the chapter describes what the drafters said about public participation in their debates with each other in both plenary and committee meetings of the Constituent Assembly. The section also includes some information from interviews that I conducted in Brazil in the course of field research in the second half of 2015.

4.7.1 *Statements in the Constituent Assembly*

A careful analysis of the transcripts of plenary, committee, and subcommittee meetings of the Constituent Assembly shows that the members of the Constituent Assembly very rarely referred to submissions from the public. A series of searches of the 9,748 pages of transcribed deliberations and speeches from the Brazilian Constituent Assembly using an exhaustive set of terms related to submissions from the public (including word-proximity searches) yields only twenty-nine such references. In the majority of these cases, submissions from the public are mentioned in passing – as one of many sources of information available to the drafters. In several other cases, the chair of a committee commended the SAIC database to the attention of the committee members. Surprisingly, among the thousands of speeches given during the drafting of the constitution, there were three occasions in which a member of the Constituent Assembly used the submissions from the public to buttress her argument.

In one of the most striking examples, Deputado Amaral Netto invoked the submissions from the public in an attempt to confer the authority of "o povo" (the people) on his position in the debate. During a meeting of the committee tasked with drafting provisions on human rights, Netto explicitly referred to the SAIC database described earlier as he sought to make a persuasive case for restoring the death penalty. Specifically, Netto described the difficulty of making concrete and credible claims about who "the people" are when politicians make a rhetorical appeal to the views of the people. Netto suggested that, when he spoke of the views of "the people," he had an authoritative source for his claim: the SAIC database:

When I speak of the people, I mean the people in general. Here is an example: the stack you see here... It contains a large number of popular suggestions favorable to the death penalty. There are 4,836 submissions, already recorded by Prodasen. Each page contains the name, the sex, the age, the profession, the origin, the neighborhood, finally, the social category of the author. This mountain of paper is surpassed only by one other, that on agrarian reform... This demonstrates the great public interest in the death penalty.[17]

Netto went on to address polling data from Gallup and *O Globo* that found that 72 percent of people in the metropolitan areas of Rio de Janeiro and São Paulo favored the use of the death penalty. An appeal to the voice of the people did not carry the day in this case. Article 5 of the constitution expressly prohibits the use of the death penalty.

In another instance, Deputada Irma Passoni complained that the paragraph that described the people as the source of the government's powers had not been amended to democratize the distribution of power, in spite of the "dozens and dozens" of submissions on the subject.[18] It is quite surprising that the drafters of the Brazilian constitution did not make more use of the submissions from the public in their arguments, but perhaps their immediate audience was not as impressed by these appeals to popular authority.

However, it was not all vain references to unread letters. During one meeting of the committee dealing with human rights, Deputado Lysâneas Maciel brought attention to an individual submission from an indigenous Brazilian (not included in the SAIC database), then to a conversation he had with a janitor, and to the larger program of public consultations that the committee had undertaken. Speaking of the many representations made to the committee by individuals and members of organizations, Maciel said: "Why do we adopt this procedure? Because, in fact, we want to make it very clear in this new Constitution that the primary source of power is the people ... Secondly, [Article 2] says that the sovereignty of Brazil belongs to the people, and only through the manifestation of their will, provided for in the Constitution, is it lawful to assume and organize power."[19] Maciel in this speech made a general appeal to the importance of input from the public as a matter of principle: The authority to make the constitution had come from the people.

Maciel went on to say: "I am quoting these facts, Mr. President, to show that in the judgment of our Subcommittee, the people, who are for the most part absent, have been heard. Proposals written on bread packaging paper – I repeat – were forwarded to the Subcommittee and taken advantage of."[20] Maciel went on to list several provisions in the draft constitution which he characterized as being responsive to the demands of the public, including popular initiatives, immediate application of direct elections for the office of president, optional voting for those between 16

[17] Amaral Netto, June 9, 1987, Ata da 12a. Reunião, Commisão da Soberania e dos Direitos e Garantias do Homem e da Mulher, Assembleia Nacional Constituinte, Brasília.
[18] Irma Passoni, September 23, 1987, 22a Reunião Ordinária, Commisão de Sistematização, Assembleia Nacional Constituinte, Brasília.
[19] Lysâneas Maciel, May 26, 1987, Ata da 3a. Reunião, Commisão da Soberania e dos Direitos e Garantias do Homem e da Mulher, Assembleia Nacional Constituinte, Brasília.
[20] Lysâneas Maciel, May 26, 1987, Ata da 3a. Reunião, Commisão da Soberania e dos Direitos e Garantias do Homem e da Mulher, Assembleia Nacional Constituinte, Brasília.

and 18, some technical changes in criminal procedure, and the right to information. Several of these demands were met in the 1988 constitution. Popular initiatives were created in Article 61. Article 14 creates a voting system much in line with what Maciel suggested. And Article 5 provides the right to habeas data and some of the other legal issues Maciel mentioned. Clearly, much negotiation over many issues took place between May 1987 and the completion of the final draft in September 1988, but these issues (which may not have been very controversial) were maintained in essentially the form that Maciel claimed met the demands of the people.

4.7.2 Statements in Interviews

One of the more challenging aspects of the research for this book was locating and interviewing members of the Constituent Assembly almost three decades after the constitution was drafted. Many of the most important actors in that process are now deceased and many others have left public life. In the end, I was able to complete fourteen interviews with politicians and their advisors who participated in the constitution-making process between 1985 and 1988. These were semi-structured interviews, lasting between twenty and ninety minutes. As was the case in my research in South Africa, respondents were (with one exception) given full anonymity and are identified here by a randomly generated four-letter alias. The respondents represent a reasonable representation of the partisan composition of the Constituent Assembly including people who had ties to the military regime and the president, and those on the far left.

In my interviews with former members of the Constituent Assembly, respondents almost universally reported that popular participation was tremendously important in shaping the constitution. They were in general less able to provide specifics about how submissions from the public influenced the text, but continually came back to the quantity of participation from individuals who wrote letters, called the Congress, or made presentations in person. One member of Congress described a "carpet of letters" that inundated the drafters (Author's interview with "RCWK," November 17, 2015). Another respondent stated: "What we had during the constitutional assembly was a nearly permanent dialogue with society, many meetings and hearings to make the constitution compatible with what Brazilians hoped for in that new political moment" (Author's interview with "AOTK," November 20, 2015).[21]

Some of the specific statements made by these drafters seem to present a much more democratic picture than other sources of information about the functioning of Brazil's political system would suggest. One respondent claimed to have consulted the people before voting in the Constituent Assembly and that they moved

---

[21] "Mas o que tivemos durante a constituinte foi um diálogo quase que permanente com a sociedade, muitas reuniões e audiências para compatibilizar o que os brasileiros esperavam daquele novo momento político."

constantly between the capital and their constituency so that they would be able to properly represent what the people wanted the constitution to say (Author's interview with "MSTH," November 18, 2015). This respondent further suggested that there are many lines in the constitution that correspond to specific demands from the people.

Another respondent (this time from a more conservative background) was similarly effusive about the importance of participation and the interaction between civil society groups and the members of the Constituent Assembly but admitted to some flaws in the execution when pressed. This member of the Constituent Assembly suggested that, in reality, the middle and upper classes were much better able to participate in politics, and further suggested that the poor were manipulated by the parties of the left (Author's interview with "KPUE," November 19, 2015).

Even President Sarney (a noted critic of the constitution at various points in its development) expressed a positive assessment of the participation from the public. He stated that he was very proud of the fact that 10 million Brazilians participated in the drafting process, even though he worried that this broad participation could lead to an unwieldy (and thus short-lived) text (Interview with the author, November 19, 2015).

Only one respondent in this series of interviews was dismissive of the role of the public, suggesting that "the people" did not really participate, but rather special interests (like labor unions), lobbied for their particular causes (Author's interview with "RLKN," December 9, 2015). Even this does not deny that there was effectual input from outside the Constituent Assembly, just that the impact came from organizations with experience, resources, and leverage. What would be clear even without a systematic review of the documentary data is that there was a great deal of organized participation, but there is disagreement among the drafters about whether submissions from individuals were taken seriously.

4.8 A NATURAL EXPERIMENT IN BRAZIL: THE AFONSO ARINOS DRAFT

Finally, one aspect of the drafting process in Brazil offers analysts the opportunity for a natural experiment that potentially sheds some light on how the participation of political parties shaped the text of the constitution. As noted earlier in the chapter, one of the first formal moves toward the drafting of a new constitution for Brazil was the appointment of an expert commission to prepare a draft of the constitution. This commission had been proposed by Tancredo Neves, but after his death, it was President Sarney who appointed the commission, which is generally called the Arinos Commission after its chairman, Afonso Arinos. The commission set about its work in two stages – first holding public hearings around the country to hear from members of the public and then writing a draft constitution in relative privacy.

While there was some overlap in the membership of the Constituent Assembly and the Arinos Commission, the basis of selection for and variation in membership provides us with something like a natural experiment in which we can test the effects of process on constitutional text. Whereas the Constituent Assembly comprised 559 politicians elected by various means, the Arinos Commission comprised 50 individuals who were selected because of their high level of professional achievement in law, business, and of course politics. Vitally for our research interests, the Arinos Commission did involve a significant amount of public participation, but did not include any representatives of political parties as such. It thus has some similarity with the Icelandic case, in that the members of the drafting body were not closely associated with political parties, but were open to input from the general public.

However, there are some complications that prevent this from being a true natural experiment. One is the fact that the Arinos draft served to some degree as a model for the final constitution. The Arinos Commission was not well liked by either politicians or the press, and President Sarney chose to bury their draft instead of moving for Congress to ratify it (as had most likely been Neves' intention). Even so, there is evidence that many members of the Congress were influenced by the draft. Arinos himself (as well as other members of the commission) also served in the Constituent Assembly the next year. This semi-ancestral relationship complicates the analysis, but to the extent it creates bias, it does so in the direction of finding less effect, not more. The form of public participation also varied between the Arinos Commission and the Constituent Assembly. As we've seen, the constitution-making process involved large-scale mobilization of members of CSOs and the use of popular amendments. In contrast, the Arinos Commission set up locations where the public could interact with them, including at least one store front, and held special meetings in various parts of the country (Author's interview with "OMAY," October 22, 2015).

In a book on the method of natural experiments, Dunning writes that natural experiments have the novel quality of being discovered, but also that the attractiveness of the method has led to a great deal of conceptual stretching (Dunning, 2012, 2–3). In a true natural experiment, the variation in the treatment variable must be near-random. In this case, the treatment variable is the participation of political parties in the drafting process. Clearly, there is variation in our case, but it is not necessarily random. Randomness in this case would require that all other details of the drafting processes would be near-identical, but that this element was different for reasons unconnected with other elements of the drafting process. Thus, the analysis here closely follows the methodology of Landemore's (2017) comparison of the expert-drafted and popularly drafted constitutions for Iceland, but it is not a true natural experiment.

As a first pass comparing the final text of the 1988 constitution with the Arinos draft, we can compare the two texts to see how much text overlaps. Surprisingly, the two documents do not differ greatly in length. The Arinos draft was over 38,000 words, while the 1988 constitution (as originally ratified) was just short of 40,000 words. Using strings of words with a length of six and allowing one imperfection per string, I find that 15 percent of the text of the 1988 constitution is composed of strings of text also found in the Arinos draft. While some of this is merely procedural language that is not of interest, many of the copied phrases are substantively interesting, especially when there are slight variations in wording between them. For example, in Article 2, the Arinos draft states that "All power comes from the people, and in their name it will be exercised." In Article 1 of the 1988 constitution, the language was changed to "All power comes from the people, who exercise it through their elected representatives or through direct means, under the terms of this constitution." The legal implications of such a change are not immediately clear, but the style of drafting indicates much more concern with precision in the 1988 constitution than in the Arinos draft, which is somewhat surprising given the larger and more chaotic drafting process in the Constituent Assembly.

In terms of formal institutions, the Arinos draft creates a parliamentary system, whereas the 1988 constitution maintains the presidential system. More specifically, the Arinos draft created a system of government in which the Congress (elected through proportional representation with 3 percent minimum threshold) would choose a prime minister. There would also be a directly elected president with essentially ceremonial functions. Much has been written about this important choice in Brazil's constitutional history (Afonso da Silva, 1990; Elkins, 2013; Cheibub et al., 2014). But for our specific purposes, it is helpful to note that 50 percent of the Brazilian public actually favored the presidential system during the constitution-making period (Globo, 1987a). In this case, it seems that the 1988 constitution is more in line with public opinion than the Arinos draft was. The parliamentary issue may be one reason for Sarney's decision to bury the draft (Reich, 2007), but the draft was also seen by many as being far too progressive on economic issues (Prado, 1987; Rosenn, 1990). The commission was itself divided between those who wanted a presidential system and those who preferred the parliamentary option. One scholar posits that the fact that the Arinos draft includes an elected president as head of state (though with few powers) is a response to the fact that the drafting took place during the outpouring of popular protest for the direct election of the president in the Diretas Já movement (Reich, 2007).

Another controversial aspect of the Arinos draft was its broad grant of powers to the state to intervene in the economy. The 1988 constitution is reasonably ambitious in this regard as well, but the lack of direct lobbying by business interests in the Arino draft may explain the greater willingness of at least the majority of the members of the commission to grant the state such a large role in planning national economic development. In a relatively broad grant of power that was then further defined in subsections, Article 319 stated that "State intervention in the economic domain may be direct or indirect, in the form of control, stimulus, direct management, supplementary action and participation in the financing of companies."

The 1988 constitution gives each level of government specific powers to take action relating to economic development, but does not include this broad grant of power. Additionally, while both the Arinos draft and the 1988 constitution include language that privileges Brazilian-owned companies, the Arinos draft's economic nationalism is much more pronounced. Both of these issues may reflect the influence of lobbying by business groups late in the Constituent Assembly process, as leaders sought to ensure that what they saw as the excesses of the left would be excised from the final draft.

In sum, there are many substantive and important differences between the two constitutions. The overall nature of the constitutions has much in common. Both are unusually long and attempt to be comprehensive. The Arinos draft was criticized as being "utopian," and so is the 1988 constitution (Prado, 1987; Rosenn, 1990). They were drafted by people of similar backgrounds and inclinations. Yet, the Arinos draft was more in line with the preferences of Brazilian academics on institutional issues and also with popular opinion on the economic ones.

4.9 CONCLUSION

It is difficult to say in absolute terms how great the impact of public participation was in the Brazilian case. On the one hand, there was an impressive record of success for groups that followed the process laid out earlier in this chapter of combining the popular amendments with public demonstrations. Interest groups that used the popular amendments achieved much of what they wanted. As noted in the section on popular amendments, nineteen amendments and sixty-two individual demands are included in the final constitution. Out of 122 possible popular amendments, that is an impressive record. However, the individual comments, either in SAIC or in letters, appear not to have an impact on their own. The demands made in the largest campaigns in SAIC fell on deaf ears. Certainly, in comparison with South Africa, the impact of public participation was far greater. As we will see, as a percentage of the total public input, there was a greater impact in Iceland. As with all of these cases, one's judgment of the efficacy of public participation depends on one's priors. If one's prior expectation is that public participation matters little, then the level of impact in Brazil may be surprisingly high. If one approaches the subject expecting that this massive investment in public participation (both on the part of the Constituent Assembly and civil society) should have markedly impacted the content of the constitution, then the impact may be disappointingly small. We can at least be relatively certain that, in the comparative terms of this book, the impact in Brazil was higher than that in South Africa, and lower than that in Iceland.

Another question concerns how much of the credit for the impact that we find in the Brazilian case can be attributed to the weakness of the political parties, and how much should be attributed to the remarkable organizational capacity of interest groups. The easy answer is that both were required – and this seems to be closest to the truth. It was necessary for this level of impact that the political parties were weak and thus less committed to a singular view of what the constitution should say. Members of the Constituent Assembly were both less well instructed by their parties than the drafters were in South Africa and also less well protected from public pressure (Schattschneider, 1942). At the same time, the constitution-making process unfolded in a moment in Brazil's history where civil society groups were flourishing as their long-pent-up energies were allowed to be manifested without fear of repression from the state. The deep inequalities of Brazilian society could be discussed openly, protested against, and hopefully rectified (at least in part) in the transformative constitution that was supposed to inaugurate a new era of democracy. The extent to which these hopes have been realized is another matter. Nonetheless, the Brazilian case demonstrates that, in cases where there is systemic weakness in the political parties and great energy and organizational capacity in civil society, we can see a significant impact from public participation.

5

Iceland: Citizen Drafters

5.1 INTRODUCTION

Following a groundswell of popular opposition to the existing political system in 2009, the people of Iceland embarked on a unique process of constitutional reform that prioritized transparency, openness, and public participation. By July 2011, the Icelanders had completed a new draft constitution through a process that has been rightly celebrated by both scholars and more casual observers the world over. It was reputed to be the world's first "crowdsourced" constitution (Morris, 2012), using internet communication technology (ICT) to involve the public directly in the drafting process. Iceland is almost uniquely suited for this kind of process with its tiny and homogeneous population, high levels of education, high level of voter turnout (averaging 88 percent since 1946), and a remarkably high level of Internet access, at 96 percent (Kelly et al., 2013). One would think that if participatory constitution-making using online tools can work anywhere, it would work here.

While Brazil and South Africa work well in a most-similar systems research design, the inclusion of the Icelandic case in a comparative study requires more justification. In colloquial terms, the Icelandic constitution-making process is usefully weird. The party-mediation thesis advanced in this book claims that constitutions that are drafted by weak parties are more likely to be influenced by input from the public than those drafted by strong parties. The argument can be usefully pushed to its limit by considering a case in which a constitution was drafted without political parties. Such cases are vanishingly rare, but Iceland provides us with such an example, and is thus an important case to consider when evaluating how public participation may be moderated by political parties.

In more scientific language, Iceland could be considered a crucial case. A finding of no impact from public participation in this case would cast doubt on the larger program of increasing public involvement in drafting processes. The combination of the case's relative simplicity and high level of participation also allow us to evaluate the impact of public participation on the drafting of a constitution without many other variables to consider (Gerring, 2007, 115–122). Furthermore, the small scale of this case (both in terms of the number of submissions from the public and the length of the constitution) allows for a more fine-grained analysis of the relationships between the texts.

In contrast with the strong parties that dominated South Africa's constitution-making process and the weak parties that drafted Brazil's constitution, representatives of political parties were explicitly excluded from the election to Iceland's drafting body. This drafting context is also important for understanding the ultimate outcome of the process, as the constitution produced by the Constitutional Council in 2011 ultimately failed to be enacted by the parliament. While we should not overemphasize the break between political elites and masses, the disconnection between these groups was important both to the protests that began this constitutional-reform process and to its ultimate failure.

The analysis in this chapter demonstrates that it was the apolitical nature of the constitution-making process, where political parties and interest groups were excluded, that led to the level of impact we observe in this case. Iceland provides us with a useful outlier in which to explore the causal process in more detail (Gerring, 2007, 37–39). Though the case is less comparable to the most-similar cases in Chapters 3 and 4, it helps us assess the theoretical claim made in this book by providing an example of a constitution drafted in a party-free context.

5.2 IMPETUS FOR REFORM: ECONOMIC CRISIS

It is helpful to begin by describing the context in which this project of constitutional reform started. Iceland was one of the worst affected countries in the banking crisis of 2008. Following a period in which government policy favored ever-greater deregulation of the financial industry, Iceland's three largest banks became preposterously overextended and collapsed in October 2008 (Sigurjonsson, 2010). The effect of this collapse was a significant economic crisis that touched the lives of the vast majority of the island's population of just over 320,000 and delegitimized the political parties and institutions in the eyes of many (Author's interview with "NRNJ," July 5, 2017, and with "YIGY," March 15, 2017). In the "pots and pans revolution," Icelanders took to the streets (cookware in hand) to demand new elections, and ultimately changes in the way their political and economic systems are governed (Castells, 2012, 34). The center-right governing coalition eventually bowed to this cacophonous expression of popular discontent, and was replaced by an interim government composed of members of the Social Democratic Alliance and Left-Green Movement parties. These two parties gained enough support in the general election of April 2009 to form a government and began to take steps toward constitutional reform (Benediktsson and Karlsdóttir, 2011).

In some sense, constitutional reform in Iceland had been a long time in coming. The current constitution had been installed as a temporary measure at the time of independence from Nazi-occupied Denmark in 1944, with multiple plans for reform or replacement failing to reform the law in the intervening years. The text of that constitution is substantially copied from the Danish constitution of 1849, with slight adaptations to the Icelandic context. As early as 1949, then President Sveinn Bjornsson, stated: "We still have a mended garment, originally made for another country, with other concerns, a hundred years ago" (quoted in Gylfason, 2016b). By 2009, the political system had evolved to the extent that the constitution no longer described how the government of Iceland actually functions, and in some respects bore little resemblance to how the law had developed. With the political system largely discredited in the eyes of the public in 2008, the time seemed right to many to push for a new constitution.[1] Beyond this, there was at that time a level of interest in constitutional matters unprecedented in Iceland's history. One participant in the process noted that the political situation in 2009 was an example of what Bruce Ackerman describes as a "constitutional moment" (Ackerman, 1998; Oddsdottir, 2014). The constitution-making process was initiated in a National Forum in 2009 and was, to some extent, completed with a referendum in 2012, but was ultimately set aside by the parliament.

5.3 THE DRAFTING PROCESS IN ICELAND

Unlike the cases of South Africa and Brazil, the constitution-making process in Iceland was directed from the grassroots. As noted earlier, it was not obvious that a new constitution would be the result of the financial collapse. However, the financial crisis was sufficiently linked to the political elite that the public response to the crisis quickly began to include the idea of major institutional changes. Many ordinary Icelanders took an interest in politics that they never had before.

The first major step in the process of reforming the Icelandic constitution was a National Forum (Þjóðfundur) organized by a group of grassroots organizations which called themselves "the Anthill" (Maurabúfan). The Anthill organized a one-day event in November 2009, for the purpose of gathering public opinion on the core values of the nation, and how Iceland's government should be reformed. The selection of delegates to this event also set the tone for much of what followed. Of the 1,500 people who attended the event, 1,200 were chosen at random from the national voters registry, while the other 300 were chosen to represent business and civil society groups (Burgess and Keating, 2013, 424).

After the success of this first National Forum, the newly elected government got involved more directly in the process and appointed a committee of seven experts to prepare the groundwork for drafting a new constitution. In November 2010, a second National Forum was held, this time a collaborative effort between the Anthill and the committee of experts. This second forum invited a similarly selected (quasi-random) group of 950. This time there was a greater focus on producing useful data

---

[1] As Machiavelli is reported to have said, "Never waste the opportunities offered by a good crisis" (quoted in Seelye, 2009).

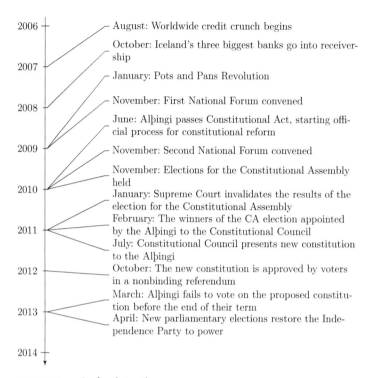

2006 — August: Worldwide credit crunch begins

October: Iceland's three biggest banks go into receivership

2007 — January: Pots and Pans Revolution

November: First National Forum convened

2008 — June: Alþingi passes Constitutional Act, starting official process for constitutional reform

2009 — November: Second National Forum convened

November: Elections for the Constitutional Assembly held

2010 — January: Supreme Court invalidates the results of the election for the Constitutional Assembly

February: The winners of the CA election appointed by the Alþingi to the Constitutional Council

2011 — July: Constitutional Council presents new constitution to the Alþingi

2012 — October: The new constitution is approved by voters in a nonbinding referendum

March: Alþingi fails to vote on the proposed constitution before the end of their term

2013 — April: New parliamentary elections restore the Independence Party to power

2014

FIGURE 5.1 Iceland timeline

from the discussions. Most importantly, the committee of experts summarized the findings of the second National Forum and published this along with a number of other resources (including two complete drafts for a new constitution) for the constitution drafters to use. This 700-page collection of resources provided the main source of information for the Constitutional Council as they began their work in Spring of 2011 (Author's interview with "XQPC," March 13, 2017). Moreover, the recommendations from this National Forum are for the most part reflected in the draft constitution produced by the Constitutional Council a year later.

The Constitutional Council (Stjórnlagaráð) was elected by means of single transferable vote in an election held in November 2010 with a slate of 522 candidates. This election was then ruled invalid by Iceland's Supreme Court, ostensibly due to problems with the design of the ballots and the voting booths, though some commentators have suggested that the action was politically motivated and facilitated by a court staffed with appointees of the then disgraced Independence Party (Gylfason, 2013b). The Alþingi (parliament) then bypassed the court by directly appointing the twenty-five people chosen by the voters to the Constitutional Council.[2] The

---

[2] Although one of the twenty-five top vote-getters declined this appointment and was replaced with the twenty-sixth-place candidate.

Constitutional Council began their work in April 2011, with a deadline to produce a draft a mere three months later.

Turnout in this election was very low (36 percent), which is perhaps not surprising given the nature of the election. The informational burden to make an informed vote was very high, with 522 candidates, none of whom was a sitting politician (though two had previously held elected office) or affiliated with any political party. The parties themselves for the most part ignored the election, with only one party providing any guidance to its members about preferred candidates (Author's interview with "GNEL," March 15, 2017). Few of the candidates spent any money campaigning. Some of the successful candidates were known already for articles they had written on politics in Iceland. All of the candidates were given time to appeal to the voters through brief radio appearances (Author's interview with "BHCQ," April 11, 2014). With so many candidates in the race, they were only permitted to answer three questions for this radio program.

Although the gender ratio on the Council was relatively representative (or at least reasonably so for a group of twenty-five), the Council was not descriptively representative in terms of education or profession.[3] The group was remarkably educated in comparison with virtually any public: Six have a PhD, eleven more have a postgraduate degree. Five of the members of the Council are university professors, four are lawyers, and two are physicians. At least eleven of the council members had previously published articles or books on constitutional issues. Thus, the group seems to have been highly qualified for the task, if not descriptively representative.

The drafting process was designed to allow for a high level of transparency at the Constitutional Council, with significant opportunity for the public to engage with the members of the Council through offering comments on the drafts and suggestions for improvements. While the work of the Constitutional Council was to some degree governed by an act of parliament passed in June 2010 (which, for example, required the plenary meetings to be open to the public), much of the detail of the process was worked out on a rather ad hoc basis (Althingi, 2010). In interviews, members of the Council suggested that there was an effort to meet the people where they were, and to make participation as simple as possible. One member of the Constitutional Council described the public consultation this way:

We were running on the ideology of programming, sort of crowdsourcing…you do things in a period and then you test it, and then you do it again, you run it again. Instead of writing a whole new program, you test it as often as you can, trying to find the bugs before they become really sort of hidden inside the whole mechanism. (Author's interview with "SBPC," April 15, 2015)

---

3 The authorizing legislation included a commitment to electing a somewhat representative Constitutional Council and also included a gender equity requirement in the allocation of the seats (Landemore, 2015). In the event, ex post balancing was not necessary as the public elected ten female council members, fulfilling the 40 percent quota.

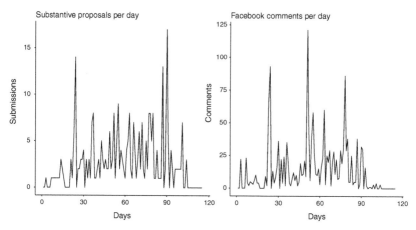

FIGURE 5.2 Public participation over time

The Council's deliberations were open to the public and live-streamed on the Internet, and minutes of the proceedings were posted later. The Council also set up accounts on social networking websites such as Facebook, Twitter, Flickr, and YouTube in order to facilitate engagement with citizens across a variety of platforms. The Council reported that they received 323 formal proposals[4] and a total of 3,600 comments (Gylfason, 2011). The 323 proposals were discussed by members of the Council and other interested people in comment threads below the proposals, with 1,575 comments posted in this way.

The varying level of public participation over time is somewhat surprising. I had expected to find that the level of participation (measured in terms of substantive proposals or Facebook comments per day) would increase over time, peaking near the time that the final draft of the constitution was to be delivered to parliament. However, to the extent that there is a trend, both the substantive proposals and commenting activity through Facebook peak around the middle of the drafting process (see Figure 1). Participation in terms of both substantive submissions and Facebook comments surged in the couple of days preceding the release of new drafts of the constitution. The commenting period closed shortly before the final draft was due, but the level of engagement seems to have been on the decline well before that.

After receiving a short extension to their original deadline, the Constitutional Council unanimously approved their draft constitution on July 29, 2011 and presented it to the parliament. Here, things slowed down considerably. A nonbinding referendum on the text was held in October 2012. In addition to voting "yes" or "no" on the draft as written, Icelanders were asked to respond to five substantive questions addressing some of the most contentious issues that came up in the two national forums, and which remained controversial during the drafting process. Reflecting

---

[4] Excluding posts by foreigners and posts that merely convey compliments to the Council, the number of substantive proposals from Icelanders was 311.

the divisions within the proposals the Council received, their final draft left several of these issues unresolved, offering ambiguous language, or allowing the legislature to make a decision.[5] Three particularly notable questions concerned language in the draft about public ownership of natural resources (a concern for the fishing industry), the decision not to reaffirm the Evangelical Lutheran Church as the national church, and changes to the electoral system.[6]

The referendum confirmed the choices made in the Constitutional Council where they had made clear statements (as in ownership of natural resources), demonstrated popular opinion about some areas where the text was left ambiguous (as on the questions of the establishment of a national church),[7] and endorsed the constitution as a whole (Robertsson, 2012). The voters approved the draft constitution with a vote of 66.9 percent in favor.

However, turnout in the referendum was around 50 percent, which is quite low compared to presidential and parliamentary elections in Iceland, which have averaged around 88 percent turnout between 1946 and 2013.[8] Turnout in parliamentary elections is of course driven in part by political party campaigns, and the lack of such mobilization efforts in this referendum could partly explain the low turnout. It should also be noted that the original plan was for the referendum to coincide with the June 2012 presidential election, but the Independence Party and Progressive Party mounted a filibuster in the parliament to prevent this from happening (Gylfason, 2016a). Iceland has had only four referendums in its history, but there were stand-alone referendums in 2010 and 2011 on legislation concerning the terms of Iceland's financial liability to foreign depositors following the banking crash, providing us with good points of comparison for turnout. The turnout rate in the 2010 referendum was 62.7 percent, and turnout in the 2011 referendum was 75.3 percent (Statistics Iceland, 2010, 2011). This indicates that turnout in the 2012 referendum was likely to be significantly lower than a parliamentary election, but it still fell short of the other referendums. Nevertheless, the outcome of the referendum might not have been much different with a higher turnout. Polling just prior to the 2012 referendum indicated that support for the draft text among all citizens was around 66 percent, which mirrors the outcome in the referendum (Market and Media Research, 2012). In addition to the parliamentary maneuvers described earlier, opponents to the new draft ran radio advertisements arguing against approval in the run-up to the referendum, which may have also contributed to the low turnout (Author's interview with "GNEL," March 15, 2017).

Following the referendum, the fate of the constitution was back in the hands of the parliament. By this point, almost four years had passed since the beginning of the

---

[5] These means of avoiding final decisions at the drafting stage have been successful in constitution-making processes in divided societies (Lerner, 2011).

[6] These are long-standing questions in Icelandic politics.

[7] Article 19 of the final draft read: "The church organization of the state may be determined by law."

[8] Voting in Iceland is not compulsory.

"pots and pans revolution," the economy had begun to improve, and it is likely that the sense of the urgent need for political reform had dissipated. Approval of the new constitution would have required an affirmative vote in the sitting parliament and a second affirmative vote in the new parliament following the Spring 2013 election (Landemore, 2015). The bill for the new constitution was not brought up for a vote on its own, and eventually failed to even be included as a last-minute amendment to a different bill before the parliament dissolved at the end of the session. One member of the Constitutional Council suggested that the parliament had reverted to its former ways, lessons from the financial crisis unlearned (Author's interview with "DLEA," March 15, 2017). In the election that followed in April 2013, the center-left coalition that came to power in the wake of the financial crisis fared poorly and the traditional center-right coalition that presided over the rampant neo-liberalism of the early 2000s was returned to power.

5.4 MEASURING PARTICIPATION

In assessing the quantity of participation, we must consider the familiar question, "compared to what?" As Iceland is a small country, the overall numbers are quite low. We can compare the level of participation in Iceland with the levels in South Africa and Brazil in a simple way by weighing the number of substantive proposals against size of the electorate. The most comparable metric here is the number of substantive proposals submitted through an official channel created for this purpose. In the case of Brazil, with 72,719 proposals from an electorate of 82,074,718, there was a participation rate of 88 proposals per 100,000 voters. In South Africa, 15,292 submissions from 22,709,152 eligible voters yielded a participation rate of 67 proposals per 100,000 voters. The comparable metric for Iceland is 311 proposals from 235,495 registered voters, with a participation rate of 130 proposals per 100,000 voters.[9] The rate of participation is clearly far higher in Iceland, but as mentioned at the outset, we should expect this in a comparison between Iceland and large developing countries. The narratives in Chapters 3 and 4 noted the non-representative nature of the participants, and this issue will be explored further later in this chapter as well.

5.5 DATA AND METHODS

The analysis that follows relies to a significant degree on two types of data: Online records generated in the drafting process and interviews with participants in the drafting process, especially the members of the Constitutional Council. Though

---

[9] It is important to note here that other forms of participation were also important in each of these cases, for example, petitions in South Africa and popular amendments in Brazil. These other forms of participation drew far higher numbers of participants. However, the submission of written proposals through an official channel is common between these three cases, and in my view provides a convenient point of reference in evaluating the comparative level of popular participation.

the Council used a number of websites to enable public engagement, the main point of contact was the Council's own website, which facilitated the posting of substantive proposals for the constitution, and public comments on these proposals through Facebook. The most important documents for this analysis are the substantive proposals submitted through the Council's website and the successive draft constitutions that the Council produced. All of these documents have been preserved online at the time of writing.[10]

For the analysis, two text files were created for each of the submissions from the public: One in the original Icelandic and a second that was automatically translated with the Web service Google Translate. Next, each proposal was manually coded according to the topics that it addressed using a coding system based on the taxonomy of constitutional topics created by the Comparative Constitutions Project (Elkins et al., 2014). This coding was accomplished through a careful reading of the English translations, with the automatic translation supplemented by the use of an Icelandic-English dictionary. These topic categorizations were used to create a dataset, to which additional variables were added, including the name of the author, date of submission, word count, number of Facebook comments responding to the proposal, number of Council members responding to the proposal in the Facebook comments, whether or not the author responded in the comment thread, the total number of proposals submitted by that author, and whether or not the author was writing in their capacity as a member of a non-governmental organization (NGO) or civil society organization (CSO). Some of the substantive proposals addressed more than one topic and were coded accordingly.

For the purposes of statistical analysis, this dataset was then altered in two principal ways. First, proposals that dealt with more than one topic were split into a proposal for each topic. Second, the categories of topics were collapsed into two new taxonomies, one with eight categories[11] and one with three.[12] This smallest categorization was the most useful for statistical analysis, given its focus on distinguishing between the effects of public participation on institutions versus rights, and was most appropriate for the small number of observations available for the study.

The drafts published by the Constitutional Council were collected in a similar way to the substantive proposals, in both Icelandic and English text files. Using some text analysis software (WCopyfind), each change between successive drafts was identified in new html files. These files with the changes highlighted were used to determine whether or not the substantive proposals led to changes in a draft of the constitution, as described in greater detail later in the chapter.

The views of the members of the Constitutional Council were vital to this analysis, and were collected through semi-structured interviews. Two interviews

---

[10] https://web.archive.org/web/*/www.stjornlagarad.is
[11] Executive branch, legislative branch, judicial branch, direct democracy, oversight institutions, fundamental rights, cultural issues, and the amendment process.
[12] Institutions, rights, and a residual category for topics not subsumed into these two.

were conducted via teleconference in 2015, and four more were conducted in person in Reykjavik in 2017. The views of several citizen-participants were also collected through semi-structured interviews. One was conducted in person in Reykjavik in 2017, and three more were conducted via teleconference. Each interview lasted between 45 and 90 minutes, and followed a list of questions prepared in advance, with the opportunity for the respondent to also suggest new avenues of conversation. The majority of the interviews were recorded in digital audio. Data from the interviews have been anonymized in the same way as in the previous chapters.

5.6 ASSESSING THE IMPACT OF PARTICIPATION

5.6.1 *The Substance of Public Participation*

As noted earlier, 311 substantive proposals were posted by Icelanders on the Council's website. Other citizens, as well as a few interested foreigners, also posted 1,575 comments about these more substantive proposals. Some concerns about the representativeness of the participants are warranted. The 311 proposals came from only 204 individuals, and the nine most active individuals combined to submit 24 percent of the proposals. All of these nine individuals were male, as were about three-quarters of all those who submitted proposals. While the age of the participants is more difficult to assess, one Icelandic scholar has estimated that 80 percent of the participants were between forty and sixty-five years of age (Helgadóttir, 2014). These dynamics tend to confirm both broader trends in offline political participation (Verba et al., 1993) and research on online political participation that suggests that dialogues are dominated by a few highly active users, and often by males (Dahlberg, 2001; Albrecht, 2006).

   The vast majority of these substantive proposals are well organized and communicated in a positive and collegial tone. Many of them are also highly informed. Some cite supporting evidence from the writings of prominent legal scholars and philosophers. Other commenters supported their claims with links to reports from NGOs, particularly International IDEA. A few Icelanders cited precedents from other national constitutions, notably the United States, Norway, Sweden, Denmark, and Finland. Depending on the issue, some commenters looked further afield, noting examples from other states that have declared neutrality, or the electoral systems of states similar in size to Iceland. International human rights treaties were also mentioned by a significant number of participants.

   Reflecting on the Constitutional Council's attitude toward the public comments and proposals, one of the Council members stated: "We were really scared when we did it first, because we thought 'this is the Internet,' people are going to lash out, and they're going to be really rude... But the actual reality was that people were really nice, and polite, clever, helpful, and brilliant" (Author's interview with "SBPC," April 15, 2015). The overall scale of the Icelandic public's involvement in

TABLE 5.1 *Distribution of topics in substantive comments*

Topic	Number suggest.	Percentage suggest. (%)	Number FB comms.	Percentage FB comms. (%)
Legislature reform	57	18.4	227	9.9
Electoral reform	56	18.1	240	10.5
Other human rights	50	16.1	228	10.0
Established church	41	13.2	433	18.9
Executive reform	39	12.6	162	7.1
Equality	25	8.1	113	4.5
Property rights	25	8.1	134	5.9
Direct democracy	23	7.4	98	4.3
Judiciary reform	18	5.8	51	2.2
Natural resources	18	5.8	46	2.0
Financial regulation	17	5.5	151	6.6
Environment protection	14	4.5	39	1.7
Neutrality/pacifism	11	3.6	36	1.6
Freedom of information	10	3.2	39	1.7
Privacy	10	3.2	37	1.6

the process is somewhat difficult to judge (more on this point later), but one can say with confidence that the engagement that did occur was of a notably high quality, as I shall explain in more detail later.

Many of the proposals addressed several issue areas and some went through large portions of the draft constitution in a point-by-point response, thus being coded as addressing a number of topics. The number of substantive proposals is at the least an indicator for the level of public interest in a given issue, and perhaps even serves as a proxy measure for how controversial a given issue area may be. Table 5.1 details the distribution of topics covered in the substantive proposals and the Facebook comment threads. Not surprisingly, emphases between the proposals and comments have a correlation of 0.86 (in terms of the number of posts per topic). There are some particularly interesting differences between the tables. One that immediately stands out is the fact that the establishment of a national church was by far the most commented-on issue (and the most contentious), while in terms of formal proposals and responses the issue only came in fourth place. Electoral reform is highly ranked in both measures. It should be noted that, while some of these topics are long-standing controversies in Iceland, others are more niche subjects. One of the members of the Constitutional Council wrote that "the people who participated in the online dialogue were a self-selecting cohort, that is generally more interested in topics such as the freedom of speech and the Internet, than the members of the general Icelandic public" (Oddsdottir, 2014, 1217).[13]

---

[13] For an analysis of the public engagement process from a communication studies perspective, see Valtysson Valtysson (2014).

5.6.2 Overall Change in the Constitutional Text

As a first cut at analyzing the impact of the public consultation process, I have measured the similarity between the 1944 constitution and the 2011 draft using two automated methods. The first way I have measured this similarity is by again using WCopyfind to identify copied strings of text. Using the original Iceland texts without translation, I find that 23 percent of the 2011 draft comes from the 1944 constitution (or from the other side 39 percent of the 1944 constitution is retained in the 2011 draft). It seems clear that the approach of the drafters in 2011 was to expand on the 1944 text. Many of these copied strings are substantively meaningful phrases, and not simply precatory or procedural language that would be common to all constitutions.

The amount of material carried over varies between the chapters of the constitution. The chapter with the largest amount of retained material is the chapter on human rights. In this chapter, the civil and political rights from the 1944 constitution are mostly carried over, though with some slight modifications. This chapter in the 2011 draft is expanded from the 1944 constitution, however, and adds new rights for children, Internet freedom, access to information, religious freedom, environmental protection, and public ownership of natural resources.[14] An analysis conducted by the Comparative Constitutions Project (CCP) shows that the current constitution includes twenty-four rights, while the draft included thirty-one. In their schema, the draft constitution dropped two rights in the area of criminal law: Right to pretrial release and the right to a fair trial, but added eight new rights that had not been included previously. The CCP report also noted that the protection against discrimination included in the new draft was one of the broadest in the world (Elkins et al., 2012).

A second – and perhaps more sophisticated – way of measuring the similarity is to develop a topic model.[15] As with the other two case studies, I have used the method of latent dirichlet allocation to identify the topics contained in the substantive proposals and in the constitutional texts. This analysis yields a similarity between the 1944 constitution and the 2011 draft of 90 percent. That is, the two texts cover 90 percent of the same topics. Additionally, assuming that there are fifteen topics covered in the substantive proposals from the public,[16] nine of these are also included in the draft constitution. Though this can actually be more informative than looking for

---

[14] Draft constitution of the Republic of Iceland, July 29, 2011, Ch. II

[15] This analysis also used the original (un-translated) texts.

[16] In a topic model using latent dirichlet allocation, values of some parameters must be set by the analyst. There are no ex ante rules about how many topics should be included. It has been my approach to run the topic model with a varying number of topics, settling on the number that produces the most intuitively sensible and coherent topics. Other approaches to topic modeling establish the number of topics in other ways (Arun et al., 2010).

matching n-grams, it still does not give us a very good substantive sense of how the texts compare. Even if we can be sure about which words have changed, we may not be sure of what the change means.[17]

5.6.3   *Verifiable Links between Proposals and the Constitution*

To determine the precise connections between public submissions and the text of the constitution, I compared the successive interim drafts of the constitution with the proposals from the public. As described earlier, I used some text analysis software to identify and highlight all wording changes between successive drafts of the constitution and sought to match these changes to individual proposals. This work principally consisted of reading a translation of each of the proposals and matching these specific demands with changes in the subsequent drafts. While the method of analysis here is not quite process tracing, it does bear some similarity to the logic of causation used in process tracing. Bennett has described four kinds of tests of causality that can be used in process tracing, which are differentiated by the degree to which they describe necessary and sufficient conditions for causation (Bennett, 2010, 210). My decision rule for finding an impact from a proposal is much like Bennett's "smoking gun test." I code a successful proposal when there is a specific demand or complaint that precedes a change in the constitutional text. Admittedly, this kind of test does not completely eliminate the possibility that the outcome we observe was brought about in some other way: It is a sufficient cause, but not a necessary cause (Collier, 2011, 827).

 Using this method, I identified twenty-nine instances where a "smoking gun test" is successful, and it seems reasonably certain that the Constitutional Council made changes in the text of the constitution in response to a public comment. In none of these cases was the precise wording suggested adopted, but the substance of the comment was incorporated into a subsequent draft of the constitution. In most examples of lawmaking there would be significant reason for skepticism about the role of proposals from the public as the causes of these changes. However, in the Icelandic constitution-making process, the nonparticipation of elites in general, but especially political parties and interest groups, isolated the drafters from other potential influences. In this context, we can be reasonably confident that these proposals from the public are indeed the causes of these changes in the constitutional text.

 Furthermore, I presented a list of these twenty-nine examples to several members of the Constitutional Council during interviews. They were generally unable

---

[17] As any student of constitutional law knows, the precise meaning ascribed by a Supreme Court Justice to a single word can have far-reaching effects. (See McCulloch v. Maryland 17 U.S. 316 [1819]; Wickard v. Filburn, 317 U.S. 111 [1942].)

to recall exactly this list, but found that the list was a reasonable recreation of what took place. They were able to recall some of the specific changes that I have included in my list. None of them suggested that I have included any spurious connections. The members of the Constitutional Council do of course have an interest in showing that they gave appropriate attention to the proposals from the public. However, at this point they are not all committed to continued efforts to pass the draft, and can discuss their work with some objectivity. Their views on the subject should be understood in that context, but are nonetheless valuable checks on the accuracy of the coding. As a further check, in interviews with several of the authors of these proposals, I queried them about their assessment of the impact that their proposals had. They were certain that their proposals were given a fair hearing, but did not feel that all of their proposals were implemented (which agrees with my coding). When pointed to evidence that their proposal resulted in a change in the draft constitution, one respondent was unwilling to claim complete credit for the change (Author's interview with "NRNJ," July 5, 2017). The full list is reproduced in the appendix to this chapter. If anything, this list may under-represent the full impact of public participation, as by its design it ignores agenda-setting effects or other potential impacts that are of a slightly nebulous nature.

Some of these changes involve rather unique provisions in the constitution and are straightforward to link to comments from the public. For example, one of the earliest proposals from a member of the public was a request to add protection for the rights of animals.[18] This was added to the constitution following the tenth meeting of the Constitutional Council. Another clear example concerns the right to access the Internet.[19] A proposal posted on June 21 discussed the importance of free access to information as a necessary condition for democracy,[20] and references a report published a month earlier by the United Nations Human Rights Commission on freedom of expression, which described access to the Internet as a human right (UNHRC, 2011). Three days later, the Constitutional Council added the right to access the Internet to their draft constitution. The day that this new draft was published, another individual wrote that he supported the addition of the right to access the Internet and suggested that this access should be uncensored.[21] The draft of the constitution published on July 12 changed the language of this provision to "unrestricted access." These examples illustrate the engagement of the Constitutional Council with the public comments and the manner in which they used that information to shape the draft constitution.

---

[18] Árni Stefán Árnason, April 6, 2011, http://www.stjornlagarad.is/erindi/nanar/item33142/
[19] If it had been approved, Iceland would have been the first country to include the protection of access to the Internet in its constitution.
[20] Þórlaug Ágústsdóttir, June 21, 2011, www.stjornlagarad.is/erindi/nanar/item33986/
[21] Svavar Kjarrval Lúthersson, June 24, 2011, www.stjornlagarad.is/erindi/nanar/item34042/

TABLE 5.2 *Simplified topics in substantive proposals*

Topic	In Proposals Number	In Proposals Percentage	In Constitution Number	In Constitution Percentage
Amendment procedures	6	1.5	0	0.0
Cultural issues	57	14.1	3	10.3
Electoral process	56	13.9	1	3.5
Executive branch	38	9.4	1	3.5
Judicial branch	18	4.5	0	0.0
Legislative branch	56	13.9	1	3.5
Direct democracy	23	5.7	4	13.8
Oversight and regulation	17	4.2	0	0.0
Rights	133	32.9	19	65.5
Total	404		29	

5.7 STATISTICAL ANALYSIS

5.7.1 *Description of the Data and Model*

As reported in Table 5.2, the qualitative analysis of the substantive proposals from the public generated a list of twenty-nine instances where a proposal is almost certain to have caused a change in the text of the draft constitution. Although this is a rather low rate (9.3 percent), it is likely higher than many observers of constitution-drafting processes would expect.[22] Based on my studies of other constitution-making processes, I consider this to be an extraordinarily high level of impact. The levels of interest from both drafters and citizens are clearly uneven across categories, but the correlation between the overall distribution of proposals and the distribution of accepted proposals is actually quite high, at 0.88. Additionally, while the numbers of both positive and negative values in this dataset are small, they are sufficient for some statistical analyses of the probability that a particular comment would be included in the text of the constitution.

We can think more systematically about the kinds of proposals that made it into the constitution with a regression model that predicts inclusion with a set of covariates that include topic dummies, and variables that capture characteristics of the suggestions and their individual contexts. Given this binary coding of the key outcome variable – whether or not a proposal was included in the constitution – I fit a probit model to estimate the values of a number of covariates that might be expected to influence the inclusion of individual proposals in the constitution. The

[22] That is 9.3 percent of the 311 proposals submitted by Icelanders. The number of observations in the rest of the paper varies as proposals are split to consider the various subject areas dealt with within individual proposals.

full model is expressed mathematically as:

$$Pr(y = 1|x) = F(\beta_0 + \beta_1[\text{days elapsed}] + \beta_2[\text{words count}]$$
$$+ \beta_3[\text{number of comments}] + \beta_4[\text{CC comments}]$$
$$+ \beta_5[\text{poster responded}] + \beta_6[\text{total posts by author}]$$
$$+ \beta_7[\text{representing NGO}] + \beta_8[\text{topic: institutions}]$$
$$+ \beta_9[\text{topic: rights}] + \beta_{10}[\text{topic: others}] + \varepsilon)$$

The intuitions in this model are as follows. The first variable is a count of the days passed since the first proposal was posted on the Constitutional Council's website – which I expected to have a negative coefficient, indicating that earlier comments are more likely to be included.[23] The second variable is the number of words in the proposal – also expected to have a negative coefficient, which would indicate that shorter proposals are more likely to be included. The next five variables all consider aspects of the comment activity that responded to the proposal: The number of Facebook comments on the proposal, the number of comments on the proposal from members of the Constitutional Council, a dummy indicating whether or not the author of the proposal responds to the comments, the total number of submissions from that individual, and whether they write on behalf of an NGO or CSO.[24] The remaining variables record the topic categories that the proposals considered.[25]

5.7.2 Results and Discussion

Coefficients for several variations of this model are reported in Table 5.3. The coefficients are reported on the main lines, with the standard errors in parentheses beneath. The estimates are fairly stable across these statistical models. The variation in the models is chiefly that, in Models 2, 3, and 4, I drop the variables for the timing and length of the proposal, and the dummy for proposals from an organized group, in an effort to investigate the variables of greatest interest in a more parsimonious equation. In Model 1, we see that the measure of time elapsed has a negative

[23] I expected that comments made earlier in the drafting period will be more likely to be accepted. The agenda at that time is more open. Additionally, drafters may be working in a more research-intensive mode early in the process, before shifting to an editing approach toward the end of the process.
[24] These variables capture information about some of my expectations (or hunches) about contextual elements that might have an impact. I expected that proposals that received attention from a higher number of members of the Constitutional Council will be more likely to have an influence on the text. Additionally, proposals that were followed by comments in which the original poster is active would be more likely to be influential, and proposals made by individuals who post multiple proposals would be more likely to be adopted.
[25] The "institutions" category includes all proposals relating to the three branches of government and to elections. The "rights" category includes all proposals having to do with human rights and duties of citizens. The "others" category includes all proposals that deal with direct democracy, amendment procedures, oversight mechanisms, and cultural issues.

coefficient, indicating that later proposals were less likely to be included in the constitution, though the effect is small. We can be quite certain that the length of the proposal had no effect on its inclusion. Also – perhaps unsurprisingly – proposals that received comments from more members of the Constitutional Council were more likely to be included in the constitution, though the total number of comments was not important. The response of the proposal author to comments on the proposal had no effect on the likelihood of its acceptance.

The most important finding in Model 1 is that proposals submitted by organized groups were *not* more likely to be influential than those submitted by individuals. On the contrary, while the coefficient is not significant, it is estimated to have a negative effect. The finding may in part be explained by some of the unique features of the drafting process. Interest groups were not allowed to participate in the process with any sort of special accommodations, and by and large abstained from participating in the open process that was available to individuals. Even so, approximately 10 percent of the proposals on the Council's website were posted by representatives of NGOs or CSOs. The results here may not be suggestive of how this dynamic works in other cases, where interest groups and NGOs are often given preferential treatment (Gylfason, 2013a).

Models 2, 3, and 4 allow us to examine the possibility that the effectiveness of public participation depends on the subject matter of the proposal, by varying the reference category for the topic variables. In Model 2, we see that, relative to the "other" category, "institutions" are less likely to be included in the constitution, and "rights" are more likely. Likewise, in Model 3, we see that proposals dealing with "institutions" and "others" are both less likely than "rights." Finally, Model 4 shows that, relative to "institutions," both "rights" and "others" are more likely to be included.

Although the probit coefficients are suggestive, their interpretation is not immediately clear, so the marginal effects of these variables are presented in Table 5.4, and Figure 5.3. Here we can see that the effects of all of these variables are quite small. The variables relating to the metadata of the proposal have such small effects that they hardly bear mention. It is notable, however, that additional comments from members of the Constitutional Council did increase the likelihood of a proposal's inclusion in the draft constitution by 1 or 2 percent. Model 1 provides a nice comparison of the relative effects of being in the "institutions" and "rights" categories, with "rights" being 5 percent more likely to be included relative to "others" (though this is not quite significant) and "institutions" about 5 percent less likely. The strongest effect in Model 4 is that of the "rights" dummy variable. In Model 4, the marginal effect of moving from the "institutions" category to the "rights" category is an increase in the probability that a proposal would be incorporated in the constitutional text of approximately 16 percent. This finding strongly confirms one of the key claims made in this chapter and also agrees with the findings of Maboudi and Nadi (2016) in the Egyptian case.

TABLE 5.3 *Probit estimates*

	Model 1	Model 2	Model 3	Model 4
(Intercept)	-1.29^{***}	-2.06^{***}	-1.58^{***}	-2.71^{***}
	(0.38)	(0.27)	(0.20)	(0.33)
Days elapsed	-0.02^{***}			
	(0.00)			
Length of proposal	0.00^{**}			
	(0.00)			
Num. Facebook comments	-0.01	-0.01	-0.01	-0.01
	(0.02)	(0.01)	(0.01)	(0.01)
Num. comms. from Council	0.17^{*}	0.20^{**}	0.21^{**}	0.20^{**}
	(0.07)	(0.06)	(0.06)	(0.06)
Orig. poster commenting	-0.21	-0.30	-0.29	-0.29
	(0.29)	(0.27)	(0.26)	(0.27)
Total submits by poster	0.05^{*}	0.04	0.04^{*}	0.04
	(0.02)	(0.02)	(0.02)	(0.02)
Submitted by NGO/CSO	-0.18			
	(0.39)			
Topic: Institutions	-0.74^{*}	-0.65^{*}	-1.14^{***}	
	(0.35)	(0.32)	(0.29)	
Topic: Rights	0.65^{*}	0.53^{*}		1.20^{***}
	(0.26)	(0.24)		(0.29)
Topic: Other			-0.44	0.72^{*}
			(0.25)	(0.32)
AIC	179.48	192.75	194.60	191.83
BIC	219.76	220.97	222.81	220.05
Log likelihood	-79.74	-89.38	-90.30	-88.92
Deviance	159.48	178.75	180.60	177.83
Num. obs.	415	416	416	416

$^{***}p < 0.001, ^{**}p < 0.01, ^{*}p < 0.05$

   Why might public participation have greater effects in the domain of rights? In many areas of the constitutional text there are clearly competing alternatives. For example, one controversial topic in the Icelandic political system concerns the number of electoral districts in their system of proportional representation. This choice has a significant impact on the balance of power between rural and urban interests in Iceland. Other politically salient decisions are essentially binary, as between a presidential system or a parliamentary system, with clear implications for many interested parties. These are areas where public participation is less likely to be influential, both because these decisions have clear costs and benefits for established elites and because the drafters are likely to encounter conflicting proposals from the public. Moreover, changes in these areas often require a cascading series of edits to maintain a coherent text. However, in the area of rights, the proposals are more likely to be additive, rather than competitive. For example, a new class of persons can be added to the equal protection clause without creating conflicts with other areas of the text (as was in fact done in the Icelandic draft).

TABLE 5.4 *Marginal effects for Model 1 and Model 4*

	Model 1	Model 4
(Intercept)	−0.082*	−0.237***
	(0.032)	(0.036)
Days elapsed	−0.001**	
	(0.000)	
Length of proposal	0.000*	
	(0.000)	
Num. Facebook comments	−0.001	−0.001
	(0.001)	(0.001)
Num. comms. from Council	0.011*	0.018**
	(0.005)	(0.006)
Orig. poster commenting	−0.012	−0.022
	(0.015)	(0.018)
Total submits by poster	0.003*	0.003
	(0.001)	(0.002)
Submitted by NGO/CSO	−0.010	
	(0.018)	
Topic: Institutions	−0.047*	
	(0.021)	
Topic: Rights	0.054	0.161***
	(0.028)	(0.045)
Topic: Others		0.087
		(0.047)
AIC	179.478	191.833
BIC	219.761	220.048
Log likelihood	−79.739	−88.917
Deviance	159.478	177.833
Num. obs.	415	416

$^*p < 0.05, ^{**}p < 0.01, ^{***}p < 0.001$

The global trend has been to increase the number of rights in constitutions over time (Law and Versteeg, 2011), suggesting that rights in constitutions may operate with a ratchet-like mechanism in which adding more rights is straightforward, but it is almost impossible to remove a right. Beyond this, it is likely that members of the public find rights more accessible than the intricacies of the translation of votes to seats in the legislature (though there were two suggestions from Icelanders that addressed exactly that).

There is further empirical support for the intuition that rights are more likely to be influenced by input from the public than other areas of the constitution. As referenced earlier, Maboudi and Nadi's (2016) study of the Egyptian constitution-making process found that public participation dealing with rights was more likely to have an effect on the text than submissions dealing with any other aspect of the constitution. This finding is further bolstered by more theoretical and empirical work in law that shows that rights are sometimes added to constitutions in order to

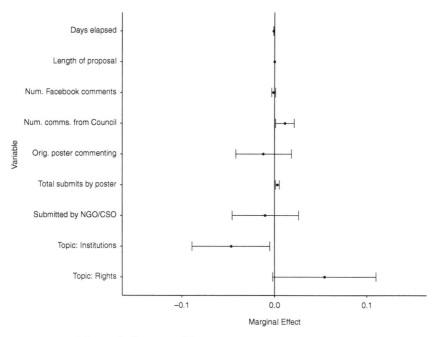

FIGURE 5.3 Marginal effects, Model 1

secure the support of politically important groups (Dixon, 2018). I take up this issue again in the cross-national analysis in Chapter 6.

There is also a more positive interpretation to put on some of the insignificant statistical results in this case. Null findings could be interpreted as evidence of fair process of evaluation of the suggestions submitted to the Constitutional Council. There is clearly little in the way of a systematic relationship between characteristics of the suggestions and the probability that they will be implemented (beyond the subject matter effect discussed earlier). Perhaps this is the best outcome and evidence that the "best" suggestions were implemented regardless of other factors.

5.8 WHY DID THE DRAFTERS GIVE EFFECT TO PROPOSALS FROM THE PUBLIC?

Having established that the Icelandic drafters not only paid attention to the proposals from the public, but also included at least twenty-nine of these proposals in their final draft, we must turn to the question of why. The explanation for this phenomenon relates to a number of elements in the context of constitution-making in Iceland, several of which have been touched on earlier in this chapter. First, the political context in Iceland between 2009 and 2012 involved a resurgence of democratic political activity alongside the delegitimation of political parties and institutions. It was this context of rejection of the political system that inspired the constitution-making process. The law that established the constitution-making process specifically forbade the president, government ministers, or members of parliament from standing for election to the Constitutional Council (Althingi, 2010, Art. 6). The law further stipulated that the members of the Council should be bound only by their own convictions and not by instructions from anyone else (Althingi, 2010, Art. 19). Alongside these legally required barriers between the Constitutional Council and the political establishment, the political parties evinced no interest in the work of the Council during its months of drafting. For the most part, civil society groups were not very active either (Author's interview with "XQPC," March 13, 2017, and "YIGY," March 15, 2017). The combination of these legal and practical factors meant that the drafters were quite isolated from the political system, and thus both more reliant on the public for information about what should go into the constitution and unmoored from any prior policy commitments.

Relatedly, many of the Council members seem to have had concerns about the legitimacy of their appointment and about the relationship between their work and the role of parliament. Although the complaints about the legality of the original election to the Constituent Assembly are not entirely convincing, the nature of the appointment process did tend to hang over the Council. The mandate of the Council was also somewhat unclear. Some members of the Council understood their role to be to draft a new constitution which the parliament would duly approve. Others understood their draft to be something that parliament would significantly amend. This difference of opinions persisted both in the Icelandic public and on the Council throughout the drafting process (Author's interview with "XQPC," March 13, 2017). Adding to this confusion about the fate of their draft in parliament was a worry on the part of some Council members that the draft could not be completed in the time parliament had allowed (Author's interview with "GNEL," March 15, 2017).[26] These considerations pushed the Council members to take steps to shore up the legitimacy of their work and to demonstrate the support of the public for their draft. Council members believed that giving significant effect to proposals from the public would give the draft sufficient legitimacy to carry it forward (Author's interview with "DLEA," March 15, 2017).

Finally, there is a real sense in which the simple explanation "No one told them not to"[27] is the truth of how the Icelandic case can be explained in relation to more traditional examples of constitution-making. The drafting process was somewhat ad hoc, without clear rules for how public input would take place or how it should relate to the drafting. In this context, the members of the Council had few reasons not to give attention to proposals from the public, and (as noted earlier) some rather strong incentives to be seen to be doing so. One member of the Council suggested

---

[26] Note that most successful constitution-making processes in recent years have taken between two and five years (Updike Toler, 2014).
[27] As proposed by one early commenter on this project.

that "There was really no cost in considering sensible suggestions" (Author's interview with "YIGY," March 15, 2017). In this relatively apolitical context, proposals from the public were much more valuable and influential than they are in most law-drafting processes.

The absence of political parties is a thread that unites these partial explanations for the high impact of public participation on the draft in Iceland. Every step of the drafting process – from the election of the Constitutional Council, to the unanimous approval of the draft – is best understood in a comparative perspective through the issue of the nonparticipation of the political parties. The individuals who were selected to draft the constitution did not have a career path typical of either politicians or the constitutional lawyers who often advise such processes. As I have argued earlier, their lack of association with a party made them more dependent on both the information contained in submissions from the public and the legitimacy that their work could gain through a close association with public participation. The negotiations between drafters were then focused on competing ideas of what would be good for Iceland and most in line with the input from the public, instead of being pitched battles between representatives of strong political parties. In this party-free context, submissions from the public took on a level of significance for the debate that would be difficult to even imagine in a case like South Africa or Brazil.

5.9 A FAILED CONSTITUTIONAL REVOLUTION?

Constitutional revolution can be a thorny concept, but may be a useful way of thinking about what was attempted in Iceland. As used here, it is meant in the sense defined by Gary Jacobsohn, which includes the idea of renewal and paradigmatic shift (Jacobsohn, 2012). This seems to be how the people of Iceland understood their broader endeavor in the aftermath of the financial crisis – rebuilding what the "banksters" (as they called them) had destroyed. In this sense, the constitutional revolution would have been deemed a success if it satisfied two conditions. First, the new constitution would have to reflect the demands of the people and not merely serve as another example of elite domination of popular preferences. Second, and perhaps most obviously, there would have to be real constitutional change. In the event, the analysis undertaken in this chapter shows that the constitutional revolution was a success with regard to the first requirement, but not the second. It is possible that the success of the constitutional revolution in achieving real, popularly motivated change in the text of the constitution ultimately doomed the draft to languish un-ratified. Change took too long, and in the interim, the old regime returned to favor with enough of the electorate to regain power.

The pots and pans revolution destabilized Icelandic politics, and we do not yet know what the new political equilibrium will look like. While the Independence Party did regain some of its vote share in the 2013 election, a number of new parties have also continued to spring up. This uncertainty persisted in national polls

TABLE 5.5 *Election results*

Party	2007 Percentage	2007 Seats	2009 Percentage	2009 Seats	2013 Percentage	2013 Seats	2016 Percentage	2016 Seats	2017 Percentage	2017 Seats
Independence Party	36.6	25	23.7	16	26.7	19	29.0	21	25.2	16
Progressive Party	11.7	7	14.8	9	24.4	19	11.5	8	10.7	8
Social Democratic Alliance	26.8	18	29.8	20	12.9	9	5.7	3	12.1	7
Left-Green Movement	14.3	9	21.7	14	10.9	7	15.9	10	16.9	11
Liberal Party	7.3	4								
Iceland's Movement	3.3	0	2.2	0						
Bright Future					8.2	6	7.2	4	1.2	0
Pirate Party					5.1	3	14.5	10	9.2	6
Dawn					3.1	0	1.7	0	0.1	0
Household's Party					3.0	0				
Iceland Democratic Party					2.5	0				
Right Green People's Party					1.7	0				
Rainbow Party					1.1	0				
Reform Party							10.5	7	6.7	4
People's Party							3.5	0	6.9	4
Centre Party									10.9	7

between 2013 and 2018. In a poll in March 2015, the Pirate Party had a plurality of support from Icelanders, beating the Independence Party with a predicted vote share of 23.9 percent, compared to 23.4 percent for Independence (Ward, 2015). One of the members of parliament from the Pirate Party, Jón Þór Ólafsson, was one of the most active participants in the online discussion in 2011, and the party has expressed strong interest in reviving the issue of constitutional reform. The Pirates led in the polls from the Spring of 2015 until the Spring of 2016, giving renewed hope to supporters of the 2011 draft constitution. As it turned out, the Independence Party won the most seats in the October 2016 election and formed a center-right coalition government with the Reform Party and the Bright Future party. Following an additional political scandal, another election took place in October 2017. This time the Left-Green Movement leader (Katrín Jakobsdóttir) formed a coalition government with the Progressive Party and the Independence Party. Through all this, changes to the constitution remained a (minor) subject of debate both within Icelandic society and in the parliament. A January 2017 poll conducted by the Social Science Institute of the University of Iceland showed that public support for both the 2011 draft (58 percent) and constitutional reform in general (66 percent) remained high (Gylfason, 2017). This level of support was relatively unchanged from 2011.

A new process for constitutional reform was taken up as a project of the Icelandic parliament in January 2018. It is likely that some constitutional reforms will result, and the 2011 draft may have some bearing on what parliament decides, but it will not form the basis of the reforms (Hudson, 2018b). Note that the government that took power in 2017 includes the Independence Party, which had opposed the 2011 draft. Following Iceland's precedent-setting innovations almost a decade earlier, the new process will involve public consultations. However, the theory advanced in this book would predict that public participation will be much less influential in this new process that is dominated by strong parties.

5.10 CONCLUSION

On the whole, Iceland's constitution-drafting process almost lived up to the hype. If not actually crowdsourced, the 2011 constitution-drafting process was a "fully open and transparent" process, as described by the Constitutional Council (Stjórnlagaráð, 2011). Council members were highly engaged with the proposals submitted to the Council website, and it is clear that many of these proposals were reflected in the text of the constitution. This really is a remarkable phenomenon. Individuals have no means of validating their claim to speak for the people, broadly understood. They also have no means of ensuring that the Council would pay any attention to their suggestion. In a strategic understanding of political behavior, this outcome does not make any immediate sense. Nonetheless, the evidence clearly indicates that the members of the Constitutional Council took public participation seriously, and included many of the suggestions of the public in the final draft. The quality of participation in this case was quite high and should lend support to initiatives toward similar processes in other cases.

The impact of public participation is almost certainly much higher here than in any other case (though measurements of this kind of impact are quite difficult, particularly when the number of comments is orders of magnitude higher). I argue that the most significant reason for the greater impact was the absence of political parties. The drafters in Iceland were not bound to follow any agenda or program for constitution change other than the mandate they were individually given by the voters. Furthermore, in the context of political upheaval in which the drafting took place, popular participation had taken on a particular significance. Yet, despite the best efforts of the members of the Constitutional Council and their allies, the constitution was not ratified. It may be the case that the kind of drafting process that facilitates a high impact from public participation also decreases the likelihood that the draft can make it through ratification in the regular legislative assembly, as none of the parties has a significant stake in the document's ratification.

The Iceland case thus advances the party-mediation thesis in two steps. First, we see the possibility that public participation can have a large impact when the drafters are not acting as members of political parties. In this context, drafters are more reliant on information directly from the public, have fewer established positions on what the constitution should say, and are not bound by any commitment to a larger political group that might restrict their freedom in drafting the text. In the later part of the process that political context changes with respect to the political parties and allows Iceland to illustrate the theory in a second way. Although the drafting took place in a party-free environment, ratification depended on action in a parliament populated by strong parties. Here we see evidence of something like the South African dynamic, where in this case strong parties prevented the passage of a constitution that went against their interest. These issues are taken up in a wider context in the next chapter.

6

Cross-National Analysis

6.1 INTRODUCTION

The three previous chapters developed context-sensitive applications of the party-mediation thesis in three cases of constitution-making. The three cases allowed us to see how public participation fares in constitution-making processes with strong parties, weak parties, and no parties. In South Africa's dynamic and participatory constitution-making process, the central contest between the two main political parties dominated, while extensive public participation had little impact on the final text. Brazil's constitution-making process utilized similar forms of public involvement, and the weakness of the political parties allowed citizens and interest groups to have a moderate impact on the constitutional text. Iceland's constitution-making process allowed us some insight into the rare circumstance in which a constitution was drafted without partisan involvement. There, we found a startlingly high level of impact from public participation – at least until the political parties reasserted themselves.

The party-mediation thesis and the three main case studies all suggest that, if this theory was tested on a much larger set of cases, we should find that constitutions drafted by weak political parties are much more likely to be impacted by public participation than cases with strong parties. This may not be a perfectly linear relationship, but on balance, the prediction is that, given similar forms and levels of public participation, we should expect to find that party strength is highly correlated with the extent of public influence on the constitutional text.

In this chapter, two approaches are used to evaluate the theory with reference to a much broader set of cases. First, the theory is tested with a statistical analysis of constitution-making processes between 1974 and 2014. Using data collected by Eisenstadt et al. (2017b) and Elkins et al. (2014), I evaluate the statistical relationship between higher levels of public participation in the constitution-making process and some quantities of interest in the constitutional texts. Despite some data limitations, the results of the cross-national analysis provide strong support for the theory and suggest that a more qualitative approach may also yield more helpful information.

Second, the chapter includes sixteen shorter case studies of the most highly participatory drafting processes as coded by Eisenstadt et al. (2017b). These case studies include the full spectrum of potential values of party strength (as coded by Bizzarro et al. [2018]). The cases were selected to include only the most participatory, and exclude cases that were not successful. On the latter point, we do not have good data on how many attempted constitution-making processes have not been successful, or even commonly accepted standards for what would count as a case. Nonetheless, the sixteen cases have a good temporal and geographic spread, though there are no cases from Asia in this sample. The case studies also give deeper insight into the mechanisms behind the statistical relationships. The case studies provide strong support for the argument that public participation is more likely to have an impact on the constitutional text in cases where the drafting process is managed by weaker political parties.

6.2 COMPREHENSIVE CROSS-NATIONAL ANALYSIS

The party-mediation thesis developed in the previous chapters suggests that the degree to which public participation has an effect on the content of the constitution *depends upon* the strength of the political parties. This theoretical framing suggests that an appropriate way to model this statistically would be through an interaction between party strength and the level of public participation in a linear regression.

The challenge in expanding the analysis is of course the coding of the dependent variable. Even in the case studies described in the previous chapters, a direct line-by-line accounting of the degree to which submissions from the public led to a change in the draft constitution was only possible in the case of Iceland, where the number of submissions from the public was relatively manageable. This technique for comparison between submissions and constitutional text used in those chapters cannot be applied to a comprehensive sample – even if the full collection of the documents generated in the drafting processes were available. Nonetheless, data are available that enable me to create a reliable proxy for the effect of public participation on the constitutional text. As described later, the inclusion of novel rights in a constitution can be used as a proxy for the impact of public participation in the constitution-making process.

6.2.1 *Data*

For data on the extent to which members of the public participated in the constitution-making process, I return to the data collected by Eisenstadt, LeVan, and Maboudi in their dataset that was discussed in Chapter 2 (Constitutionalism and Democracy Dataset [CDD]; Eisenstadt et al., 2017b). However, there is no dataset that includes a direct measure of the extent to which public participation has had an impact on the content of a constitution. Indeed, it is difficult to imagine the resources that would be required to systematically measure this for any statistically useful number of cases.

Because even a partial measurement of the real dependent variable of interest (impact on the constitutional text) is not possible for a representative sample of cases, we must use some proxy for the true dependent variable of interest (impact on the text). The case studies described in this book and other previously published empirical research suggest that the aspect of the constitution that is most likely to be influenced by submissions from the public is the protection of rights (Maboudi and Nadi, 2016; Hudson, 2018a; Maboudi, 2019). However, we know from both simple intuition and empirical research that constitutions have been including more and more rights over time. Indeed, Law and Versteeg (2011) have described a "generic core" of constitutional rights that are likely to be found in any constitution. This should lead us to assert that a submission from a citizen calling for a right to free expression and the inclusion of such a right in the constitution are unlikely to be causally related. We would expect to find that right in the constitution regardless of the content of the submissions from the public. Yet, the existence of this generic core points us toward a more fine-grained proxy for the impact of public participation: The inclusion of unexpected or novel rights. As an example, as noted in the previous chapter, Iceland's 2011 draft added at one point a right to access the Internet in response to input from the public. This article was later expanded further in response to more input from the public to encompass "unrestricted" access to the Internet. This right is clearly well beyond the generic core and offers a small insight into the kinds of "boutique" rights (if you will) that would offer evidence of impactful public participation.

I implement a simple rule to establish which rights would count as being outside the "generic core," and thus giving us some useful indication that the catalog of rights in a particular constitution responds to public input: Rights found in less than half of the constitutions currently in force (ca. 2016) are counted as novel.[1] The rights included in the variable "novel rights" are listed in Table 6.1. These rights vary from the relatively common right to equal remuneration to the very rare right to bear arms.[2] The more substantively interesting rights in the list include the right to a safe and healthy workplace, the right to a reasonable standard of living, and the right to access higher education. These rights form a common part of the demands made by citizen-participants in constitution-making processes.

These data are then supplemented with other data that measure covariates of interest. Clearly, for the theory advanced in this book, we need to have a measure of party strength. In this case some conceptual thinking is required, as the

---

[1] Data from Elkins et al. (2014).

[2] On this last right, while the right to bear arms is not novel in the sense of being new, it is rare and sometimes demanded by citizens. In South Africa, for example, there was a very vocal lobby for the right to bear arms (Murray, 2001, 821).

TABLE 6.1 *Distribution of novel rights in national constitutions*

Right	Number	Percent
Right to just/fair/equal remuneration	91	46.4
Guarantee of child rights	86	43.9
Right to asylum	82	41.8
Right to strike	80	40.8
Right to access government information	75	38.3
Right to a safe/healthy workplace	73	37.2
Prohibition of slavery	73	37.3
Right to rest and leisure	73	37.3
Right to establish a business	73	37.3
Right to academic freedom	65	33.2
Right to matrimonial equality	61	31.1
Right to found a family	59	30.1
Right to shelter	54	27.6
Right to protection from libel	53	27.0
Right to inherit	53	27.0
Consumer rights	46	23.5
Right to renounce citizenship	46	23.5
Right to conscientious objection	44	22.4
Right to government funded health care	41	20.9
Right to reasonable standard of living	41	20.9
Right to a free/competitive market	40	20.4
Right to transfer property	32	16.3
Right to free development of personality	30	15.3
Right to group self-determination	26	13.3
Right to enjoy benefits of science	22	11.2
Right to access higher education	18	9.2
Right to marry	16	8.2
Right to transfer property after death	14	7.1
Right to bear arms	3	1.5

exact conceptualization of party strength that I have adopted throughout the book to this point has not been comprehensively measured. A related concept that is well developed in cross-national empirical work is that of the effective number of parties (Laakso and Taagepera, 1979). This concept has much in common with the way that Ginsburg (2003) describes party strength. However, a much closer analogue to the concept of party strength that is key to the theory developed in this book can be found in the work of Bizzarro et al. (2018). In their data (part of the larger V-Dem project), Bizzarro et al. (2018) use an expert survey to measure the strength of political parties across several decades and across all independent states. The concept of party strength that they operationalize is centered on the organizational capacity of the political parties. This again differs somewhat from the concept of real interest in this research, but it is close enough that it should at the very least be highly correlated with the latent concept of party strength that is of primary interest.

6.2.2 *Statistical Analysis*

The basic relationship of interest is that between the aggregate level of public participation in the drafting process (including everything from electing the drafters to
a ratifying referendum) and the number of novel rights included in the constitution
(as a proxy for effective participation). The party-mediation thesis suggests that the
effect of participation is conditional on the strength of the political parties involved
in the drafting process. This suggests that the regression model should be as follows:

$$Y = \alpha + \beta_1[participation] + \beta_2[partystrength]$$
$$+ \beta_3[participation] * [partystrength] + \epsilon$$

However, to fully understand this key relationship of interest, in the models presented in Table 6.2 I also include a number of control variables. I control for
the overall level of democracy (polyarchy) in the political system, expecting that
democracies are in general more likely to include rights in their constitutions than
non-democracies (Davenport, 1999; Reif, 2000). I also expect that a history of conflict may have various impacts on the constitution-making process (Widner, 2005,
2008) and control for the mean level of conflict intensity in the three years prior
to the promulgation of the new constitution (data from the Uppsala Conflict Data
Program (UCDP) and International Peace Research Institute, Oslo (PRIO)). Other
forms of political action could also have an impact on the inclusion of several of the
social and economic rights of interest, and I therefore also control for the number of
national strikes in the three years prior to promulgation (Tilly, 2004; Tarrow, 2011).
Finally, expecting that national wealth could affect approaches to rights protection
(Blanton and Blanton, 2007; Englehart, 2009), I control for GDP per capita (average
of three years prior to promulgation, in thousands of US dollars).

The models shown in Table 6.2 and Figure 6.1 are linear regressions with different combinations of variables. The second and fourth models are most important
for the theory, since they include an interaction effect between party strength and
public participation. Turning first to the simplest model with no interaction or
control variables (Model 1), the null hypotheses would be that there is no relationship between party strength, or participation, and the content of the constitution.
This overly simple model would lead us to reject the null hypothesis in the case
of participation; however, we cannot reject the null regarding party strength. The
level of participation has a significant and positive effect on the inclusion of novel
rights. Model 3 tests the same predictors with added controls as discussed earlier.
While participation retains its positive and significant effect, it is clearly outclassed
by the association between polyarchy and the inclusion of novel rights. However, these models fail to account for the party-mediation theory developed in this
book.

Models 2 and 4 seek to statistically test the party-mediation thesis by modeling
an effect of participation that is dependent on the strength of political parties. In

TABLE 6.2 *Regression models: Inclusion of novel rights*

	Dependent variable:			
	Novel rights in constitution			
	(1)	(2)	(3)	(4)
Participation	0.458***	0.793***	0.430***	0.986***
	(0.121)	(0.281)	(0.156)	(0.321)
Party strength	1.226	2.904*	−0.222	2.898
	(0.913)	(1.563)	(1.254)	(2.005)
Participation x party		−0.683		−1.232*
		(0.518)		(0.625)
Polyarchy			3.424**	3.538**
			(1.585)	(1.556)
Conflict intensity			0.223	0.126
			(0.447)	(0.441)
Strikes			0.151	0.271
			(0.189)	(0.195)
GDP pc			−0.077	−0.063
			(0.050)	(0.050)
Constant	2.001***	1.251	1.401**	0.036
	(0.530)	(0.776)	(0.638)	(0.934)
Observations	108	108	82	82
R^2	0.158	0.171	0.294	0.329
Adjusted R^2	0.142	0.148	0.238	0.266
Residual Std. Error	2.215	2.207	2.141	2.101
	(df = 105)	(df = 104)	(df = 75)	(df = 74)
F Statistic	9.822***	7.174***	5.211***	5.193***
	(df = 2; 105)	(df = 3; 104)	(df = 6; 75)	(df = 7; 74)

Note: *p<0.1; **p<0.05; ***p<0.01

Model 2, we find that the interaction is not significant. Interestingly, this model shows that, in the rare event of a process with zero participation, stronger parties include a few more novel rights than weaker parties. However, this model does a relatively poorer job of describing the dynamics of a constitution-making process than Model 4, where controls are introduced.

In Model 4, we find that the interaction between party strength and public participation is negative and significant ($p = 0.052$). The effects of increased participation are not continuous across all values of party strength. The best way to understand this interaction effect is through a plot of the predicted values under

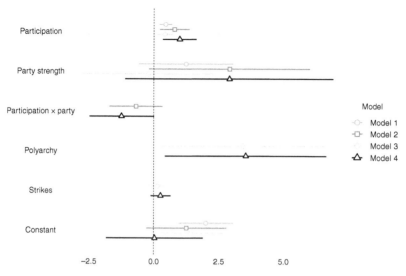

FIGURE 6.1 Point estimates (Models 1–4)

different conditions (see Figure 6.2). For both comparatively weak parties and parties of average strength, increased public participation in the constitution-making
process positively affects the number of novel rights included in the constitution.
For example, in a case with parties that are one standard deviation below the mean,
a highly participatory process would be expected to result in a constitution that
includes four more novel rights than would be included without participation.
Even in a case with average parties, a highly participatory process would be predicted to result in a constitution with at least two more novel rights. However, for
strong parties, the effect of increased participation is significantly muted. For parties that are one standard deviation stronger than the mean, the prediction would
be that one out of every two highly participatory processes would gain a novel
right.

The statistical analysis presented here provides strong support for the party-
mediation theory. While increased levels of public participation are likely to
influence the constitution (at least in the domain of rights), this effect is dependent on the strength of the political parties involved in the process. However, there
are some limitations in this analysis. While the proxy variable of novel rights is supported by both prior empirical work and normative accounts of public participation,
it is still not a direct measurement of the outcome of interest. The number of observation is also small due to missing data for some cases. The fact that we find such a
strong effect in spite of these limitations suggests that there is substantial empirical
support for the party-mediation theory. In the next section, the interaction between
public participation and party strength is further investigated through a series of case
studies.

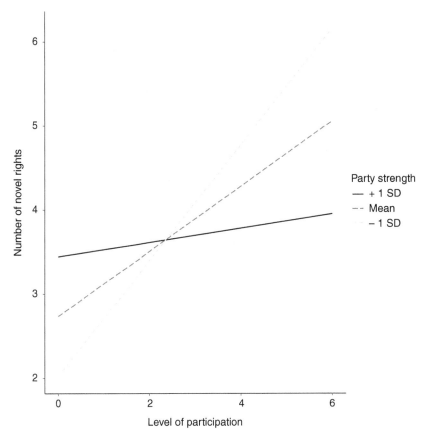

FIGURE 6.2 Interaction between participation and party strength (Model 4)

6.3 QUALITATIVE ASSESSMENT OF SELECTED CASES

To put flesh on the bones of this statistical analysis, we can look at the key cases in more detail. The theory has little to say about cases in which there was very little participation. However, the cases with a high level of participation could potentially provide a great deal of useful information about the dynamics between public participation and political negotiation. To that end, this section includes a brief analysis of *all* cases of constitution-making between 1974 and 2014 that involved a high aggregate level of public participation.

The CDD dataset includes a variable that records the aggregate level of public participation in the drafting process, combining each of the three stages of the process in one variable. Using this measure, there are eighteen cases with at least a score of five (out of a maximum of six). Sixteen of these cases are dealt with in this

TABLE 6.3 *Case selection and party strength*

Year	Country	Party strength
1978	Spain	0.965
1997	Poland	0.882
1992	Lithuania	0.797
1991	Romania	0.714
2014	Tunisia	0.618
1998	Ecuador	0.564
2010	Kenya	0.556
2012	Egypt	0.555
1987	Nicaragua	0.549
1998	Albania	0.514
2008	Ecuador	0.486
1992	Paraguay	0.457
1992	Togo	0.42
1995	Uganda	0.388
1991	Colombia	0.305
1990	Benin	0.253

chapter.[3] For each of these cases, there is also data from Bizzarro et al. (2018) on party strength. The party strength variable has a potential range of 0–1, and within this small sample of eighteen cases, there is significant variation, with a mean of 0.58, minimum of 0.25, and maximum of 0.97. This wide variation within a small sample provides us with an opportunity to arrange the cases along the scale of party strength and evaluate the extent to which public participation made a difference for the content of the constitutional text in each case, thus supplementing the statistical models described earlier with more nuanced assessments of particular cases of interest. Each case is considered briefly, with the cases ordered from strongest parties to weakest parties.

Spain 1978

Spain had a somewhat closed constitution-making process, with the original draft being completed in conditions of secrecy by a committee of just seven politicians. The Cortes (parliament), acting as a constituent assembly, subsequently confirmed the draft and submitted it for popular approval in a referendum. This procedure left little space for formal popular consultation, although the people were given the

---

[3] One of these eighteen is a case where the new constitution has actually not yet been ratified. Although a new draft was approved by Tanzania's constituent assembly in 2014, a promised referendum was delayed several times. It is unclear if this constitution will be voted on at all, so the case study would necessarily be incomplete. Another case is South Africa, which has been considered at some length earlier in the book and is therefore not discussed here.

opportunity to reject the completed text. From the perspective of popular participation, there are a number of problems with this process, but it created a relatively
stable constitution.

Political reform in Spain started with very slow steps during Francisco Franco's
dictatorship, and significant steps were taken within a few months of his death
in 1975. In 1976, King Juan Carlos appointed a new prime minister, Adolfo
Suarez, who quickly presented a new fundamental law that began Spain's transition to democracy by reforming the Cortes (Bonime-Blanc, 2010). This first step
toward reform set the tone for the rest of the process and is a laudable approach
in that Suarez was able to work within the existing structure of the Franquist
regime. This gave the democratization process legitimacy with supporters of the
old regime, bringing them into the process and preventing spoiling (Gunther,
1985, 46). These reforms were then approved by a majority of Spanish citizens
through a popular referendum. Suarez continued with further reforms, culmi-
nating in free elections in June 1977. The Spanish transition to democracy is
remarkable and relatively rare in that every step was completed within the legal
framework that already existed (Rosenfeld, 1998; Gunther et al., 2004; Comella,
2013).

It was unclear at the time of the election whether a regular Cortes was being
elected or a constituent assembly (Bonime-Blanc, 1987, 35). Although the party system was still in its infancy, with hundreds of brand new parties vying for power, the
elections were generally viewed as a success and resulted in broad enough representation in the Cortes to be legitimate as a constituent assembly (Rosenfeld, 1998, 1911).
The election system sought to balance representing new parties with the desire to
limit the number of effective parties. This was reasonably well accommodated in the
Congress of Deputies (although the larger parties were overrepresented), but representation in the Senate included only half of the parties that had seats in the lower
house (Gunther, 1985, 49). Suarez's party, the Union of the Democratic Center
(UCD), won the most seats in the new parliament and was in favor of having a regular Cortes that would also write a constitution (Bonime-Blanc, 1987, 36). The UCD
got its way, over the objections of the leftist parties, and parliamentarians agreed on
a seven-phase approach to constitution-making. The process not only empowered
political parties at the expense of the people, but it especially empowered the older
and larger parties.

The first and most important step was the drafting of the constitution by a subcommittee of the Cortes (Bonime-Blanc 1987, 36). This group was composed of seven
members of the Cortes, representing five parties: Three from the UCD and one
each from each of the next most popular parties. The subcommittee was well suited
to its task. The members of the subcommittee were both popularly elected representatives and constitutional lawyers (Hyden, 2010). Thus, they were able to bring
both subject matter expertise and popular legitimacy to the process of constitutional
drafting. Meeting in secrecy, the subcommittee was able to produce a complete

preliminary draft in about eight months (Bonime-Blanc, 1987, 38). However, this closed drafting obviously left no space for effective public engagement.

After this very narrow and closed part of the process, there was a steady broadening of participation. The second phase of the process involved turning the draft over to a larger committee of the lower house (Congress of Deputies) of the Cortes for amendments and revision. This group produced a new draft that was handed on to the full Congress of Deputies for approval in the third phase. Having received approval here, the fourth phase required approval by a committee from the upper house (Senate) of the Cortes. This committee was presented with 1,254 amendments (Bonime-Blanc, 1987, 39), but still managed to complete its work in about a month. The fifth phase required the approval of the full Senate. After this, the process narrowed briefly as a small, joint committee of the Congress and Senate met in secret talks to reconcile the different versions of the constitution that had been passed by the two chambers. The text that this committee produced became the final draft of the constitution. In the seventh phase, this final draft was passed by both houses of the Cortes and was submitted for the approval of the people in a popular referendum. The constitution was approved by 87.7 percent of those who participated in the referendum or 59 percent of the total Spanish electorate (Bonime-Blanc, 1987, 42). The text received royal assent in December 1978 and became law.

While coded as highly participatory due to the election of the drafting body and ratification through a popular vote, the Spanish case involved few opportunities for public participation during the critical drafting stage. The opportunity to veto the draft is certainly a powerful opportunity for public input, but this veto is almost never used (Elkins and Hudson, 2019). What we find instead is a constitution-making process that was effectively managed by strong parties, shutting out popular participation.

Poland 1997

Poland's postcommunist constitution-making process features some notable similarities with the process in South Africa. Most notably, the process involved an interim constitution (1992), before a final constitution was ratified in 1997 (Přibáň, 2004). The timeline of this two-stage process nearly mirrors what happened in South Africa. Moreover, the constitution-making process was undertaken by the parliament, alongside its other legislative tasks. Osiatynski has noted that the process of constitution-making was delayed by the comingling of "ordinary politics" and constitution-making (Osiatynski, 1997). Obviously, there are a great many differences in other matters of substance, but these are striking parallels.

Political parties played an interestingly role in the transition to democracy in Poland. In the early days of the transition, it was hoped in some quarters that a party-less democracy could be created (Osiatynski, 1997). This was not the case, as Poland quickly developed a strong party system, dominated by parties that were organized from the top down and disconnected from social movements. These were not propitious conditions for strong public influence on the development of the constitutional text.

Under a just-adopted election law, a new parliament was elected in 1993, with a coalition of postcommunist parties in power and parties allied to the democracy movement "Solidarity" in the opposition. A number of parties (particularly on the right) failed to reach the 5 percent minimum threshold for representation and proceeded to challenge the legitimacy of the parliament to draft a new constitution (Wyrzykowski, 1997). As a consequence, the constitution-making process involved a compromise between the governing and opposition parties. The parliament provided for public participation through the submission of drafts from civil society groups that could manage to establish support for the draft from at least 500,000 people (Poplawska, 2008). Using this procedure, the Solidarity movement drafted its own "Citizens' Constitution" (Millard, 2002). Yet, the constitution-making process was dominated by a process of elite negotiation, with the only influential voices from outside coming from academic and legal experts (Poplawska, 2008). In the end, the constitution was approved in a referendum by a narrow majority of 53 percent, while turnout was notably low at only 43 percent (Osiatynski, 1997).

Given the party-dominated nature of the drafting process, to what extent does the 1997 Polish constitution reflect input from the people? Analyses of the drafting process, and in particular the work of Poplawska (2008), suggest that, whatever the official level of public input, the constitution was scarcely touched by citizen participation. On the contrary, the constitution reflected a process of elite negotiation. Although the use of a ratifying referendum suggests that there was an opportunity for effective public participation, the fact that it was passed with the support of less than a quarter of the eligible voters suggests that, even in the end, the people had very little say. Poplawska (2008, 285) concludes: "There is no doubt that, in the light of Polish experiences, broad pre-constitutional social consultations cannot be regarded as an important causative factor, actually influencing the contents of fundamental law."

Lithuania 1992

Although, according to the V-Dem measure of party strength, Lithuania had strong parties during the period of constitution writing in the early 1990s, accounts of the political history of that period tell a somewhat different story. According to Krupavicius (1998), the transitional period was marked by the emergence of a reform movement (Sąjūdis), which quickly splintered into a number of new political parties. By the time the new constitution was ratified, there were more than thirty registered political associations and parties in Lithuania (Krupavicius, 1998, 10).

Whatever the true measure of party strength or institutionalization in postcommunist Lithuania, the drafting of the constitution actually took place in a manner that makes this issue of lesser importance. Much like in the Brazilian case, a sort of predraft was prepared by a committee selected from the ranks of the legal and a political elite (Gelazis, 2001, 169). This draft was intended to be the basis of the later process that would elaborate the final constitution. One and a half years later, the constitution itself was drafted by another nonpartisan commission. This second drafting process was remarkably fast, lasting just over eight months (Pettai and Kreuzer, 1999). The last stages of the drafting process involved efforts from Sąjūdis to influence the draft from outside the government and push back from within the government. Despite continuing dissatisfaction with both the draft and the process, the Supreme Council (interim governing body) approved the draft and sent it to the voters for a referendum. The whole process was rushed through in an effort to accomplish some legal aspects of the transition away from rule by the USSR and toward membership in the EU without any unnecessary delay.

The case is scored as highly participatory since there were referendums at the beginning of the process and again at the end. However, much like in the Spanish case, the actual drafting of the constitution was accomplished without much public input, in a process that utilized a small committee of experts (Mikkel and Pettai, 2004). Indeed, Gelazis (2001, 166) writes: "Public debate of the draft was remarkably limited and brief and referendum participants were basically expected to vote for any draft that was put before them." While the process can be characterized as involving significant contestation between political parties (both inside and outside the legislature), the rushed nature of the process meant that even these negotiations were in some sense perfunctory and the draft was pushed to voters in great haste. Thus, in the Lithuanian case, we can be sure that public participation contributed little to the development of the constitutional text, yet some form of participation (voting in a referendum) was necessary both to shape the initiation of the drafting process and to ratify the final text. Largely in line with the theory presented in this book, the constitution-making process was managed by the political parties, leaving little room for effective public engagement.

Romania 1991

Like Lithuania, Romania completed the constitutional aspect of its transition toward democracy with remarkable speed. Romania was actually able to ratify a new constitution less than two years after the end of the socialist regime. However, the speed of the transition is closely linked to its deficiencies in actually replacing the socialist regime. In the immediate aftermath of the collapse of the regime, many of the formerly socialist elites took steps to preserve their status in the political elite by forming a new political party, the National Salvation Front (FSN). This party dominated the constitution-making process and was largely successful in shaping the text (Parau, 2013). Indeed, the larger political context in some ways preserved the dynamics of contestation (such as they were) of the socialist era, as the FSN replaced the regime as the primary opponent of civil society – with similar imbalances in power between a single strong political actor and a number of weaker opposing organizations (Pietraru, 1997, 324). Blokker (2012) describes the transition as being ephemeral, as both the holders of political power and the political practices they employed were barely changed by the ostensible revolution.

Nonetheless, elections for a constituent legislature were held in May 1990. The constitution was drafted by a committee of twenty-three members of this bicameral legislature, with the added participation of five constitutional law experts who were chosen by the political parties. In a context in which public law had been little studied for many years, these legal scholars had a significant influence on the development of the constitutional text (Parau, 2013). In their assessment of the failures of this drafting process, Gherghina and Hein (2016, 178) write that "the commission sessions were not open to the public and many decisions were not even transparent for the other members of parliament... In sum, the constitution-making process did not meet democratic – not to mention deliberative – standards by far." Pietraru concludes that civil society had been effectively excluded from the constitution-making process (Pietraru, 1997, 327).

However, the constitution was drafted by an elected body and was ratified by the people in a binding referendum. Thus, while the case meets some basic thresholds to qualify as a case of participatory constitution-making, the historical record shows that the effectual opportunities for participation were not available. The constitution-making process was instead dominated by one strong party (FSN). The Romanian experience again illustrates that formally participatory mechanisms are of little value when strong political parties are the central participants in the process.

Tunisia 2014

Tunisia's 2014 constitution-making process is the first of the cases that falls below the threshold of being a case where strong parties were participants. Instead, while Tunisia has several reasonably well-established political parties, they are coded by Bizzarro et al. (2018) as having relatively low organizational capacity. In the constitution-making process, we can observe some stark differences from the strong party cases discussed earlier, many of which may be attributed to this comparative weakness in the political parties. In the case of Tunisia, we are uniquely fortunate, as this is the one of only two cases for which there is systematic empirical evidence of the extent to which public participation had an impact on the text of the constitution. The careful analysis of this case by Maboudi (2019) is one of the few benchmarks we have for the impact that public participation can have in a constitution-making process.

The political context in which the constitution was drafted in Tunisia was not especially propitious for political party development. During the reign of authoritarian President Ben Ali, Tunisia was economically liberal, but politically repressive (Cross and Sorens, 2016). Though they had little prospect of achieving political power at the time, the development of various social movements during the authoritarian era laid the groundwork for political party formation during the revolution of 2010–2011. This is best exemplified by the rapid success of the main Islamist party,

Ennahda, in transforming itself into a political party and quickly vying for control of the government (Ghannouchi, 2016). Following the elections for the Constitutional Assembly in October 2011, Ennahda formed a coalition with two center-left secular parties (Congrès pour la République and Ettakatol) to govern during the transition as the constitution was drafted. As the constitutional drafting process unfolded, other new political parties became more professionalized and organized themselves better both within the party and between parties (Hartshorn, 2017, 414). This makes the measurement of party strength in this case a moving target, but it comports with the quantitative assessment of Tunisia as having the strongest parties within the "weak" category in this chapter.

The constitution-making process was not designed to facilitate public participation from the outset. Instead, the coalition led by Ennahda moved to open the process to public involvement only after the publication of the first draft. As Maboudi (2019, 3–4) describes it, this decision had both positive and negative effects for the political parties concerned. Although the party had itself grown from the social movement milieu as the main actor in the political process of drafting a constitution, Ennahda found itself in competition with more liberal/secular social movements as the more public-facing battles over constitutional content unfolded. In a surprising move, it was Ennahda and not the comparatively weaker opposition parties that pushed for public involvement in the constitution-making process midstream (Maboudi, 2019).

The move did not entirely succeed for Ennahda. Citing an interview with a leader of one of the opposition parties in the constituent assembly, Maboudi (2019, 4) states: "Ennahda wanted to impose its views on the constitution but as they faced increasing opposition from citizens, they realized they were going to lose their electoral support; hence, they revised their position on several controversial issues." This dynamic in Tunisia illustrates how parties of moderate strength engage with public participation in constitution-making. On the one hand, they have clear ideas about their desired constitutional content and enough discipline within the drafting body to see their preferred procedural rules adopted. On the other hand, they are exquisitely aware of how changes to the constitution relate to their fragile plurality of support in the voting population. Thus, they are more likely to respond to pressure from outside the drafting body and revise their proposals in response to input from the public.

Maboudi (2019, 11) finds, in the end, that up to 43 percent of the proposals from the public in the Tunisian case are reflected in the constitutional text. It should be noted, however, that the method used for this measurement precludes a verifiable one-to-one causal relationship between submissions from the public and constitutional content. Instead, this reflects a topical correspondence between what was suggested and what was included in the constitution (with many submissions on the same topics). In his assessment, this high level of impact can be attributed in part to procedural rules that forced the largest party (Ennahda) to make compromises with the smaller parties. Without discounting the procedural drivers of consensus between the parties, I would further argue that Ennahda's openness to changing the drafting process to even allow for significant public consultations is closely related to its status as a new and relatively weak party.

Ecuador 1998 and 2008

Ecuador appears twice in these case studies, as the country drafted a new constitution in 1998 and then again in 2008. As measured by Bizzarro et al. (2018), the parties were comparatively weaker in 2008 than in 1998, so we begin with the earlier case. Proceeding solely in terms of party strength (as I have done with the rest of the cases), Ecuador's 2008 constitution-making process would come later, between Albania (1998) and Paraguay (1992).

Pachano describes the recent decades in Ecuadorian politics as being characterized by a crisis of representation, but suggests that, at the same time, Ecuador's political system has been highly open to social movement activity (Pachano, 2012, 88). The 1997–1998 constitution-making process emerged from a moment of increased instability in Ecuadorian politics, in which social movements asserted their power in a new way. The instability began when the protest movement "Frente Patriótico" organized a sufficiently large protest to force the Congress to remove the president (Abdalá Bucaram) from office and replace him with Fabián Alarcón. Under the leadership of the Federation of Indigenous Peoples of Ecuador (CONAIE), civil society groups pressured the government to begin a process of constitutional reform, organized under the slogan "ni una assemblea más sin nosostros" (not another assembly without us; Segura and Bejarano, 2004, 222). A referendum in May 1997 bestowed both electoral legitimacy on the replacement of the president and on the convocation of a constituent assembly.

The constitution-making process was characterized by a contest between the traditionally dominant parties in Congress and the social movements outside. Fearing that the dominant parties were shaping the process in a way that would exclude them, CONAIE and its allies organized their own (unofficial) constitution-making body in October, hoping that their complete draft would have some agenda-setting effects for the official drafting process (Mijeski and Beck, 2011, 52). However, in November, the Congress attempted to avoid a complete overhaul of the constitution by passing a limited set of reforms. This was ultimately unsuccessful, and a complete constitution was drafted by an elected Constitutional Assembly that completed its work in May 1998. In these events, social movements pushed forward an agenda for constitutional change that outpaced what the established political parties wanted (Segura and Bejarano, 2004, 222), and their later support for constitutional change may have been an attempt to keep up with public demand. The events of 1997–1998 in Ecuador are an example of a constitution-making process that was driven from the grassroots and not a project of elite drafting that was adapted to popular demands later on.

The very existence of the 1998 constitution and the process through which it was drafted are examples of the power of social movements and public participation at that moment in Ecuadorian politics. However, the text of the 1998 constitution was something of a hybrid between two approaches to constitution-making that were prominent at the time and in the years that have followed. On the one hand, it followed some of the dictates of the Washington Consensus (Williamson, 2009), but also responded to demands from social movements, such as the expansion of collective rights (Pachano, 2012). Perhaps relatedly, the constitution did not establish harmonious institutions that would tend to stabilize the political system, and it lasted only a decade. One of the most visible areas where the constitution was clearly influenced by public participation (chiefly through CONAIE and the newly formed political party Pachakutik) was the revision of the first article to recognize that Ecuador is a "multicultural and multinational state" (Mijeski and Beck, 2011, 51). While not completely following the language that CONAIE preferred, the constitution of 1998 did describe Ecuador as "multicultural and multi-ethnic." Furthermore, the constitution included a chapter on indigenous collective rights that was unprecedented in its comprehensiveness, and embrace of indigenous understandings of land, education, and health. As in many other cases, the impact of public participation was for the most part confined to issues of rights, while business associations were successful in protecting their interests in other parts of the text (Andolina, 2003).

The 1998 constitution lasted only ten years, being replaced in 2008 by Ecuador's twentieth constitution since independence. The 2008 constitution was the fulfillment of an election campaign promise made by Rafeal Correa during the 2006 presidential election. According to Bizzarro et al. (2018), the political parties were even weaker in 2008 than in 1998, and it is easy to see why. Although Correa shared some goals with Ecuadorian social movements (including CONAIE) in terms of opposing neoliberalism and expanding the provision of social services, he was in conflict with the major social movements from the beginning (de la Torre, 2014). Fundamentally, Correa had pitched himself as an opponent of the "partidocracia" that had long dominated Ecuadorian politics (de la Torre, 2014), and throughout his time in office he was in fact able to sideline the traditional parties (Becker, 2013). In their place, Correa's new party, the Alianza País (Country Alliance), dominated the elections to the 2007 constituent assembly (with nearly 70 percent of the popular vote), but was in fact a "very loose and diverse grouping" (Becker, 2011, 49). With such complete dominance of the electoral space, Correa's party found its main opposition in the same social movements that had intervened in the 1998 constitution-making process.

As Martínez Dalmau (2016) notes, the 2008 constitution-making process was highly democratic at least in its procedures. There was a sense in which constituent power was "activated" by a referendum that called for the drafting of a new constitution. The constituent assembly was directly elected to serve that purpose. The drafting process could be characterized as popular and consultative. Finally, the new constitution was approved in a referendum. As noted earlier, this was also a constitution-making process that featured weak parties, albeit with one party dominating the membership of the constituent assembly. The potential conflict between this dominant party and the social movements (especially CONAIE) provides us with an excellent opportunity to observe the extent to which a weak party (Alianza País) with a dominant position within the drafting body incorporates input from the public.

The constitution-making process in fact featured stronger centralized control than one might have expected. However, indigenous groups in particular were able to achieve a number of significant changes in the constitution that corresponded to some long-held demands. In an assessment of the role of indigenous movements in the constitution-making process, Becker writes that "the constitution represented significant and dramatic gains for indigenous aspirations" (Becker, 2011, 57). One of the major successes for the CONAIE and its allies was the inclusion of the word "plurinational" in the first article of the constitution. Just as in 1998, their preferred language for describing the nature of the Ecuadorian population was not realized, but the inclusion of this word was seen as a major symbolic victory (Becker, 2011, 53–54). Similarly, indigenous languages were recognized in the new constitution, but not given the full official status that indigenous social movements had demanded (Becker, 2011, 56). Furthermore, the new constitution went much further than its predecessor in recognizing the collective rights of indigenous communities, Afro-Ecuadorians, and other groups. Beyond the indigenous communities, other long-held goals for the political left in Ecuador were realized in the new constitution, including expanding governmental powers to regulate natural resources, transportation, and telecommunications (Becker, 2013). The constitution was supported in the end by many social movements and was passed with a high level of support in a ratifying referendum (almost two-thirds).

In spite of the potential for domination of the constituent assembly by the governing party, social movements (and in particular indigenous movements) were able to achieve a number of significant changes in the constitution. Despite its numerical strength, the larger weaknesses of the unstable coalition that formed Alianza País left it vulnerable to pressure from outside the constituent assembly. In the literature on the Ecuadorian case, there is little to suggest that individuals had any success in proposing constitutional content, but we can be quite confident that the constitution-making process was responsive to demands from the public that were articulated through social movements. While the differences in context prevent us from saying too much on this point, we can also see that the 2008 constitution (under weaker parties) gave the social movements more of what they had asked for than the 1998 constitution had.

Kenya (2005 and) 2010

Kenya's 2010 constitution is a remarkable document and the product of a long, difficult, and at points violent process of constitutional reform. It is possible to draw some neat boundaries around the constitution-making process that led to the 2010 constitution. The process formally began with the passage in December 2008 of the Constitution of Kenya Review Act. Here, the Kenyan parliament outlined a multistage process through which a new constitution would be drafted. The process would include extensive involvement from legal scholars, negotiations between rival political parties, feedback from interested members of the public at an intermediate stage, and a final choice on the constitution to be made by the electorate in a nationwide referendum (Murray, 2013). The Act also set out a number of significant restrictions on the amount of time that various stages could take – thus forcing compromise and a result of some kind.

However, such a short story would of course be incomplete. The constitution-making process of 2008–2010 responded in many ways to the failures of the 2001–2005 constitutional reform process and to the violence that followed the election of 2007. Kramon and Posner (2011) describe the constitution-making process in Kenya as having unfolded in three major stages between 2000 and 2010: (1) The work of the Constitution of Kenya Review Commission (CKRC) in 2000; (2) the period between the unification of the main opposition parties in the National Rainbow Coalition (NARC) in 2002 and the violence following the 2007 election; (3) the period between the negotiations that ended that violence and the ratification of a new constitution in 2010.

A full accounting of this decade in Kenya's history is of course beyond the scope of this short section. The key facts for understanding the main period of interest include the following points. The constitutional reform process of 2000–2010 was part of the longer process of transitioning from the single-party state that had existed for most of Kenya's postindependence history toward a competitive democracy. That dominant party, the Kenyan African National Union (KANU), had continued to rule after the single-party provision was removed from the constitution in 1991 and first lost power in 2002. Indeed, the CKRC was appointed even before KANU lost power, although President Daniel arap Moi sought to scuttle the project when the committee produced a draft that was not in line with the ruling party's objectives (Kramon and Posner, 2011). The 2002 electoral defeat was at the hands of NARC, a union of the National Alliance of Kenya (NAK), the Liberal Democratic Party (LDP), and the Democratic Party. The NARC was a marriage of necessity and featured continued power struggles between Mwai Kibaki and Raila Odinga (who had both led their own party before joining forces in the NARC). Odinga had supported Kibaki as the NARC presidential candidate in return for the promise of appointment as prime minister. Fulfillment of such a promise depended on constitutional reform (Barkan, 2004). None of these parties would qualify as "strong." Most of the political parties in Kenya over the past three decades have been the personal vehicle of a particular leader and feature strong ethnic identification (Elischer, 2013, 43–99).

It was in this fraught political context that Kenya's 2002–2005 constitutional reform process took place. Interrupted by an election, the process that began with the CKRC was followed by the deliberations of a group of politicians from various levels and representatives of interest groups in the National Constitutional Convention (NCC) at Bomas between 2003 and 2004. The NCC included an ambitious program of public consultations, but was also marred by Kibaki's supporters' decision to exit the process and prepare their own draft ("Wako draft") when the NCC ("Bomas draft") did not follow their preferred institutional arrangements regarding devolution and the structure of the executive (Chege, 2008). It was the "Wako draft" that was placed before the voters in the 2005 referendum and rejected by a vote 57 percent against. Kibaki had supported the draft, while Odinga had opposed it. The NARC (as many expected) did not last long in its original form, and the 2007 election featured a contest between Odinga (now of the Orange Democratic Movement – ODM) and Kibaki (now also leading a new movement, the Party of National Unity – PNU). Political violence accompanied both the election campaign and the announcement of the results. Almost 600 people were killed before the election (Cheeseman, 2008) and more than 1,300 people were killed after it (Brown and Sriram, 2012).

These events provide the necessary context in which to evaluate the impact of public participation in the constitution-making process of 2008–2010. No doubt the postelection violence created a greater sense of urgency in the drafting process (Brown and Sriram, 2012). Wamai (2014) in fact characterizes the mediation process that ended the violence and created a power-sharing agreement between Kibaki and Odinga as a constitutional moment. This power-sharing agreement itself required a constitutional amendment, which was passed by the parliament unanimously and with great dispatch.

The Kenyan case is an interesting example of elite accommodation and bargaining in a context of weak parties. Murunga (2014, 158) presents the constitution-making process as a struggle between two elite groups, with the structure of the executive, devolution, rights, and security as the key points of conflict. These four areas in fact cover a great deal of constitutional ground. The process was designed with a number of immovable deadlines that would force compromise. There was less direct public involvement in this drafting process than there had been in the 2002–2005 process, and the drafters of the latter process in fact drew upon the archives from their predecessors to gain a greater understanding of the issues that mattered to Kenyans (Murray, 2013). However, the Committee of Experts that was tasked with the majority of the drafting work drew upon the knowledge and views of a reference group of leaders of CSOs, engaged in public education initiatives, and also received more than 25,000 submissions from the public (Saati, 2015, 158).

There was apparently no consensus on many issues either in the material from the public or among the major parties. Kramon and Posner (2011) suggest that what the public most wanted was to see the process of constitutional reform completed.

Research on the latter drafting process in Kenya has not prioritized evaluation of the impact of public participation on the constitutional text. There are certainly some echoes of the South African drafting process in Kenya, as despite the high level of public participation, the focus was on the negotiations between the political parties. While the ODM and PNU are not coded as strong parties by most metrics, like the ANC and NP in South Africa, they negotiated with a clear view of how the constitutional text would shape their immediate political future. Comparing the two drafting processes in Kenya, Macharia and Ghai (2017, 97) find that "A process controlled by politicians and political interests ends up with a political compromise which does not prioritize the views of the public. The CKRC-led process was multi-interest and multi-sectoral compared to the CoE process." Despite some victories for popular participation (such as the protection of the right of the people to participate in the process of policy development via Article 10), it does not seem that public participation had a direct impact on the 2010 Kenyan constitution.

Egypt 2012

Egypt's 2012 constitution was not in force very long, but the drafting process is instructive. The 2012 constitution was drafted as what might have been the final step in the revolution that began in Tahrir Square in January 2011. Unfortunately, the constitution-making process (in its various stages) dominated the short-lived presidency of Mohammed Morsi, who was overthrown in a coup d'etat in July 2013. Following the coup, a new constitution was drafted and ratified in 2014. In all, the 2012 constitution was in force for only 190 days.

The constitution-making process was governed by a 2011 constitutional declaration made by the Supreme Council of the Armed Forces (which ran the country between the ouster of Hosni Mubarak and the 2011 elections; Gebaly, 2012). In the 2011 election, two Islamist party alliances won the majority of the seats in the legislature (People's Assembly). The Muslim Brotherhood's electoral wing (Freedom and Justice Party – FJP) led a grouping called the Democratic Alliance that dominated the election, finishing with 235 seats (224 for the FJP), accounting for 47.2 percent of the seats in the legislature. The second Islamist alliance was more conservative, led by the Al-Noor Party. Al-Noor accounted for another quarter of the seats in the legislature (Hassan, 2013).

Under the authority of the 2011 declaration, the Constituent Assembly was initially selected by the newly elected legislature in March 2012. The legislature decided to appoint a mixed assembly, with half (50) of the seats in the Constituent Assembly chosen to represent the balance of power in the legislature and the other half of the seats to be occupied by leaders from various sectors of civil society and the government (Johnson, 2015). Initially, this process resulted in sixty of the seats being occupied by members of the Islamist parties or their supporters (Ottaway and Brown, 2012). However, secularist parties were successful in challenging the unrepresentative nature of the Constituent Assembly in court and having a new (slightly more representative) Constituent Assembly appointed in its place (Johnson, 2015). The new Constituent Assembly included thirty-nine members of the legislature (itself dissolved soon after) and sixty-one representatives of civil society groups and governmental institutions (Maboudi and Nadi, 2016). The new Constituent Assembly had less than six months left before the deadline for completing a new constitution and submitting it to the voters in a referendum.

One of the five committees of the Constituent Assembly was tasked with facilitating and processing input from the public (called the Drafting and Research Committee). The committee engaged in outreach through both public consultations and broadcasts of its hearings, and also received input from the public in the form of 35,000 written submissions (Maboudi and Nadi, 2016). In one of the first moves toward online participation in a constitution-making process, the Constituent Assembly also created a website that hosted drafts of the constitution and allowed public feedback (in the form of both comments and up/down votes) on the drafts. The data from this website were extensively studied by Maboudi and Nadi (2016), providing us with excellent analysis of the extent to which public participation had an impact on the development of the constitutional text.

Maboudi and Nadi (2016) find that public input had a significant impact on the development of the constitutional text in Egypt, at least up until a certain point in the process. In this context of deep uncertainty about the status of the legislature, a recently elected president, and a still-powerful military, public input reached a rather fragile Constituent Assembly. The manner in which party strength influenced the drafting process in Egypt was determined in part by Assembly rules that followed a decision-making process that emphasized consensus and reserved voting for breaking deadlocks (Johnson, 2015). In effect, this forced smaller parties (secularists) to choose their battles carefully and made their eventual boycott of the process more likely. Between September and November 2012, representatives of most non-Islamist parties withdrew from the constitution-making process, frustrated by their inability to influence the text (Maboudi and Nadi, 2016).

However, before the boycotts began, there were some signs that public participation was having an impact on the constitutional text. The Drafting and Research Committee used a four-stage process to collect, sort, summarize, and distribute information from the public that had been collected through the various means of participation (including phone, fax, email, paper, and through the Assembly's website; Maboudi and Nadi, 2016, 720–721). As each new draft of an article was posted online, the processing of data from the public was repeated. In all, 803 draft articles were posted to the Assembly's website, generating 572,000 votes and 78,000 comments (Maboudi and Nadi, 2016, 720–721). Based on an extensive statistical analysis of the patterns of both participation and change in the draft articles, Maboudi and

Nadi (2016) find that articles that received many "dislike" votes were likely to be revised by the drafters, while those with more "likes" were changed less often. However, they also find that, after the boycott of the process by the non-Islamist parties, the effect of public participation significantly declined. Maboudi and Nadi argue that the public participation is more likely to have an impact when there is consensus among the elite about the process itself. A counter argument more in line with what is suggested by the larger narratives of this book is that public participation had an impact as long as there was real division within the drafting body. When the non-Islamist parties exited the process, there was no longer any need to pay attention to the input from the public – the Islamist parties knew what they wanted the constitution to say.

Nicaragua 1987

Nicaragua's 1987 constitution (an amended version of which is currently in force) was drafted during a period of arbitrary rule by the Front Sandinista de Liberación National (FSLN – "Sandinistas"). The FSLN had come to power in 1979, overthrowing the Somoza regime, and had quickly suspended the existing constitution. The 1986–1987 constitution-making process was part of a larger effort to normalize their rule and end the civil war with the US-backed Contras. However, the drafting took place under a state of emergency that had initially been decreed in 1982. Many important civil liberties had been suspended in 1982, temporarily reinstated for the elections of 1984, and then suspended again in October 1985 (The Associated Press, 1985). The state of emergency continued for another year after the ratification of the constitution (Preston, 1987). Thus, despite the highly participatory drafting process, the degree to which the process was democratic by any normal understanding of the word is highly questionable. Measurement of party strength is once again problematic. While, by the organizational strength measurement of Bizzarro et al. (2018), the political parties were rather weak, we might question whether that really tells us much about how the Sandinistas and the opposition parties engaged with each other in the constitution-making process.

The elections of 1984 were the first since the FSLN seized power in 1979, and selected both a new president and a National Constituent Assembly. In that election, the FSLN received just over two-thirds of the popular vote and was awarded 63.5 percent of the seats in the Assembly, with the remaining seats distributed among a number of much smaller opposition parties (Walker and Williams, 2010). In this election (as in the years immediately before), the FSLN operated in some ways as a sort of umbrella organization for a number of social movements that supported the party, perhaps contributing to some organizational weakness (Walker and Williams, 2010). The members of the Assembly then selected from among themselves a twenty-two-person Special Constitutional Commission (whose partisan composition roughly reflected the larger Assembly) to begin the drafting process in April 1985 (Morgan, 1990). From there, the process that the Assembly followed

included a central role for public participation. The Commission invited presentations from civil society before beginning its draft. Following the completion of
an initial draft in February 1986, the Commission distributed 150,000 copies of the
draft throughout the country (Walker and Williams, 2010).

The most important aspect of the participation program was a series of seventy-
three public meetings (cabildos abiertos) that were held in various places across
Nicaragua, targeting in most cases a local community, but there were seven cabildos that focused on the concerns of Nicaraguan women (Morgan, 1990). In all,
the Assembly estimated that 100,000 Nicaraguans participated in the meetings, with
2,500 making a statement and 1,500 written submissions were also received (Lobel,
1987; Morgan, 1990). The larger Cold War context of Nicaragua's constitution-
making process is clearly visible in the differing reports of public participation in
the drafting process. The US State Department (no friend of the FSLN) described
the cabildos in rather dismissive terms. Concretely, the State Department stated: "In
reality, a local FSLN organization... selects those who attend the town meetings and
then joins them in drafting questions. Access to the microphone is controlled by the
Sandinista party... They have been little more than support sessions for Sandinista
ideology and politics" (United States Department of State, 1987, 3). A contemporary
account of the drafting process that is generally quite friendly to the FSLN coun-
tered this view, stating that "discussions at many of the cabildos were wide ranging
and unorchestrated" (Lobel, 1987, 851). Although conceding that opposition parties
generally viewed the cabildos with suspicion, one more recent account suggests that
"Most independent observers of the public forums agree, however, that the discussions were generally quite dynamic and freewheeling" (Walker and Williams, 2010,
489).

Following the period of public consultations, a new commission of the National
Constituent Assembly set about revising the draft in light of the input received
from the public in the cabildos. By most accounts, public participation was relatively impactful in this process. The constitution was revised in response to public
input on a number of fronts, including gender equality, violence against women,
the rights of prisoners, indigenous rights, citizenship, and recognition of God
(Boudreaux, 1987; Lobel, 1987; Walker and Williams, 2010). None of these changes
affects larger issues of an institutional nature, following the pattern observed in
a number of other cases. Summarizing the drafting process, Morgan (1990, 26)
describes the constitution as "a product of compromise and pragmatism." The
National Constituent Assembly finalized the draft in November 1986 and it became
law in January 1987. The final version of the constitution still failed to gain support
from representatives of a number of opposition parties (Boudreaux, 1987).

The place of the Nicaraguan case within the theory of party-mediated drafting
advanced in this book is somewhat difficult to determine. On the one hand, the
process was highly participatory and most scholars agree that the final text of the
constitution reflects a number of changes in response to input from the public.

In this regard, it agrees with the prediction that in cases with weak parties we will find a larger impact from public participation. On the other hand, the somewhat authoritarian context in which the drafting took place makes it difficult to determine the true nature of the participatory process and its relationship to the political parties. To what extent can genuine political participation take place under a state of emergency with many civil liberties suspended? However, Walker and Williams (2010, 498) praise the FSLN's approach to the constitution-making process as rejecting Nicaragua's history of elite pact-making and embracing an inclusive process and making concessions to the concerns of the opposition parties. On the whole, the Nicaraguan constitution-making process seems to be a case where weak parties were receptive to public input, and crafted a text that reflected the concerns raised in public consultations.

Albania 1998

Albania followed a comparatively lengthy process in transitioning from a single-party communist system to a multiparty democracy. While an interim set of constitutional laws called the "Major Constitutional Provisions" was implemented prior to the first free elections in 1991, it was not until 1998 that a new constitution was ratified. There was little organized dissent under communism in Albania, and as Austin and Ellison (2009, 179) put it: "Albania had an anti-communist revolution because everyone else was having one." The 1991 election took place in this context of a half-hearted transition, and returned the communist party (formally known as the Party of Labor, but soon renamed the Socialist Party) to power. However, responding to public pressure from urban areas, the Party of Labor soon invited the main opposition party (Democratic Party) to join them in a coalition government of "national salvation" (Austin and Ellison, 2009). In the midst of a major economic crisis, the coalition government fell apart and new elections were held in March 1992 (Pashko, 1993). The new elections brought the Democratic Party to power with 57.3 percent of the seats, while the Socialist Party received a strong opposition mandate with 23.7 percent (de Nève, 2010, 133). Even as Albania's party system quickly solidified into a two-party contest between these two parties, neither party could be characterized as strong in any meaningful sense throughout the decade (de Nève, 2010). Both parties had remarkably long-tenured leaders, with Fatos Nano of the Socialist Party and Sali Berisha of the Democratic Party alternating in power from 1991 until the early 2000s.

The Major Constitutional Provisions were always intended to be temporary and themselves called upon the parliament to establish a drafting process, which parliament did in 1993 (Carlson, 2010). The 1993–1994 drafting process was characterized by domination by the Democratic Party government. Not only was the drafting process controlled by the government, but the government also changed the ratification procedure. Assuming that it would not be able to reach the two-thirds supermajority in the legislature that was required by the Provisions, the government passed a law that changed the ratification requirement to a simple majority in a nationwide referendum (Carlson, 2010). However, this was not successful either. In a referendum in 1994, the government's proposed constitution was rejected by the voters. The Principles remained in place, establishing a semi-presidential system with a very powerful president and an increasingly high level of corruption (Case, 2001).

Albania held new elections in 1996. Having had its constitution defeated in 1994, the Democratic Party feared another failure in the parliamentary election (Austin and Ellison, 2009, 185). The election featured widespread manipulation and even physical violence against opposition party supporters. One observer at the time called it a "travesty of all the hopes pinned on it" (Pettifer, 1996, 388). The result was a crushing majority for the Democratic Party. However, on top of the questionable legitimacy of its mandate, the government quickly faced insurmountable economic challenges. The Democratic Party government had presided over a financial system that had facilitated the creation of massive pyramid schemes that began to collapse in late 1996. In early 1997, the government resigned amid riots, and the country quickly descended into near-anarchy in which approximately 2,000 people were killed (Jarvis, 2000). In the elections that followed in June 1997, the Socialist Party was returned to power with a large majority of the seats in the parliament (65 percent; de Nève, 2010, 133).

In the wake of the violence and economic crisis that led to the election, the international community (and especially the Organization for Security and Co-operation in Europe – OSCE) took an interest in assisting Albania with stabilization, including constitution drafting (Aucoin, 2004). In this context, the ratification of a new constitution was seen as an important step in improving Albania's reputation internationally, and the constitution-making process received financial support from the US and German governments, and from the OSCE (Carlson, 2010). In September 1997, the parliament passed a resolution (Decision 339) that laid out the major contours of the constitution-making process. While a parliamentary Constitutional Commission was the major official actor in the drafting process, a unique independent organization supported by both the Albanian Ministry of Institutional Reform and a number of international donors took on an influential role in organizing public participation and contributing information to the drafters. This Administrative Center for the Coordination of Assistance and Public Participation (ACCAPP) was especially active in providing news and education about the constitution-making process, and also in arranging the means of public participation.

The participation program was designed to involve a preliminary stage in which the ACCAPP would collect input from the public about the potential content of the constitution, and a second stage in which a draft would be circulated and more public input on the draft would be collected. One of the international legal experts who advised the constitution-making process has noted that, in the first phase, much of the participation came from NGOs, while in the latter phase more individual citizens participated (Frasheri, 2011). The parliamentary commission agreed to a full draft of the constitution in August 1998, and the more focused phase of the participatory process began. While the ACCAPP held public meetings and solicited comments from the public in other fora, the Democratic Party and its members for the most part refused to take part (Carlson, 2010). The Democratic Party did not recognize the legitimacy of the Socialist Party government, and viewed the process as "controlled and manipulated by the Socialists and their allies" (Frasheri, 2011, 100). Despite the lack of bipartisan consensus, the participation process is reputed to have been a success. The prioritization of education in the process may have allowed for more meaningful participation (Saati, 2015, 97). Based on an inside view of the drafting process, Carlson (2010, 317) asserts that the Constitutional Commission considered hundreds of changes proposed by members of the public, and that "more than 50 proposed changes, affecting more than 45 of 183 total articles, were accepted." This is a notably high level of impact from public participation.

   To what extent can we attribute this high impact to the nature of the political parties in the process, and the interaction between them? We know that both the major parties were quite weak, although power has continued to alternate between them. It is notable that, while even the then ruling Socialist Party was organizationally and ideologically weak, it clearly dominated the political space during the drafting process due to both its numerical superiority in the parliament and the decision of the Democratic Party to essentially boycott the process. Several factors may have pushed the Socialist Party to be receptive to public input. One, of course, is the high level of involvement in the drafting process of international legal experts, the OSCE, and the Venice Commission. However, a more compelling explanation is a continued worry about the local legitimacy of the constitution, drafted as it was in the wake of a major crisis and without the participation of the major opposition party. In this context, signals that the public had an active and effective role in the drafting process could have been an important source of legitimation.

Paraguay 1992

Having endured the regime of the longest-tenured authoritarian in the region, Paraguayans experienced a strange form of democratic transition in 1989. After taking power in a coup in 1954, Alfredo Stroessner and the Asociación Nacional Republicana (Partido Colorado) had ruled Paraguay without any serious challenge for thirty-five years. However, the 1989 coup was more about preserving the existing order than facilitating change. As leader of the coup, another leader of the Partido Colorado, General Andrés Rodríguez, took power and maintained the central role of the Partido Colorado in government. With the exception of the 2008–2013 term, a member of the Partido Colorado has been president of Paraguay from 1953 to the present, while the party has also maintained a strong presence in both chambers of the bicameral legislature. As Riquelme and Riquelme (1997, 52) describe it: "The transition process in Paraguay took place without any negotiations between the government and the opposition. The agenda was decided by the military, and implemented through one of its major brokers, the Colorado Party." Other scholars give a more central role to the Partido Colorado than to the military (Abente-Brun, 2008), but in either case, the opposition was not the key actor in the transition. It was in this context of a dominant party revising the terms of its hegemony that the 1992 constitution was drafted.

The first election after the 1989 coup featured a somewhat changed partisan landscape, however. During the Stroessner era, there was first a period of single-party rule, followed by a noncompetitive multiparty system. While there were officially recognized opposition parties during the latter period, some opposition parties continued in an "irregular" status and did not participate in the electoral process. Riquelme and Riquelme (1997, 48) characterize the party system that was established after the 1989 coup as a "semi-competitive multi-party system." A new election shortly after the 1989 coup made it clear that there were now two major parties: The Partido Colorado and the Partido Liberal Radical Auténtico (PLRA). The PLRA had until then been one of the "irregular" parties and had a surprising success in the 1991 municipal elections, potentially due to a high level of factionalization within the Partido Colorado (Valenzuela, 1997). However, with the active assistance of the military, the Partido Colorado was able to win a clear majority in a special election for the constituent assembly that same year (Riquelme and Riquelme, 1997). The Partido Colorado was able to secure 55.1 percent of the vote and 62 percent of the 198 seats in the National Constituent Convention, while the PLRA was the most numerous opposition party with 27.8 percent of the seats (Nohlen, 2005; Claude, 2012). The transition had succeeded in creating a "protected democracy," in which electoral outcomes could still be managed (Loveman, 1994).

Nonetheless, the parties worked together to at least some extent in the constitution-making process. Riquelme and Riquelme (1997) report that the parties worked together on issues of mutual interest in the constitution. This led to a constitution that was far more progressive than the one it replaced. Despite its numerical superiority and the ongoing support of the military, Colorado was still a weak party by most metrics. As Molinas et al. (2004) note, "the presence of internal factions created room for strategic alliances with opposition forces." They go on to describe the way that the parties worked together to pursue decentralization in the constitution. This context of weak parties created space for effective public participation – at least in some areas.

There are more concrete examples of how groups outside the National Constituent Convention were able to shape the content of the constitution. As Bareiro and Soto (1997) write, women were able to achieve some progress on issues of gender equality in the constitution. Although women made up a very small minority of the membership of the Constituent Convention, many of the female members of the drafting body worked together with feminist NGOs in a multiparty "Women's Forum for the Constitution" to create concrete proposals on gender for the constitution. A number of these were adopted by the Constituent Convention, including a guarantee of gender equality and a prohibition on gender discrimination, as well as affirmative rights to protection from domestic violence, reproductive freedom, and state action to remove obstacles to gender equality (Bareiro and Soto, 1997, 93). These constitutional provisions were the result of collaboration between the feminist groups outside the Constituent Convention and supportive members of the parties within the Convention.

Indigenous groups also achieved some success in the constitution-making process. While indigenous groups were unsuccessful in an effort to gain a block of voting roles in the National Constituent Convention, something like official observer status was created. The partisan nature of the indigenous-supporting coalition in the Convention is interesting. While the PLRA was clearly the prodemocracy party, in this area it was the Partido Colorado that took a more progressive approach and supported indigenous causes in the constitution (Kidd, 1997). With the support of organizations like the Instituto Paraguayano del Indígena (INDI), a number of indigenous rights were recognized in the constitution. The six articles of the constitution that are devoted to indigenous concerns include recognition of the status of indigenous peoples, the right to preserve indigenous identity and culture, traditional governance of indigenous communities, communal ownership of land, political participation rights, and exemption from military service.

However, there were clear limits to the ability of the public and the opposition parties to influence the content of the constitution. The Partido Colorado presented a united front on issues that affected its interests and those of the military (Riquelme and Riquelme, 1997). Despite the partial success for women and indigenous groups, landless peasants were for the most part shut out of the constitution. The landholders association was able to successfully influence the draft, blocking meaningful land reform. Instead, the constitution established a process for expropriation with full compensation that has been exploited by many land owners to sell unproductive land at above-market prices (Lambert, 2000, 388). In these ways, the constitution realized some progressive features in response to public input, and yet blocked any institutional features that would either endanger the Partido Colorado's political dominance or threaten the economic interests of the country's military-connected elite.

Togo 1992

Togo's 1992 constitution marked a significant step in a rapid process of democratization following the overthrow of the single-party dictatorship that had ruled the country since 1967. In 1963, only a few years after Togo had gained its independence from France, Gnassingbe Eyadéma led a military coup. After four more years of civilian rule, Eyadéma led another coup in 1967, and this time took the presidency for himself, suspended the constitution and dissolved the existing political parties. Eyadéma was somewhat slow to institutionalize his rule, founding a political party (Rassemblement du Peuple Togolais – RPT) in 1969. What is most noteworthy, however, is Eyadéma's disinterest in formal legal change. As van Rouveroy van Nieuwaal (1992, 31) writes: "Unlike many others this particular military regime apparently did not feel any immediate need to provide a legitimate basis for its authority through a constitution." It was not until 1979 that a new constitution was drafted to institutionalize the single-party dictatorship. The 1992 constitution-making process with which we are concerned here took place as the Eyadéma regime engaged in a process of transition to a multiparty system. However (despite a brief ban), the RPT continued to dominate Togolese politics until it was transformed into a new ruling party in 2012.

The 1992 constitution was drafted by a National Conference that met in the summer of 1991. Togo had been caught up in a wave of political contestation that had been sweeping through francophone Africa, perhaps inspired in part by the transitions taking place in the former USSR (Heilbrunn, 1993; Weyland, 2014). In April, Eyadéma had agreed to permit the formation of opposition parties, and agreed to a National Conference in June (Ellis, 1993). Similar National Conferences were taking place in Benin, Mali, Gabon, Niger, and Zaire (Nzouankeu, 1993). Eyadéma and the RPT intended the National Conference to have a rather minor role. Its members had been appointed by the government and included many members of the RPT (75 percent of the 1,000 members), but also a great many people from civil society organizations that were opposed to the Eyadéma regime (Heilbrunn, 1993). There was also a regional and ethnic division in the National Conference, as many of the members were from the southern Ewe ethnic group, while Eyadéma's supporters were mainly from the northern Kabye ethnic group. The National Conference quickly embraced what many of its members perceived to be an opportunity for revolutionary political change, declaring the National Conference to have sovereign authority and suspending the 1979 constitution. This provoked a walkout on the part of the RPT (Heilbrunn, 1993). The National Conference went on to ban the RPT and appointed a new government under the leadership of a new Prime Minister, Joseph Kokou Koffigoh (Ellis, 1993).

Although this case is coded by Eisenstadt et al. (2017b) as highly participatory, there was actually very little substantive participation from the broader public in the constitution-making process. The National Conference was appointed, not elected, and made no effort to collect the views of the Togolese people as it drafted a new constitution (Heilbrunn, 1993, 289). The constitution was drafted by the opposition rather than the RPT, but the one-sided and closed nature of the drafting process makes it less comparable to the other cases that have been considered in this chapter. The fact that Eyadéma continued to control the armed forces throughout the process constrained the National Conference, and led to a constitution that ultimately did not challenge Eyadéma's regime. As Heilbrunn (2019, 207), writes: "In effect, he indulged the delegates' ambitions to draft a lengthy constitution as long as they never really challenged his or his clan's prerogatives. In this fashion, Eyadéma placated international demands that he reform the Togolese state, while

reserving powers for himself that were consistent with an extreme dictatorship."
Ultimately, the public participated in a constitutional referendum, approving the
new constitution with an improbably high level of support of 99 percent (Qvortrup,
2014, 279). In some senses, this case underlines some of the challenges of using
large-N cross-national data to understand the impact of public participation in
constitution-making processes. The case certainly has weak parties, but its participatory credentials are questionable. With no real participation, there is no impact
to find.

Uganda 1995

Uganda's 1995 constitution has its roots in the rise to power of the National Resistance Movement (NRM) in 1986. Constitutional reform had long been part of the
NRM platform, but it still took the movement under the leadership of President
Yoweri Museveni a few years to properly begin this process (Moehler, 2008, 52).
The constitution-making process was intended to be fairly quick, but ended up taking six years. There is some suggestion that this was intentional, giving the NRM a
longer period in office before facing elections (Tripp, 2010; Furley and Katalikawe,
1997). Whatever the real factors in drawing out the process, by the time the constitution was ratified in 1995, the process had become one of the longest and most
expensive on the continent, but also one of the most broadly participatory.

The Ugandan constitution-making process unfolded in a number of clearly
identified and (despite logistical challenges) well-planned steps. Simplifying
Moehler's (2008, 54–55) breakdown of the process, the major stages were: Planning and publicity, education, popular consultation, analysis, comparative study,
and drafting. The education stage, beginning in August 1989, was the most time
consuming. According to Justice Odoki, the chair of the Uganda Constitutional
Commission (UCC) that undertook much of the drafting works, the original plan
for the education stage was to have seminars at the district level and have those
trained at these more central meetings educate the people in the villages. This
proved impossible in practice, and the education stage was expanded to involve
seminars in each of the 717 subcounties in the country (Odoki, 2005, 85).

During the consultation stage, the members of the UCC again visited each of the
subcounties, holding meetings with the public, and collecting memoranda from
various groups. The process of collecting the views of the people also relied heavily
on the party structures of the NRM, called Resistance Councils (RC; Odoki, 2005,
137). It should be noted that, while the NRM had not outlawed opposition parties,
it had severely restricted the activities that parties could undertake (Tripp, 2010,
161–162). The majority of the memoranda that the UCC collected came from the
various levels of RCs, although there were a significant number of submissions from
both private citizens and civil society groups (Moehler, 2008, 57). Some opposition
parties (notably the Uganda People's Congress) charged that the UCC was engaged
more in pushing NRM views than in listening to the people, and the UCC's own

reports note that the process was more educative and consultative (Furley and Katalikawe, 1997, 251, 253). The level of public participation, however, was really quite remarkable. Even critics of the process and its outcomes credit the NRM with organizing broad participation in the process (Tripp, 2010, 163). Moehler (2008, 57) reports that 13.6 percent of the population took part in the process at least through attendance at a local meeting. This is an impressive statistic in comparison with other constitution-making processes around the world.

The analysis stage began in October 1991. Justice Odoki refers to this stage as a search for consensus and describes it as the most important part of the process (Odoki, 2005, 155). The UCC translated all of the memoranda into English, and then undertook a statistical analysis to determine the popularity of various possible constitutional provisions. After describing the process of looking for the consensus view on each of the twenty-nine issue areas the NRM had identified, Odoki stated that "This elaborate system of analyzing people's views was put in place to allay the fears and suspicions of the people that their views would be ignored or rigged out" (Odoki, 2001, 273). In his book-length narrative of the constitution-making process, Odoki (2005) spends a great deal of time explaining the care that was taken to accurately gauge the consensus view through analysis of the memoranda collected by the UCC. However, critics of the process have noted that memoranda on contentious issues could have been vetted at a lower level by the RCs, and that the UCC may have been biased in favor of the single-party movement (Tripp, 2010, 163). So, while the Ugandan case illustrates a significant effort to involve the public in the process, it is uncertain how much the consultations really affected the text.

It was originally the intent of the NRM to ratify the constitution through the National Resistance Council (NRC) and the National Army Council, both NRM bodies, but it became clear during the popular consultations that this would not be acceptable to the majority of the population (Moehler, 2008; Tripp, 2010, 579). The selection of the Constituent Assembly mirrored the achievements and shortcomings of the earlier parts of the process. There were popular elections for most of the seats, supplemented by appointment of representatives of designated groups such as women from each district, youth, and trade unions. However, there were restrictions on campaigning and other activities – notably anything resembling political party organization – that appear designed to give the NRM an advantage (Moehler, 2008, 62–63). One observer has noted that this was the first opportunity for the NRM to officially enact a legal ban on opposition party activity (Tripp, 2010, 165). Even the seemingly positive appointment of representatives for potentially marginalized groups had the effect of allowing the NRM to appoint its supporters to the Constituent Assembly.

The Constituent Assembly debated the text prepared by the UCC for a period of seventeen months, receiving several extensions on its term during those months. Moehler reports that many Ugandans held very positive views about the Constituent Assembly, and 21.1 percent of those Moehler surveyed followed the debates

(Moehler, 2008, 64). There were significant clashes within the Constituent Assembly between supporters of a multiparty system and those supporting the movement system set up by the NRM (Tripp, 2010). In the end, the movement system won, setting Uganda up for the NRM domination that continues to this day. The final text ratified by the Constituent Assembly retained 80 percent of the material in the draft prepared by the UCC (Moehler, 2008, 65). Depending on one's evaluation of how much popular participation fed into the UCC, this could be good or bad. However, the most likely outcome is that the 1995 constitution was only moderately impacted by the public participation process. Some scholars are more skeptical. After noting some positive aspects of the process, Furley and Katalikawe (1997, 252–253) write:

However, a close examination of the available evidence suggests that far from being based on the people's views, the people's constitution is a product of the country's elites: it was designed, written and promulgated by them. It simply could not be otherwise. The people were of course, consulted, they even sent their representatives and delegates to the Constituent Assembly, but by then the game was already up.

Viewing the full constitution-making process, it appears that, although the NRM would reject the idea that it was a political party, it functioned during the constitution-making process much like a strong party in many respects.

Colombia 1991

The process that created Colombia's 1991 constitution is notable for at least two reasons. First, it was a response to both popular and elite demand. After a failed elite-driven constitutional revision process in 1989, law students (and others) demanded constitutional reform through a popular process in 1990 (Banks and Alvarez, 1991). Second, the constitutional replacement in this case required a break in legality. The new constitution was adopted in a process that did not conform to the requirements for constitutional revision in the then effective 1886 constitution, yet enjoyed a high initial level of sociological legitimacy due to the participatory nature of the drafting process. Banks and Alvarez (1991, 43) thus describe the 1991 constitution as "perhaps illegal but nonetheless valid." This is therefore a case in which public participation was necessary to legitimate a process with at the very least questionable legal authority. This was understood from the beginning, as the Supreme Court was called upon to rule on the legality of a plebiscite on calling a constituent assembly in 1990. In that ruling, the Court argued that "the people... is the primary constituency from which all constituted and derivative powers emanate" (Landau, 2011, 617).

It is also a case in which a constitution was drafted during a shift in the party system. Colombian politics had stabilized in the mid-twentieth century through the establishment of a pact between the Partido Liberal Colombiano (PLC) and Partido Social Conservador (PSC) called the "Frente Nacional." This pact came to an end with the election of 1974 (Paredes and Díaz, 2007). Even after 1974, the two major parties continued to dominate the elections (and especially the Liberal party), but in 1990 a third party candidate (Álvaro Gómez Hurtado of the Movimiento de Salvación Nacional – MSN) came in second place. The new constitution in 1991 continued to weaken the two main parties. According to Dargent and Muñoz (2011), "The resulting Colombian party system has weak and fluid political linkages, paling by comparison to its previous institutionalization." Nevertheless, at the time of drafting, the political system was still largely controlled by the two major parties. It is also notable that the process involved little participation from most of the armed groups that had contributed to decades of political violence in Colombia, although demobilized guerrillas were allowed four seats in the Constituent Assembly. The guerrilla group M-19 (19th of April Movement) was a notable exception as it demobilized and participated as a political party in the constitution-making process (Dávila Ladrón de Guevara, 2015).

Following the 1990 election, the leading political parties agreed to a process for constitutional reform that would entail the election of a seventy-member Constituent Assembly, the drafting of a number of amendments with a limited scope, and judicial review of the proposed amendments. This agreement was given effect through a presidential Decree, which was then itself subject to judicial review. Surprisingly, the majority of the justices ruled that the limits on the scope of the amending powers of the Constituent Assembly were unconstitutional (Banks and Alvarez, 1991). As noted in the abovementioned quotation, this ruling rested on a view of constituent power that admitted few limits. The National Constituent Assembly was elected from a single nationwide district, and was therefore dominated by reformists and included few regionally based politicians (Dargent and Muñoz, 2011). The members of the Constituent Assembly included twenty-five from the PLC, nineteen from M-19, eleven from the MSN, nine from the PSC and its allies, and six from smaller parties (including two representatives of the indigenous peoples of Colombia; Santos Pérez and Ibeas Miguel, 1995, 366). No single party had a strong enough position to accomplish anything without significant multiparty support. Additionally, the low level of turnout in the election (27.1 percent) suggested to some that the Assembly lacked broad support and legitimacy (Dávila Ladrón de Guevara, 2015).

In line with the use of popular sovereignty as a source of legitimation for the constitution-making process, there was a high level of popular participation in the drafting of the constitution. The Constituent Assembly received 230,000 submissions from individuals and CSOs during in-person workshops on the constitution (Garcia-Guadilla and Hurtado, 2000, 10). These workshops were organized by municipalities, CSOs, universities, and indigenous groups (Jiménez Martín, 2006). Additionally, groups and individuals contributed 100,569 proposals for constitutional content, generating 131 legislative proposals in the Constituent Assembly (Dugas, 1993, 57).

Unfortunately, it is not clear how many of the proposals that had their origins in submissions from the public were successfully added to the constitution. Jiménez Martín (2006) argues that, despite the high level of participation, political elites dominated the actual drafting, and the constitution was little influenced by popular deliberation. However, Bernal (2019) states: "The Constituent Assembly included many of the citizens' proposals in the final constitutional text." Colombian voters had no opportunity to effectively express their own view of the degree to which they had been heard, as the constitution was ratified and given effect by the National Constituent Assembly, subject only to a procedural verification from the Supreme Court of Justice (Fox et al., 2010).

As one would expect based on the larger measurement of party strength, the political parties generally had a very low level of cohesion or discipline in the Constituent Assembly, although the M-19 movement was an exception to this as well (Dávila Ladrón de Guevara, 2015). Yet, the constitution-making process has been described as an elite pact (Dávila Ladrón de Guevara, 2015). Garcia-Guadilla and Hurtado (2000) characterize the process as a contest for power between the old elites (Liberal and Conservative parties), and the rising parties and movements (M-19, MSN). These accounts suggest that, although these were weak political parties in the broad sense, the old parties of the Frente Nacional did manage to organize themselves to preserve at least some of the institutional arrangements that were significant to them. It is likely that public participation had some impact on the constitutional text, but the precise level of impact is unclear. As with other cases, the subject matter of submissions from the public often concerned issues of rights, especially social and economic rights (Fox et al., 2010, 473).

Benin 1990

The constitution-making process in 1990 in Benin will be familiar already, as it was the Beninese process that inspired the events in Togo that were described earlier. Benin had been governed since 1972 by Mathieu Kérékou and the Parti de la révolution populaire du Bénin (PRPB). By the late 1980s, the socialist government of the PRPB had reached a point where it could do very little to address significant economic problems and faced increasing demands for change from the Beninese people. In the face of widespread protests in Benin in December 1989, the French government made further economic aid conditional on political change (Reyntjens, 1991). Student movements also made a series of demands, including a new constitution and multiparty elections (Heilbrunn, 1993). In response, Kérékou called for a National Conference that met for ten days in February 1990.

Establishing the pattern that Togo would soon follow, the National Conference quickly made a declaration of its sovereignty, suspended the constitution, established a provisional government (the High Council of the Republic – HCR), and appointed a Constitutional Commission to draft a new constitution. While the National Conference as a whole had concluded earlier, a draft constitution was completed by the Commission in April 1990 (Gisselquist, 2008). From there, the constitution was passed to the HCR for further changes.

The constitution was drafted in a very short period (nineteen days), leaving little opportunity for processes of public engagement at least during the work of the Constitutional Commission. However, even during the single-party regime of the PRPB, there was a strong tradition of holding at least nominal consultative processes (Seely, 2009, 144). The HCR commissioned a short program of public education and consultation that took place in June 1990, with small teams of officials visiting each of the administrative regions of the country (Seely, 2009, 83). Three issues were of particular interest for the HCR as it sought input from the public: The structure of the executive, age limits for the head of state, and whether public education should be free and obligatory. Public input was especially informative on the last issue (Gisselquist, 2008, 797). Participants in the consultations also supported an age limit for the president, but such a measure was deeply unpopular with some senior politicians who had influence in the HCR (Seely, 2009, 84). The HCR approved a final draft constitution in August 1990.

The new constitution was submitted to the Beninese people in December 1990, in a referendum that included an unusual and innovative voting procedure. The drafters of the constitution had left an age limit for candidates for the presidency (thus excluding Benin's former presidents) for the voters to decide (Seely, 2009, 79). Thus, voters could choose between three colored ballots, with options fully approving the constitution with age limits, approving without age limits, or rejecting the constitution. Seventy-three percent of the voters chose to approve the constitution with an age limit, while almost 20 percent approved the constitution without it. Less than 7 percent of the voters rejected the constitution (Heilbrunn, 1993, 294–295). A vote to reject the constitution was understood by the HCR to be a vote in favor of a semi-presidential system in place of the presidential system created by the proposed constitution (Seely, 2009, 87).

Given the pace of drafting, it is not likely that public consultations had a very significant impact on the constitutional text. However, the public certainly contributed to the resolution of the critical issues that had divided the elite drafters, most notably the issue of the presidential age limit that was resolved in the referendum. The role of party strength is unclear in this case. The previously dominant PRPB had been rendered very weak indeed by the pace of the transition. A number of political parties were formed around the time of the National Conference (Seely, 2009, 87), but they obviously had little time to organize themselves to participate effectively in the constitution-making process between February and August 1990. This is not quite a case without parties, but the process was dominated by political elites with some personal standing, and not by interparty negotiations. In this case, public participation was an effective mechanism for resolving disputes among the elites who dominated the constitution-making process.

6.4 CONCLUSION

The mixed methods analyses in this chapter largely confirm the theory that constitution-making processes that feature weak parties are generally more likely to be influenced by public participation than those that feature strong parties.

Despite some limitations, the statistical analysis that began the chapter provided strong support for the party-mediation thesis. The interaction between strong parties and public participation (at an aggregate level) tends to decrease the number of novel rights included in a new constitution. The analysis showed that the effects of participation are dependent on the strength of the political parties. In cases with weak parties, the effects of participation are positive, but in cases with strong parties, the effect is negligible. Figure 6.2 provides an excellent depiction of the argument of the entire book in one frame.

The case studies provide even firmer support for the theory. The coverage of the case studies was limited to those cases that included a high level of public participation, but still included a wide range in terms of party strength as measured by Bizzarro et al. (2018). In cases with strong parties (e.g., Spain and Poland), there was very little impact on the constitution from an ostensibly participatory process. In contrast, the cases with weak parties (e.g., Egypt, Nicaragua, Colombia) showed a relatively high level of impact from public participation – at least within certain limits. In each case, even the weak parties were able to protect many of their prerogatives while allowing public input to influence the draft in less politically sensitive areas. Benin also highlighted a more institutionally effective example of public participation, as the elite drafters turned to the public to resolve an impassable issue, the question of an age limitation for presidential candidates. This approach has also been used in Iceland (2012) and Bolivia (2009) (Qvortrup, 2014, 258, 267), where specific questions were addressed to the public in addition to asking for approval of a new constitution.

However, as noted earlier, the case studies also cast some doubt on the usefulness of the quantitative measures of participation in some circumstances. Some of the cases that are coded as highly participatory turn out to have relatively little citizen involvement (e.g., Togo and Benin). One might wonder how much the process in Togo (where an appointed body drafted a constitution with relatively little public input) is comparable to Uganda (where consultations happened over a much longer period of time). The case studies also illustrate the various ways in which public participation can be implemented, and the fact that even seemingly similar procedures can be turned to different ends. For example, many experts would agree that education programs are an important aspect of a participatory constitution-making process (Brandt et al., 2011; Dann et al., 2011). This would be equally true in Canada or in Cameroon. However, in some of the cases, it seems that the education program was intended to help citizens arrive at the position of the dominant party (e.g., Uganda) rather than to give them the knowledge necessary to reason through the complexities of constitutional design.

7

Public Participation in Constitution-Making Reconsidered

7.1 INTRODUCTION

The preceding chapters have covered a lot of territory, from Paraguay's 1992 constitution-making process to Iceland's experience in 2011, and many points in between. As we have seen, public participation is a growing part of constitution-making processes and is likely to play an increasingly important role as technologies for public engagement advance. This move toward public involvement has included recognition of an international legal right for the public to be consulted, diverse means of consultation, and strong evidence of significant public interest in participating. What had been missing in our knowledge up to this point was a careful analysis of the extent to which public participation actually impacts the constitutional text. This book has sought to significantly advance our understanding in this area.

The empirical analyses in this book have investigated the extent and quality of public participation across a host of cases, and especially with regard to nineteen highly participatory cases of constitution-making. Further, I have sought to measure the impact of that participation with reference to the constitutional texts. In the three main case studies, new textual and interview data were employed to carefully ascertain the extent to which public participation influenced the constitution. The analysis showed that the level of impact was quite high in Iceland's rather unique constitution-making process and surprisingly low in South Africa's much celebrated experience. The Brazilian case was more complex, with significant impacts from public participation in the area of rights, but not on the major issues of controversy in the text. Beyond the case studies, a creative approach to large-N cross-national analysis of the relationship between participation and constitutional content yielded a strong result, showing that the effects of participation are dependent on the strength of the political parties that are involved in the drafting process. Taken together, both the case studies and the cross-national statistical analysis support the party-mediation thesis. This chapter synthesizes the findings of the previous chapters and outlines some of the broader implications that they raise.

The book concludes with some practical reflections on how this new understanding of the relationship between political parties and public participation should inform the design of constitution-making processes.

7.2 REVIEWING THE EVIDENCE

While the three main cases are significantly separated in time and geography (three continents and over twenty years), the forms of public participation are quite similar, as are the progressive intentions of many of the drafters. It also bears noting that the technology used in each of these cases was a significant advance on all the cases before it. Brazil's SAIC database was very impressive for the time, allowing the interested reader to quickly determine the level of support for various kinds of constitutional provisions across demographic categories. South Africa's extensive use of television and radio repeats the work in outreach conducted in Brazil, and went even farther as the first constituent assembly to post its work-in-progress on the Internet. Iceland's use of social media and live streaming to facilitate public engagement was very natural in its time, but was still a groundbreaking advance in transparency and participation that has inspired similar campaigns in Mexico City and Chile.

While each case has its own unique historical and political context, they share a common theme of political renewal after a major moral or constitutional failure. The degree of failure differs greatly – from the abuses of apartheid to the much less concerning collapse of a financial system. But the new constitutions drafted in the processes considered in this book each respond to a moment of political crisis and renewal. And each of the new constitutions sought to revolutionize the political system to varying degrees.

Though the cases differ in many aspects that complicate the analysis, the variation on the key independent variable would be difficult to achieve with any other trio of cases. South Africa's ANC is surely one of the most disciplined parties in the democratic world, while Brazil's political parties' endemic weakness endures to this day. Putting these three cases together maintains, to a significant degree, the level of public participation, while including a great deal of variation in the strength of political parties. The outcome in Brazil seems to some degree dependent on the unique innovation of the popular amendments. Yet, in the South African case there were presentations by interest groups, mass demonstrations (though fewer), and petitions. Drafters could be quite certain that the majority of the members of the public had a particular view about issues like capital punishment, and yet chose not to follow the wishes of the public in the constitution. Petitions are not very different from popular amendments, but in South Africa the petitions had no effect. This suggests that the explanation for the effectiveness of the popular amendments in Brazil was not due solely to this procedural innovation, but was facilitated by the political context. Certainly, there are other explanatory factors that may matter a great deal – the ambitions of presidents, for example. However, taken together, these cases present strong evidence for the contention that the strength of political parties is the key variable explaining the variation in levels of impact in constitution-making processes.

South Africa's constitution makers invested significant amounts of time and money in facilitating public participation, only to see the text be developed in terms of compromises between two very disciplined and programmatic political parties. Brazil's frenetic drafting process witnessed a remarkable level of public engagement in many ways, and the weakness of the political parties created a space in which the demands of civil society groups could be turned into constitutional text. Iceland's decision to draft a nonpartisan constitution led to a drafting process in which public input was both highly valued and unhindered. Leaving aside the larger judgments of the quality of these constitutions for a moment, we can say with some confidence that strong parties are inimical to effective public participation.

Moreover, beyond these three cases, this book has presented evidence of similar dynamics between public participation and party strength in cases as diverse as Spain (1978) and Benin (1990). The strong parties in cases like Spain, Romania (1991), Lithuania (1992), and Poland (1997) managed the constitution-making process in ways that favored their interests. While there were significant opportunities for public participation (particularly through referendums), these public inputs had little or no impact on the constitutional text. The dynamics were different in cases with weaker parties. As Maboudi (2019) showed in his study of Tunisia (2014), it is possible for public participation to make a difference. There, as in Nicaragua (1987), Albania (1998), Ecuador (1998 and 2008), and Egypt (2012), weak parties were forced to make concessions to public pressure and alter their constitutional projects. There were also cases that complicated the picture. For example, Uganda's 1995 constitution was drafted after an extensive participation process featuring a dominant party that was organizationally weak. Yet, scholars of Ugandan politics suggest that the constitution was an elite creation, little influenced by public input (Furley and Katalikawe, 1997). On the whole, however, the shorter case studies provided further evidence in support of the party-mediation thesis developed in this book.

Finally, the cross-national statistical analysis that began Chapter 6 provided further support for the party-mediation thesis. As simply illustrated in Figure 6.2, the effects of public participation depend on the strength of the political parties involved in the drafting process. The statistical models showed that, in general, higher levels of public participation are associated with the inclusion of more novel rights in the constitution (a good proxy for the effect of public input). However, this generally positive impact is vastly altered by different levels of party strength. For cases with parties weaker than average, increased participation leads to the inclusion of more novel rights. In contrast, in cases with parties at least one standard deviation stronger than the sample average, increased participation has almost no effect. This finding provides strong support for the party-mediation thesis, showing that, whatever the normative appeal of public participation may be, its practical effects on the constitutional text are determined by political party strength.

7.3 BROADER IMPLICATIONS

Everything that we have seen in this book so far pushes us to think about broader questions with implications for several areas of research. In particular, five issues come to mind: (1) the quality of the constitutional text, (2) the quality of democracy, (3) the legitimacy of the constitution, (4) the role of political parties, and (5) areas of public participation beyond constitution-making. I will address each of these in turn in the subsequent paragraphs, reflecting primarily on the ways in which the three main case studies inform our views about these issues.

The quality of a constitutional text is a difficult thing to measure and it has not been a focus of analysis in this book. Nonetheless, it is appropriate to make a few comments on the issue here, as the quality of the constitution produced is in part a reflection of the relative success or failure of the process, and relates in part to the impact of public participation. There are, of course, different ways in which the quality of a constitution could be conceptualized. One view centers on the coherence of the constitution and the extent to which the text accomplishes the tasks normally associated with a constitution, such as constraining the use of power and fostering deliberation (Holmes, 1988; Elster, 2000). Another, more normative concept emphasizes the extent to which the constitution fulfills some moral goal, such as protecting the rights of vulnerable people or ameliorating sources of injustice (Sunstein, 1991; Fabre, 2000). Reviewing much of the literature on constitutional design, Carey (2009) accounts for these views and others, suggesting that the three key desideratum in a constitution are (1) democracy, (2) temperance, and (3) durability. I will take up the connection with democracy momentarily, and first turn to some variations on what Carey means by temperance and durability.

Early evaluations of new constitutions by legal scholars most often focus on the temperance dimension. By this, Carey (2009, 157) meant the degree to which the constitution establishes an effective division of powers and encourages reasoned deliberation in decision-making processes. On this basis, the South African constitution is widely recognized by scholars as an exemplary text (Simeon, 1998; Sunstein, 2001; Kende, 2003; Alence, 2004). The late US Supreme Court Justice Ruth Bader Ginsburg once infamously implied that the South African constitution might be better than the American constitution as a model for other countries writing a new charter. She said: "That was a deliberate attempt to have a fundamental instrument of government that embraced basic human rights, had an independent judiciary... It really is, I think, a great piece of work that was done" (Keating, 2012). Legal scholar Cass Sunstein called the South African charter "the most admirable constitution in the history of the world" (Sunstein, 2001, 416). Its domestic reputation began on a very high note, but has since faced increasing criticism, as a younger generation faces a lack of progress toward social justice, and unfulfilled promises for social and economic transformation in the two decades since the end of apartheid (Terreblanche, 2015; Mthombothi, 2017). The extent to which this can be blamed on the constitution itself is a matter of current debate in South Africa (Calland, 2017). If we look at the text through the lens of the content as inventoried by the Comparative Constitutions Project (CCP), we see that it is a reasonably comprehensive text and provides extensive human rights protections. Furthermore, the text provides for a number of very serious checks on the abuse of government power through the Chapter 9 institutions, such as the Public Protector.

The Brazilian constitution is by comparison less temperate. It is famously long (currently 64,488 words – surpassed only by India, Nigeria, and several US states) and yet was incomplete in many ways when it was ratified. As noted in the chapter on this case, President Sarney was unsparing in his criticism of the text at the close of the drafting process, asserting that the constitution would make the country ungovernable. That has not turned out to be the case, but the constitution contained many internal contradictions and was not truly workable as initially ratified. In fact, to this day, some relatively routine legislative actions (e.g., changing the rate of taxation on ethanol [de Moraes and Zilberman, 2014, 114]) require regular constitutional amendments. The Brazilian constitution is famously detailed, including provisions on many topics not addressed by most other constitutions, such as the right to food (Art. 6) and an entire section on sports (Chapter III, S. III). In the CCP inventory of textual content, the text is highly comprehensive (ranked 20th in scope and 10th in the number of rights).

The Icelandic draft constitution of 2011 was not quite as spartan as the text it was intended to replace, but was still quite short (slightly over 8,000 words) and less detailed than most constitutions currently in force. While it added some new rights, it still failed to address some important topics in constitutional law, such as the rights of those accused of crimes, economic freedoms, and social rights. In its brevity, it has of course missed some other things, and critics of the text noted imprecise language at various points (Guillenchmidt et al., 2013). However, it responded to input from the public in adding new mechanisms for direct public involvement in making legislation and created new rights as yet unheard of in other countries, such as the right to access the Internet. Landemore (2016) has argued that the 2011 draft that was studied here was both better than the constitution it would have replaced and better than a draft produced by an expert committee. However, the expanded processes for direct democratic participation in policy-making could have made for a less temperate constitution.

Following Carey (2009, 158), the third outcome of interest for a constitution is its durability. Here, the three main cases discussed in this book may have less to tell us; however, the limited data suggest that perhaps strong parties draft more durable constitutions. Iceland's 2011 draft of course fails immediately here, never having been ratified and put to use. Brazil and South Africa's constitutions have endured several decades now, including guiding their respective states through major constitutional crises, such as the impeachments of two presidents in Brazil (Collor and Rousseff) and the attempted removal of one president in South Africa (Zuma). While both countries face serious challenges to their democratic institutions, the replacement of either constitution in the next few years appears to be a remote possibility.

One could expand on the simple idea of constitutional durability in the sense of a constitution that has not been replaced, and consider durability in the sense of a constitution persisting in its original form. On this score, South Africa has been more successful. The South African constitution has been amended only seventeen times since it became law in 1997, although that number tends to undercount the substantive changes as each amendment made several alterations to the constitution. These amendments have primarily been of a minor nature, however, dealing with issues like appointment processes and terms of office for a variety of officials. More interestingly, five of the amendments have dealt with the possibility for a member of the National Assembly or a provincial legislature to change their political party without giving up their seat. This was not possible under the original constitution and remains contrary to the constitution today. In stark contrast, the constitution of Brazil has been amended more than 100 times since it was ratified in 1988. Again, many of these amendments are of a relatively minor nature. As the Brazilian constitution is so detailed, matters as trivial as the admission of foreign professors and students to Brazilian universities have been the subject of constitutional amendments (EC 11/1996). More politically important amendments have reduced the term of office of the president, changed the immunities of legislators, and reformed some aspects of the judiciary. On this basis then, the South African constitution appears to be more durable than that of Brazil.

For many scholars, the most important thing that a constitution can achieve is the maintenance of a democratic system of government. This book has not been concerned in the main with the quality of democracy either before or after these new constitutions were produced. In other works cited here – principally Eisenstadt et al. (2015, 2017a) and Saati (2015) – that was the main outcome of interest, and I have little to add to their systematic analyses. However, the importance of this issue demands some critical reflections on how these cases fit into the larger picture.

In two of the cases considered here, Brazil and South Africa, the new constitution was drafted during a transition to democracy. In both cases, the level of democracy is better by most metrics now than it was prior to the ratification of the new constitution. However, both countries remain deeply flawed in their practice of democracy today. Furthermore, in both cases the defects of democracy are related to the political parties that dominated the analysis here. In the case of Brazil, the systemic weakness of the political parties continues to support a personalistic and at times corrupt style of politics. While in South Africa, the ANC's apparently unbreakable hold on power has led to concerning levels of corruption in some quarters and a related lack of accountability for the government. It seems unlikely that the situation would be any different if the constitutions had been drafted without public input. What is clear is that the foundational aspects of the party system and axes of political contestation retain many features of their earlier iterations. These two cases cast some doubt on the larger endeavor of connecting the quality of democracy with the features of the constitution-drafting process. Instead, more fundamental features of the political context shape them both.

In this respect, the Icelandic case has little of a concrete nature to tell us. The country has had very high levels of democracy for decades, and since the constitution has not yet entered into force, it has had no impact on the level of democracy.[1] One might, however, speculate about how democracy in Iceland might have been changed if the constitution had been ratified. The draft contained a number of features of direct democracy that could have deepened Iceland's democracy, involving citizens in the business of government in new ways. To the extent that these democratic innovations were added to the constitution in response to input from the public, this hypothetical improvement in democracy would have been linked to the participatory nature of the drafting process. However, for the time being this remains entirely speculative.

One of the most important contributions that this book has made is to provide some empirical data that are relevant to theoretical arguments about constitutional legitimacy. Participatory processes are (at least theoretically) strongly associated with perceptions of legitimacy in the constitutions they produce (Chambers, 2004). Indeed, this dynamic of participation as a legitimating force has been developed in a host of political contexts (Scharpf, 1998; Fung, 2015; Yang, 2016). Fallon (2005) helpfully distinguished between three concepts of constitutional legitimacy: legal, sociological, and moral. Here, I am most interested in the sociological legitimacy of the constitution, the extent to which the constitution "is accepted (as a matter of fact) as deserving of respect or obedience" (Fallon, 2005, 1790). The connection between public participation and assumptions about sociological legitimacy in the constitutional context is a matter of the highest importance and demands further empirical research on at least two accounts.

The first is a worry that gains in the perception of the sociological legitimacy of a constitution are based on false statements on the part of constitution makers and inaccurate judgments on the part of the public. It is clearly in the interests of politicians to give the impression that public participation was far more meaningful than it actually was. The various advertising slogans with which I began this book all attest to ways in which constitution makers create an impression that input from the public will have an influence on the constitutional text. A similar impulse may

---

[1] Though some would argue that the decision of parliament not to ratify the new constitution was a democratic failure (Gylfason, 2013b; Lessig, 2016).

be behind some of the rather fulsome statements made by Brazilian politicians in the interviews conducted for this book.

At the same time, for a citizen-participant, the informational burden in assessing the impact of participation means that they have little to go on beside the claims made by these politicians. As reported in Chapter 4, Brazilians who had participated in the constitution-making process had generally positive evaluations of the role of public participation, in spite of more negative views of both the constitution and the political system. An exception to this might be the writer of numerous letters to the drafters of the interim constitution in South Africa that was reported in Chapter 3. That individual paid close attention and pressed the drafters to take account of his input. In my view, this kind of close attention and follow-up is extraordinary, and most participants would have little sense of how much attention both their own input and the larger volume of ideas from the public received. The fact that such participation can legitimate a constitution without actually affecting the text presents a troubling puzzle.

We still have few empirical benchmarks for the extent to which public participation has actually had an impact on constitution-making processes. Understanding the extent to which constitutions really do respond to public input is a key background condition that should inform our normative views of the role of public participation in constitution-making. Alongside the recent work of Maboudi (2019), the three main case studies in this book should serve to re-calibrate our expectations about how much a constitution can be expected to reflect direct public input. In my view, Iceland presents an almost ideal case for effective participation, and it is unlikely that the almost 10 percent efficacy rate reported there will be matched elsewhere in the world. It is a remarkable achievement in one sense. But does the fact that 90 percent of the submissions from the public were not implemented undercut the contribution that this participation may have made to the legitimacy of the draft constitution?

The second concern impacts the successors to this drafting generation: How long does this boost to sociological legitimacy last? As noted earlier, the South African constitution is now facing some criticism from South Africans who believe that the compromises made in the drafting process have served to limit the degree and pace of economic and social transformation in the country. In defending the constitution against this charge, one South African academic pointed to the participatory nature of the drafting process as a bulwark of legitimacy for the constitution, such that its legitimacy had until recently been beyond question (Calland, 2017). This may suggest that the duration of the legitimacy bonus is about a generation – in line with Thomas Jefferson's suggestion about the ideal life span of a constitution (nineteen years; Kurland and Lerner, 1986, 392–397).

Turning to larger normative issues, we should also be concerned about whether or not constitution drafters really *should* be implementing the ideas that come to them from the public. This is a matter with which scholars with an interest in deliberative and epistemic democracy are vitally concerned. In each of the three cases that were studied in depth, the patterns of participation were far from random. From Rio de Janeiro to Reykjavik, men were more likely to participate than women. Moreover, participants with higher levels of wealth and education were also overrepresented. The potential of democratic innovations that rely on self-selected participants to skew the picture of the public mind and increase polarization has been noted for some time (Sunstein, 2003; Karlsson, 2012). This of course matters for the degree to which such participation should be understood to legitimize the constitution. There are more sophisticated ways to involve the people in a constitution-making process, including sortition or "liquid democracy" (Landemore, 2020a); however, these have not been used in a constitution-making process to this point. Assuming a self-selected sample of the population is participating, it may indeed be the case that a contest between political parties creates a debate with greater democratic legitimacy than the citizen-participants can provide.

Finally, the connection between the legitimating effects of participatory drafting and the larger concept of constituent power also deserves some attention. The concept of constituent power was considered in some depth in Chapter 2, and it continued to dwell in the background of each of the case studies. A cynic might suggest that constituent power arises whenever it is needed: If a constitution is to be replaced, then the body that undertakes the work is accorded constituent power in order to carry it out. Legal scholars differentiate between original and derivative constituent power (Roznai, 2017, 113) and suggest that original constituent power is the only sufficient authority to fundamentally alter (dismember or replace) a constitution (Albert, 2017). The most compelling demonstration of original constituent power is a highly participatory drafting process.

Albert (2019, 72–73) describes the dynamics in which I am interested here in an artful way:

Where the political class recognizes the validity of a constitutional change and the people approve or acquiesce to it, that change may have a claim to legitimacy though not necessarily to legality: a constitution can therefore simultaneously be illegal yet democratically legitimate. In the case of creating a new constitution, the range of valid exercises of constituent power is boundless. There are no rules of process to legitimate the outcome; the very fact that a popular choice has been made is its own source of legitimation.

The empirical question that lurks behind this idea of popular approval or acquiescence is the degree to which the kinds of participatory mechanisms currently in use (e.g., written submissions, popular consultations, and referendums) really demonstrate popular support. In other work (with Zachary Elkins), I have questioned the relationship between referendums and substantive choice on the part of voters (Elkins and Hudson, 2019). The evidence presented in this book should also drive us to reconsider the extent to which participatory drafting processes should be understood as demonstrations of popularly legitimated constituent power.

Political parties featured prominently in the causal narrative developed in this book, and the findings reported may contribute to our normative views on the subject. The dominant normative position on party strength for more than a century has been that democracy is nearly impossible without political parties, and moreover that stronger parties are better for democracy (Wilson, 1885; Schattschneider, 1942; Fiorina, 1980). Most of these early and influential works were written in the context of the USA. Further abroad, the picture has been slightly more complicated while still in the main supporting strong political parties as being more effective in supporting accountable and democratic government. There have been some examples of the deleterious effects of overly strong parties (Coppedge, 1997; Siljanovska-Davkova, 2013), but also arguments that stronger parties would be a healthy change in many democratizing countries (Mainwaring and Scully, 1995b; Fish, 1998; Lipset, 2000). Surveying a great deal of recent empirical literature, Stokes (1999) suggests that the question of whether or not political parties are on balance good or bad for democracy has not yet been settled. More concerning for present purposes, scholars have for the most part avoided the question of the appropriate role of political parties in constitution-making processes.

These broader concerns are of course relevant to the party-mediation thesis articulated in this book. If strong parties are effective in providing meaningful and accurate representation of the interests of voters (Rosenbluth and Shapiro, 2018), then additional self-selected participation may contribute little of value. As noted earlier, after all, the self-selected participants in a constitution-making process are often unrepresentative of the population. If a political party has an effective organizational structure and provides good representation of popular interests, there does not seem to be any reason to supplement that with further participation. Yet, it could also be the case that the interests of "discrete and insular minorities," or even majorities that are "anonymous and diffuse" may not be well represented by political parties (Ackerman, 1985, 724). Balancing these concerns might suggest the normative desirability of strong parties supplemented by mechanisms for direct input from groups and individuals who do not feel well represented by an electoral outcome. However, the party-mediation thesis would suggest that these latter inputs are unlikely to find their way into the constitution in a context of strong parties.

By contrast, if the parties are weak, then additional participation may serve a salutary function in providing a quality of representation that was lacking in the electoral arena (Arce, 2010). The evidence presented in this book shows that constitution-making processes in the context of weak parties are also more likely in fact to include direct input from the public in the constitutional text. Thus, constitution makers representing weak parties are both more reliant on the information conveyed in submissions from the public and more likely to include these ideas in the constitutions they draft. On the surface, this seems like an effective way to counter-balance the representational shortcomings of weak parties. However, the dynamic may still produce lower-quality representation than may be offered by strong political parties.

Perhaps adding to the long-standing view that stronger parties are better for democracy, the evidence presented earlier further suggested that strong parties may draft better constitutions. While further empirical work should be done on this question, the insight follows naturally from the broader idea of strong parties as effective channels of representation and interelite contestation. This adds even more urgency to the argument that democratization and state-building processes should prioritize the development of strong political parties (Reilly, 2013).

The ideas articulated in this book also have further implications beyond the immediate context of the drafting of new constitutions. Constitution-making processes are in fact quite rare. Although those of us who study constitution-making processes find several new and interesting cases ongoing each year, compared to most political phenomena, new constitutions occur with a rarity that is almost unique in politics. While their importance commands our attention, a theory of the relations between public participation and political outcomes such as the one advanced in this book should have implications for how we understand the more mundane political interactions that dominate the actual practice of politics in most countries. As we know, local politics have much more impact on the daily lives of individuals than the mega-politics of constitutional reform. How does what we know about the interaction between citizen demands and elite politics in constitution-making processes inform our expectations for the local level?

Some of the most celebrated opportunities for citizen involvement in local politics are the innovative participatory budgeting processes (PB) that were pioneered in Porto Alegre, Brazil, and have since spread to many other parts of the world (Goldfrank, 2012). However, PB almost invariably involves a small portion of the city budget, and often a choice between particular projects that have already been selected through a less participatory process (Stewart et al., 2014). This seems quite different from the ostensibly open agenda that characterizes the way that citizens engage with big questions in constitution-making processes.

A closer parallel may be the citizens' assemblies at the local level that have been proliferating over the past several years. Notable examples that appeared in the months immediately prior to the publication of this book include a new regional citizens' assembly for the German-speaking minority in Belgium (The Economist, 2019), an assembly to consider climate change in the United Kingdom (Montlake, 2020), and a series of deliberative events across France to address the issues raised in the "yellow vests" protests (Landemore, 2019).

These local citizens' assemblies are much more like the open invitations for citizen participation in constitution-making processes. Here, we have individual contributions to large and complicated subjects, but with the focus on what may be done at the local level. There is some international variation in the extent to which political parties are active in local politics, but where they are present, there is a strong link between the theory advanced in this book and local politics. The clearest implication from the processes studied in this book is that the relationship between a citizens' assembly and any elected legislature must be carefully managed. If a partisan legislature acts after popular consultations, it is unlikely to adopt very much of what was decided in the popular consultation. If a process for popular consultation is to have much power, some precommitment from the other relevant institutions is a must.

7.4 GUIDANCE FOR CONSTITUTION MAKERS

To this point, I have avoided directly addressing ground-level practical implications and have not offered much that might be useful to those actually involved in the drafting of new constitutions. Assuming that designers of constitution-making processes genuinely seek to have effective input from the public, each case should be seen in somewhat cautionary terms, and yet each also offers some positive lessons.

Turning to the cautionary side, there are a number of points that become clear from these cases. First, one should be very alive to the possibility that public consultations will produce such a volume of material that it will be very difficult to properly process and distill. Even in Iceland, with its small number of submissions, it was a significant added burden for the drafters to consider input from the public in addition to the usual discussions within the drafting body. When we consider cases like Brazil – with over 72,000 submissions – it becomes obvious that the task of processing the written material from the public and making it useful to the drafters requires a significant investment in human and technological resources. The 2018 constitutional amendment consultations in South Africa (on revision of Section 25 of the constitution) produced more than 700,000 submissions from the public (Timeslive, 2018) in a matter of months. It is inconceivable that the drafters of this rather limited amendment will read even a small percentage of these. If all the drafters consume is a summary table of the content of these submissions from the public, one has to ask if a written submission is of any more value than a petition or an opinion poll. It is certainly possible that consuming information from the public in this way would actually be injurious – resembling the data from a poll with a representative sample, but including only the views of an interested minority.

Second, one should consider the extent to which public participation can reasonably be expected to make a difference and pitch the appeal for public comments in light of this. If, for example, issues of interest to both the parties and politicians are of such weight and immediacy that no volume of comments from the public could change the outcome, one should perhaps consider whether having a public consultation process is effective or honest. It could be that inviting members of the public to speak on the issue (even if they are not heard) will yield a boost to perceptions of legitimacy, but that is a matter for future research. The current South African experience suggests that such legitimacy bonuses have a relatively short life span.

There are also some clear positives in this story. The Icelandic case demonstrates that it is possible to draft a constitution in conditions of real-time transparency. Transparency is a growing area for international activism, and we should expect that demands for transparency in constitution-making processes will be on the increase in the years to come. The debate on this issue is certainly not settled, as the South African case demonstrates the value of giving drafters space to decide contentious issues in privacy. However, Iceland's experience also shows that drafting need not take place in a closed room with no public record of the proceedings. Live streaming of plenary sessions is most likely the way of the future. The effective combination of legal drafting and boots-on-the-ground activism in Brazil suggests an effective path for organizations seeking to effect constitutional change. The concrete proposal of constitutional text backed by massive demonstrations of public support for those proposals creates a situation in which the outcome of that activism is clear to many – both politicians and the public. Unlike isolated letters from individual constituents, or even signatures on petitions, these clear demands backed by public pressure create conditions under which it may be costly for politicians to ignore the voice of the people. Beyond this, we should be encouraged to find that members of the public can contribute to a constitution-making process a great deal with impressively well-informed and carefully written submissions. The cases considered here were not filled with the kinds of cranks that many politicians assume would turn up in an open consultation.

In a constitution-making process, there are many matters that political actors can determine. They can decide on the nature and composition of the drafting body, the rules of procedure, and the ratification process. But they cannot make changes to the political culture by fiat. As much as constitution-making processes can mark a clear break with the past and the dawn of a new era in a country's history, no one can alter the larger social and political context. There is then an element of path dependency in this. In countries with long histories of strong parties, it is difficult to see how public participation could be made effective. The South African drafters said very hopeful things about public participation at the time, but both the analysis conducted here and their own reflections years later show that public participation did not make a great deal of difference. If public participation is to be meaningful in countries with that kind of political context, it may be necessary to follow Iceland, and elect a special assembly without the participation of parties. However, this too comes with risks – most importantly that the constitution will not be passed into law if established political groups have no stake in its ratification. Also, there are some indications that a constitution drafted in such a way may have blind spots with regard to the pressing issues of governance.

These reflections on the practicalities of public participation in constitution-making call for a certain humility. We seek to engineer various aspects of the process (both in constitution-making and elsewhere), tinkering with mechanisms of consultation and new technologies for public input, while the larger political foundations on which these structures are built persist unchanged. No amount of finessing the proportions of the windows will alter the political and economic foundations of the edifice.

This book has touched on a number of themes – the advantages and disadvantages of strong parties, the competence of average citizens as drafters of constitutions, the ability of drafters to take public input into account, and the possibility that public participation may produce more heat than light. We have seen that public participation really can make a difference in the constitutional text when the political context provides an opening. I have stressed the importance of political parties throughout, and maintain that the variation in party strength is the key explanatory factor. The findings here suggest that a more clear-eyed approach to popular participation is required both in scholarship and in practice. Public participation is but one part of a momentous period in a country's political history and its effectiveness cannot be assumed.

Appendices

TABLE A1 *Gender of SAIC participants*

Gender	# in SAIC	% in SAIC	% in population	Ratio
Male	45,119	65.58	49.3	1.32
Female	23,679	34.42	50.7	0.68
Not specified	3,881			

TABLE A2 *Ages of SAIC participants*

Age	Count	Percentage
10–14	4,904	7.21
15–19	11,569	17.02
20–24	8,982	13.21
25–29	8,754	12.88
30–39	13,518	19.89
40–49	8,801	12.95
50–59	6,093	8.96
Over 59	155	0.23
Not specified	4,703	

TABLE A3 *Occupations of SAIC participants*

Industry	Count	Percentage
Agriculture, fishing, and extractive industries	3,691	5.85
Manufacturing industry	1,745	2.77
Construction industry	1,248	1.98
Other industrial activities	1,775	2.81
Trade in goods	4,284	6.79
Service sector	9,346	14.81
Public administration	11,363	18.01
Social activities	2,573	4.08
Transportation industry	950	1.51
Communication	2,578	4.09
Other activities	23,534	37.30
Not specified	9,589	

TABLE A4 *Education level of SAIC participants*

Level of education	Number	Percentage
Illiterate	686	1.01
Primary education incomplete	20,993	30.85
Secondary education incomplete	12,769	18.76
Secondary education complete	13,191	19.38
Tertiary education incomplete	7,011	10.30
Tertiary education complete	11,128	16.35
Post-graduate degree	1,726	2.54
Not specified	4,624	

TABLE A5 *Income level of SAIC participants*

Income brackets	Count	Percentage
Without income	14,364	22.14
Up to the minimum salary	11,625	17.92
Between 1 and 2 MS	10,123	15.60
Between 2 and 3 MS	7,416	11.43
Between 3 and 5 MS	7,713	11.89
Between 5 and 10 MS	7,516	11.58
Between 10 and 20 MS	4,170	6.43
More than 20 minimum salaries	1,892	2.92
Not specified	7,793	

TABLE A6 *Residences of SAIC participants*

Residence	# in SAIC	% in SAIC	% in population	Ratio
Urban	58,988	88.69	67.7	1.31
Rural	7,520	11.31	32.3	0.35
Not specified	5,867			

TABLE A7 *Geographical distribution of SAIC submissions*

States	# in SAIC	% of SAIC	% of population	Ratio
Distrito Federal	1,879	2.59	0.99	2.60
Roraima	106	0.15	0.07	2.15
Paraná	9,682	13.32	6.40	2.08
Minas Gerais	10,960	15.08	11.27	1.34
Mato Grosso do Sul	1,095	1.51	1.16	1.30
Santa Catarina	2,777	3.82	3.04	1.26
Paraíba	1,932	2.66	2.32	1.15
Goiás	2,163	2.98	2.67	1.12
Piauí	1,389	1.91	1.81	1.06
Alagoas	1,253	1.72	1.66	1.04
Amapá	110	0.15	0.15	1.02
São Paulo	14,721	20.25	20.95	0.97
Rio Grande do Sul	4,420	6.08	6.56	0.93
Rio Grande do Norte	927	1.28	1.60	0.80
Pernambuco	2,902	3.99	5.15	0.77
Espírito Santo	947	1.30	1.70	0.76
Ceará	2,445	3.36	4.44	0.76
Mato Grosso	521	0.72	0.97	0.74
Maranhão	1,808	2.49	3.38	0.74
Rio de Janeiro	4,843	6.66	9.48	0.70
Bahia	3,540	4.87	7.92	0.61
Sergipe	424	0.58	0.95	0.61
Amazonas	522	0.72	1.20	0.60
Rondônia	152	0.21	0.42	0.50
Acre	83	0.11	0.25	0.45
Pará	891	1.23	2.90	0.42
Tocantins	0	0.00	0.61	0.00
Not specified	190	0.26	0.00	

APPENDIX TO CHAPTER 5

TABLE A8 *Changes in drafts in response to submissions from the public*

Date	Participant name	Change in draft constitution
6-Apr-11	Árni Stefán Árnason	Draft 10[a] adds a provision to protecting the rights of animals.
14-Apr-11	Olgeir Gestsson	Draft 7 adds provisions against government ministers voting as MPs.
15-Apr-11	Hjalti Hugason	Draft 11 places the religious articles in the human rights section, and adds protections for a broader category of organizations.
17-Apr-11	Lúðvíg Lárusson	Draft 7 bans conscription.
18-Apr-11	Herdís Þorvaldsdóttir	Draft 15 adds specific protections for vegetation, soil, etc. and promises that previous damage will be repaired.
28-Apr-11	Hans Tómas Björnsson	Draft 7 bans discrimination on the basis of genotype.
28-Apr-11	Samtök hernaðarandstæðinga	Draft 7 bans conscription.
29-Apr-11	Kristinn Már Ársælsson	Draft 12 adds language requiring the government to keep minutes of meetings and to make this public.
29-Apr-11	Kristinn Már Ársælsson	Draft 12 adds requirements about publishing information about financial contributions to candidates and parties.
29-Apr-11	Kristinn Már Ársælsson	Draft 12 adds language on referenda and initiatives in line with this proposal.

[a] In this table, draft numbers refer to the number of the council meeting. Not all meetings produced a new draft. The first new draft was published after the fourth meeting (Draft 4), the next was published after the seventh meeting (Draft 7).

Date	Name	Proposal
2-May-11	Valdimar Samúelsson	Draft 4 changes the language on gender discrimination in line with this proposal.
5-May-11	Sigurður Jónas Eggertsson	Draft 10 adds new provisions to the article on education that is in line with this proposal.
8-May-11	Bergsteinn Jónsson	Draft 8 changes child rights language in line with this proposal.
9-May-11	Þórlaug Ágústsdóttir	Draft 17 introduces new language in the preamble that reflects this proposal.
9-May-11	Guðmundur Hörður Guðmundsson	Draft 10 adds language on environmental protection that includes the interests of future generations, as proposed here.
15-May-11	Hjörtur Hjartarson	Draft 18 lowers the necessary threshold for a popular initiative from 15 to 10 percent, as proposed here.
20-May-11	Örn Leó Guðmundsson	Draft 10 includes the fact that the natural resources are the "everlasting" property of the people, as proposed here.
27-May-11	Frosti Sigurjónsson	Draft 18 lowers the necessary threshold for a popular initiative from 15 to 10 percent, as proposed here.
27-May-11	Smári McCarthy	Draft 15 removes language allowing police to attend public assemblies and replaces this with language about restrictions in a democratic society.
30-May-11	Kristinn Már Ársælsson	Draft 11 removes some speculative language about the ability of the Althingi to hold secret meetings.
16-Jun-11	Jón Guðmundsson	Draft 17 changes the provision on freedom of association in line with this proposal.
21-Jun-11	Þórlaug Ágústsdóttir	Draft 14 adds a right to access the Internet.
23-Jun-11	Sigrún Helgadóttir	Draft 15 makes changes to the protections of nature and the environment in line with this proposal.
24-Jun-11	Svavar Kjarrval Lúthersson	Draft 16 makes Internet access unrestricted.
28-Jun-11	Nils Gíslason	Draft 16 removes the phrase "ever expanding" from the discussion of human rights protections, as was proposed here.
1-Jul-11	Sigurður Hr. Sigurðsson	Draft 16 requires asylum seekers to receive a speedy trial.
4-Jul-11	Svavar Kjarrval Lúthersson	Draft 16 changes referendum language to follow this proposal.
5-Jul-11	Daði Ingólfsson	Draft 18 removes government protection of religious groups, as proposed here.
5-Jul-11	Jakob Björnsson	Draft 16 changes language on the preservation of natural resources in line with this proposal.

FULL LISTS OF TOPICS

TABLE A9 *Distribution of topics in public comments*

Topic	Number	Percentage
Legislature reform	57	18.39
Electoral reform	56	18.06
Other human rights	50	16.13
Established church	41	13.23
Executive reform	39	12.58
Equality	25	8.06
Property rights	25	8.06
Direct democracy	23	7.42
Judiciary reform	18	5.81
Natural resources	18	5.81
Financial regulation reform	17	5.48
Environmental protection	14	4.52
Neutrality/Pacifism	11	3.55
Freedom of information	10	3.23
Privacy	10	3.23
Taxation	8	2.58
Const. amend. rules	6	1.94
Citizenship	5	1.61
Health rights	5	1.61
Subsistence rights/Min. wage	5	1.61
Dignity	4	1.29
Official language	4	1.29
Animal welfare	3	0.97
Education	3	0.97
Right to life	3	0.97
Shelter	3	0.97
Children's rights	2	0.65
Free expression	2	0.65
Intellectual property	2	0.65
Right to public assistance	2	0.65

TABLE A10 *Distribution of topics in Facebook comment threads*

Topic	Number	Percentage
Established church	433	18.92
Electoral reform	240	10.48
Other human rights	228	9.96
Legislature reform	227	9.92
Executive reform	162	7.08
Financial regulation reform	151	6.60
Property rights	134	5.85
Equality	113	4.94
Direct democracy	98	4.28
Judiciary reform	51	2.23
Natural resources	46	2.01
Freedom of information	39	1.70
Environmental protection	39	1.70
Privacy	37	1.62
Neutrality/Pacifism	36	1.57
Animal welfare	32	1.40
Official language	31	2.35
Const. amend rules	27	1.18
Education	25	1.09
Subsistence rights/Min. wage	24	1.05
Taxation	22	0.96
Citizenship	17	0.74
Health	16	0.70
Dignity	15	0.66
Intellectual property	11	0.48
Children's rights	10	0.44
Free express.	10	0.44
Right to public assistance	6	0.26
Shelter	5	0.22
Right to life	4	0.17

EXPANDED STATISTICAL MODELS

TABLE A11 *Statistical models with expanded topics*

	Model 1	Model 2	Model 3	Model 4
(Intercept)	−1.53***	−1.29***	−2.69*	−2.89**
	(0.38)	(0.38)	(1.12)	(1.03)
Days elapsed	−0.02***	−0.02***	−0.02***	−0.02***
	(0.01)	(0.00)	(0.01)	(0.01)
Wordcount	0.00*	0.00**	0.00**	0.00**
	(0.00)	(0.00)	(0.00)	(0.00)
Num. FB comms.	−0.01	−0.01	−0.00	−0.00
	(0.02)	(0.02)	(0.02)	(0.02)
C.C. memb's commenting	0.19*	0.20*	0.20*	0.19*
	(0.09)	(0.08)	(0.08)	(0.08)
Orig. poster commenting	−0.29	−0.25	−0.28	−0.27
	(0.31)	(0.29)	(0.30)	(0.30)
Tot. submits by same ind.	0.04	0.04*	0.05*	0.05*
	(0.02)	(0.02)	(0.02)	(0.02)
Submit. by interest group	−0.15	−0.13	−0.17	−0.17
	(0.41)	(0.38)	(0.41)	(0.41)
Topic: Amendment	0.26		−2.94	
	(0.74)		(572.78)	
Topic: Culture	0.50		1.35	1.55
	(0.31)		(1.12)	(1.02)
Topic: Electoral system	−0.33		0.52	0.73
	(0.40)		(1.19)	(1.09)
Topic: Executive branch	0.17		0.84	1.03
	(0.44)		(1.10)	(1.00)
Topic: Legislative branch	−0.05		0.75	0.94
	(0.41)		(1.09)	(0.99)
Topic: Direct democracy	1.21**		1.97	2.18*
	(0.39)		(1.13)	(1.02)
Topic: Oversight and reg.	−0.82		−3.50	
	(0.79)		(312.09)	
Topic: Rights	0.79**	0.63*	2.07	2.27*
	(0.27)	(0.26)	(1.09)	(0.98)
Topic: Institutions		−0.75*		
		(0.35)		
AIC	174.32	179.56	184.10	180.24
BIC	234.06	219.85	248.55	236.64
Log likelihood	−71.16	−79.78	−76.05	−76.12
Deviance	142.32	159.56	152.10	152.24
Num. obs.	309	415	415	415

*** $p < 0.001$, ** $p < 0.01$, * $p < 0.05$

APPENDIX TO CHAPTER 6

TABLE A12 *Summary statistics, Models 1–4*

Statistic	N	Mean	St. dev.	Min.	Max.
Novel rights	145	3.448	2.339	0.000	9.000
Aggregate participation	143	2.441	1.767	0.000	6.000
Party strength	116	0.497	0.243	0.003	0.965
Polyarchy	143	0.327	0.219	0.018	0.891
Conflict intensity	149	0.345	0.563	0.000	2.000
Strikes	123	0.485	1.146	0.000	7.000
GDP pc (thou. USD)	141	2.380	5.357	0.092	39.587

Bibliography

Abente-Brun, D. (2008). Paraguay: The Unraveling of One-Party Rule. *Journal of Democracy* 20(1), 143–156.

Ackerman, B. A. (1985). Beyond Carolene Products. *Harvard Law Review* 98(4), 713–746.

Ackerman, B. A. (1991). *We the People: Foundations*. Cambridge, MA: Belknap Press of Harvard University Press.

Ackerman, B. A. (1998). *We the People: Transformations*. Cambridge, MA: Belknap Press of Harvard University Press.

Ackerman, L. W. H. (2004). The Legal Nature of the South African Constitutional Revolution. *New Zealand Law Review* 2004, 633–680.

Afonso da Silva, J. (1990). Presidencialismo e Parlamentarismo no Brasil. *Revista de Ciência Política* 33(1), 9–32.

African National Congress (1989). Constitutional Guidelines for a Democratic South Africa. *South African Journal on Human Rights* 5(2), 129–132.

Agência Estado, Rio (July 18, 1987). Nas Ruas do rio, a passeata das emendas. *Estado de São Paulo*, 7, http://www2.senado.leg.br/bdsf/handle/id/134826.

Albert, R. (2017). Constitutional Amendment and Dismemberment. *Yale Journal of International Law* 43, 1–84.

Albert, R. (2019). *Constitutional Amendments: Making, Breaking, and Changing Constitutions*. Oxford: Oxford University Press.

Albrecht, S. (2006, February). Whose Voice Is Heard in Online Deliberation? A Study of Participation and Representation in Political Debates on the Internet. *Information, Communication & Society* 9(1), 62–82.

Alence, R. (2004, July). South Africa After Apartheid: The First Decade. *Journal of Democracy* 15(3), 78–92.

Almond, G. A. (1958). Research Note: A Comparative Study of Interest Groups and the Political Process. *The American Political Science Review* 52(1), 270–282.

Almond, G. A. and S. Verba (1963). *The Civic Culture: Political Attitudes and Democracy in Five Nations*. Princeton, NJ: Princeton University Press.

Althingi (2010, June). Lög nr. 90, 16 June 2010, www.althingi.is/altext/stjt/2010.090.html.

Ames, B. (2002a). *The Deadlock of Democracy in Brazil*. Ann Arbor, MI: University of Michigan Press.

Ames, B. (2002b). Party Discipline in the Chamber of Deputies. In S. Morgenstern and B. Nacif (Eds.), *Legislative Politics in Latin America*, pp. 185–221. New York: Cambridge University Press.

Andolina, R. (2003). The Sovereign and Its Shadow: Constituent Assembly and Indigenous Movement in Ecuador. *Journal of Latin American Studies* 35(4), 721–750.

Arato, A. (2000). *Civil Society, Constitution, and Legitimacy.* Lanham, MD: Rowman & Littlefield Publishers.

Arce, M. (2010, September). Parties and Social Protest in Latin America's Neoliberal Era. *Party Politics* 16(5), 669–686.

Arun, R., V. Suresh, C. E. V. Madhavan, and M. N. N. Murthy (2010, June). On Finding the Natural Number of Topics with Latent Dirichlet Allocation: Some Observations. In *Advances in Knowledge Discovery and Data Mining*, pp. 391–402. Berlin, Heidelberg: Springer.

Asmal, K. (2006). Guest Lecture Series of the Office of the Prosecutor, the Hague, www.icc-cpi.int/NR/rdonlyres/895EC486-C209-4AD8-8D7F-00EB250D03BC/0/Asmal.pdf.

Assembleia Nacional Constituinte (1987, May). *Diário Da Assembleia Nacional Constituinte (Suplemento).* Brasilia: Assembleia Nacional Constituinte.

Aucoin, L. (2004). The Role of International Experts in Constitution-Making: Myth and Reality. *Georgetown Journal of International Affairs* 5(1), 89–95.

Austin, R. C. and J. Ellison (2009). Albania. In L. Stan (Ed.), *Transitional Justice in Eastern Europe and the Former Soviet Union: Reckoning with the Communist Past*, pp. 176–199. Abingdon: Routledge.

Backes, A. L. and D. B. de Azevedo (2008). *A Sociedade No Parlamento: Imagens Da Assembléia Nacional Constituinte de 1987/1988.* Brasilia: Câmara dos Deputados.

Baiocchi, G. (2001). Participation, Activism, and Politics: The Porto Alegre Experiment and Deliberative Democratic Theory. *Politics & Society* 29(1), 43–72.

Banks, A. M. (2007). Expanding Participation in Constitution Making: Challenges and Opportunities. *Wm. & Mary L. Rev.* 49, 1043–1069.

Banks, W. C. and E. Alvarez (1991). The New Colombian Constitution: Democratic Victory or Popular Surrender. *University of Miami Inter-American Law Review* 23(1), 39–92.

Bannon, A. L. (2007). Designing a Constitution-Drafting Process: Lessons from Kenya. *The Yale Law Journal* 116(8), 1824–1872.

Banting, K. G. and R. Simeon (1985). Introduction: The Politics of Constitutional Change. In K. G. Banting and R. Simeon (Eds.), *The Politics of Constitutional Change in Industrial Nations: Redesigning the State*, pp. 1–29. New York: Palgrave Macmillan.

Bareiro, L. and C. Soto (1997). Women. In P. Lambert and A. Nickson (Eds.), *The Transition to Democracy in Paraguay*, Latin American Studies Series, pp. 87–96. London: Palgrave Macmillan.

Barkan, J. D. (2004). Kenya after Moi. *Foreign Affairs* 83(1), 87–100.

Beall, J., S. Gelb, and S. Hassim (2005). Fragile Stability: State and Society in Democratic South Africa. *Journal of Southern African Studies* 31(4), 681–700.

Becker, M. (2011, January). Correa, Indigenous Movements, and the Writing of a New Constitution in Ecuador. *Latin American Perspectives* 38(1), 47–62.

Becker, M. (2013). The Stormy Relations between Rafael Correa and Social Movements in Ecuador. *Latin American Perspectives* 40(3), 43–62.

Benediktsson, K. and A. Karlsdóttir (2011). Iceland Crisis and Regional Development – Thanks for All the Fish? *European Urban and Regional Studies* 18(2), 228–235.

Bennett, A. (2010). Process Tracing and Causal Inference. In H. E. Brady and D. Collier (Eds.), *Rethinking Social Inquiry: Diverse Tools, Shared Standards*, pp. 207–220. Lanham, MD: Rowman & Littlefield Publishers.

Benomar, J. (2004). Constitution-Making After Conflict: Lessons for Iraq. *Journal of Democracy* 15(2), 81–95.

Bernal, C. (2019). How Constitutional Crowdsourcing Can Enhance Legitimacy in Constitution Making. In D. Landau and H. Lerner (Eds.), *Comparative Constitution Making*, pp. 235–256. Cheltenham: Edward Elgar.

Bertoncelo, E. R. E. (2009). "Eu quero votar para presidente": Uma análise sobre a Campanha das Diretas. *Lua Nova: Revista de Cultura e Política* 76, 169–196.

Bishop, P. and G. Davis (2002). Mapping Public Participation in Policy Choices. *Australian Journal of Public Administration* 61(1), 14–29.

Bizzarro, F., J. Gerring, C. H. Knutsen, A. Hicken, M. Bernhard, S.-E. Skaaning, M. Coppedge, and S. I. Lindberg (2018). Party Strength and Economic Growth. *World Politics* 70(2), 275–320.

Blanton, S. L. and R. G. Blanton (2007). What Attracts Foreign Investors? An Examination of Human Rights and Foreign Direct Investment. *The Journal of Politics* 69(1), 143–155.

Blei, D. M., A. Y. Ng, and M. I. Jordan (2003). Latent Dirichlet Allocation. *Journal of Machine Learning Research* 3(4/5), 993–1022.

Blokker, P. (2012). Constitution Making in Romania: From Reiterative Crises to Constitutional Moment. *Revista Română de Drept Comparat* 3(2), 187–204.

Bonavides, P. and P. de Andrade (1989). *História Constitucional Do Brasil*. Brasilia: Paz e Terra.

Bonime-Blanc, A. R. (1987). *Spain's Transition to Democracy: The Politics of Constitution-Making*. Studies of the Research Institute on International Change, Columbia University. Boulder, CO: Westview Press.

Bonime-Blanc, A. R. (2010). Constitution Making and Democratization: The Spanish Paradigm. In L. E. Miller (Ed.), *Framing the State in Times of Transition: Case Studies in Constitution Making*, pp. 417–432. Washington, DC: United States Institute of Peace Press.

Boraine, A. (2014). *What's Gone Wrong? South Africa on the Brink of Failed Statehood*. New York: New York University Press.

Botha, H. (2010). Instituting Public Freedom or Extinguishing Constituent Power? Reflections on South Africa's Constitution-Making Experiment. *South African Journal on Human Rights* 26(1), 66–84.

Boudreaux, R. (1987, January). God Kept in Nicaragua Charter: Sandinistas Compromise Somewhat to Win Approval. *Los Angeles Times*, www.latimes.com/archives/la-xpm-1987-01-09-mn-2856-story.html

Brady, H. E., S. Verba, and K. L. Schlozman (1995). Beyond SES: A Resource Model of Political Participation. *American Political Science Review* 89(2), 271–294.

Brandão, L. C. (2011). *Os Movimentos Sociais e a Assembleia Nacional Constituinte de 1987–1988: Entre a Política Institucional e a Participação Popular*. Ph.D. thesis, Universidade de São Paulo, São Paulo.

Brandt, M., J. Cottrell, Y. Ghai, and A. Regan (2011). Constitution-Making and Reform Options for the Process. Technical Report, Interpeace, Geneva.

Brooks, H. (2015). *In Opposition and in Power: The African National Congress and the Theory and Practice of Participatory Democracy*. Ph.D. thesis, University of the Witwatersrand, Johannesburg, South Africa.

Brooks, H. (2018). Differential Interpretations in the Discourse of "People's Power": Unveiling Intellectual Heritage and Normative Democratic Thought. *African Studies* 77(3), 451–472.

Brown, S. and C. L. Sriram (2012, April). The Big Fish Won't Fry Themselves: Criminal Accountability for Post-election Violence in Kenya. *African Affairs* 111(443), 244–260.

Burgess, S. and C. Keating (2013). Occupy the Social Contract! Participatory Democracy and Iceland's Crowd-Sourced Constitution. *New Political Science* 35(3), 417–431.

Cairns, A. C. (1988). Citizens (Outsiders) and Governments (Insiders) in Constitution-Making: The Case of Meech Lake. *Canadian Public Policy/Analyse de Politiques* 14, Supplement S121–S145.

Calland, R. (2017, March). South Africa's Constitution Is under Attack. *The Mail & Guardian*, https://mg.co.za/article/2017-03-20-south-africas-constitution-is-under-attack/.

Cardoso, E. and A. Urani (1995). Inflation and Unemployment as Determinants of Inequality in Brazil: The 1980s. In R. Dornbusch and S. Edwards (Eds.), *Reform, Recovery, and Growth: Latin America and the Middle East*, pp. 151–176. Chicago, IL: University of Chicago Press.

Carey, J. (2009). Does It Matter How a Constitution Is Created? In Z. D. Barany and R. G. Moser (Eds.), *Is Democracy Exportable?*, pp. 156–177. New York: Cambridge University Press.

Carey, J. and A. Reynolds (2007). Parties and Accountable Government in New Democracies. *Party Politics* 13(2), 255–274.

Carlson, S. N. (2010). The Drafting Process for the 1998 Albanian Constitution. In L. E. Miller (Ed.), *Framing the State in Times of Transition: Case Studies in Constitution Making*, pp. 311–331. Washington, DC: United States Institute of Peace Press.

Case, A. (2001). Election Goals and Income Redistribution: Recent Evidence from Albania. *European Economic Review* 45(3), 405–423.

Castells, M. (2012). *Networks of Outrage and Hope: Social Movements in the Internet Age.* Cambridge, UK; Malden, MA: Polity Press.

Ceka, B. (2013). The Perils of Political Competition: Explaining Participation and Trust in Political Parties in Eastern Europe. *Comparative Political Studies* 46(12), 1610–1635.

Chambers, S. (2004). Democracy, Popular Sovereignty, and Constitutional Legitimacy. *Constellations* 11(2), 153–173.

Cheeseman, N. (2008, July). The Kenyan Elections of 2007: An Introduction. *Journal of Eastern African Studies* 2(2), 166–184.

Chege, M. (2008, October). Kenya: Back from the Brink? *Journal of Democracy* 19(4), 125–139.

Cheibub, J. A., Z. Elkins, and T. Ginsburg (2014). Beyond Presidentialism and Parliamentarism. *British Journal of Political Science* 44(3), 515–544.

Chiaretti, D. (1987, February). Rio e São Paulo, o desconhecimento da Constituinte. *Gazeta Mercantil*, 28.

Choudhry, S. and M. Tushnet (2020, May). Participatory Constitution-Making: Introduction. *International Journal of Constitutional Law* 18(1), 173–178.

Christiano, C. (February 15, 1987). Caça a jacare no livro paulista. *Folha de São Paulo*, 9.

Claude, L. L. (2012). Historia constitucional del Paraguay (período 1870–2012). *Revista Jurídica* 3(1), 173–291.

Cobb, R. W. and C. D. Elder (1983). *Participation in American Politics: The Dynamics of Agenda-Building.* Baltimore, MD: Johns Hopkins University Press.

Collier, D. (2011). Understanding Process Tracing. *PS: Political Science & Politics* 44(4), 823–830.

Collier, D. and S. Levitsky (1997). Democracy with Adjectives: Conceptual Innovation in Comparative Research. *World Politics* 49(3), 430–451.

Colón-Ríos, J. I. (2012). *Weak Constitutionalism: Democratic Legitimacy and the Question of Constituent Power.* New York: Routledge.

Comella, V. F. (2013). *The Constitution of Spain: A Contextual Analysis.* Oxford: Bloomsbury Publishing.

Constitutional Assembly (1995, August). Transcript of Public Hearing on Social and Economic Rights. Technical report, Constitutional Assembly, Cape Town.

Constitutional Committee (1994, September). Minutes of Fourth Constitutional Committee Meeting. Technical report, Constitutional Assembly, Cape Town.

Constitutional Committee (1995, April). Minutes of Seventh Meeting of the Constitutional Committee. Technical report, Constitutional Assembly, Cape Town.

Coppedge, M. (1997). *Strong Parties and Lame Ducks: Presidential Partyarchy and Factionalism in Venezuela.* Palo Alto: Stanford University Press.

Corrigan, T. (2018, May). Expropriation without Compensation: Non-participatory Participation. *Daily Maverick,* www.dailymaverick.co.za/article/2018-05-16-expropriation-without-compensation-non-participatory-participation/.

Cox, G. W. (1997). *Making Votes Count: Strategic Coordination in the World's Electoral Systems.* Cambridge; New York: Cambridge University Press.

Crisp, B. F. (1997). Presidential Behavior in a System with Strong Parties: Venezuela, 1958–1995. In S. Mainwaring and M. S. Shugart (Eds.), *Presidentialism and Democracy in Latin America,* pp. 160–198. New York: Cambridge University Press.

Cross, E. and J. Sorens (2016). Arab Spring Constitution-Making: Polarization, Exclusion, and Constraints. *Democratization* 23(7), 1292–1312.

Currie, Iain, and Johan de Waal, eds.(2001). The New Constitutional and Administrative Law: Constitutional Law. Vol. 1. Cape Town: Juta.

Dahl, R. A. (1971). *Polyarchy: Participation and Opposition.* New Haven, CT: Yale University Press.

Dahlberg, L. (2001). Computer-Mediated Communication and The Public Sphere: A Critical Analysis. *Journal of Computer-Mediated Communication* 7(1), Online.

Dalton, R. J. (1985). Political Parties and Political Representation: Party Supporters and Party Elites in Nine Nations. *Comparative Political Studies* 18(3), 267–299.

Dalton, R. J. (2004). *Democratic Challenges, Democratic Choices: The Erosion of Political Support in Advanced Industrial Democracies.* Oxford: Oxford University Press.

Dann, P., M. Riegner, J. Vogel, and M. Wortmann (2011, November). Lessons Learned from Constitution-Making: Processes with Broad Based Public Participation. Technical Report Briefing Paper No. 20, Democracy Reporting International.

Dargent, E. and P. Muñoz (2011). Democracy against Parties? Party System Deinstitutionalization in Colombia. *Journal of Politics in Latin America* 3(2), 43–71.

Davenport, C. (1999). Human Rights and the Democratic Proposition. *Journal of Conflict Resolution* 43(1), 92–116.

Dávila Ladrón de Guevara, A. (2015). *Democracia pactada : El Frente Nacional y el proceso constituyente de 1991 en Colombia.* Travaux de l'IFEA. Lima: Institut français d'études andines.

Davis, G. (1996, November). ANC to Act over Abortion Vote. *The M&G Online,* http://mg.co.za/article/1996-11-15-anc-to-act-over-abortion-vote/

de Klerk, E. (1995, July). Email: Subject: Gun Control, University of Cape Town Special Collections, BC 114: Constitutional Assembly Papers; A3 Correspondence 1995–1996.

de la Torre, C. (2014). The People, Democracy, and Authoritarianism in Rafael Correa's Ecuador: The People, Democracy, and Authoritarianism in Rafael Correa's Ecuador: Carlos de la Torre. *Constellations* 21(4), 457–466.

de Mendonça, M. X. (March 2, 1987). Governo de SP reune em livro propostas para a nova carta. *Folha de São Paulo,* a4.

de Moraes, M. A. F. D. and D. Zilberman (2014). *Production of Ethanol from Sugarcane in Brazil: From State Intervention to a Free Market.* Heidelberg: Springer Science & Business Media.

de Nève, D. (2010). Albania. In D. Nohlen and P. Stöver (Eds.), *Elections in Europe: A Data Handbook*, pp. 125–148. Baden-Baden: Nomos.

de Vos, P. and W. Freedman (Eds.) (2014). *South African Constitutional Law in Context.* Cape Town: Oxford University Press.

Devenish, G. E. (2012). The Republican Constitution of 1961 Revisited: A Re-Evaluation after Fifty Years. *Fundamina* 18(1), 1–14.

Diamond, L. and R. Gunther (2001). Types and Functions of Parties. In L. Diamond and R. Gunther (Eds.), *Political Parties and Democracy*, Journal of Democracy Book, pp. 3–39. Baltimore, MD: Johns Hopkins University Press.

Dixon, R. (2018). Constitutional Rights as Bribes. *Connecticut Law Review* 50(3), 767–818.

Dryzek, J. S., A. Bächtiger, and K. Milewicz (2011). Toward a Deliberative Global Citizens' Assembly. *Global Policy* 2(1), 33–42.

Dugas, J. (1993). *La Constitución de 1991: un pacto politico viable?* Bogotá: Department de Ciencia Política, Universidad de los Andes.

Dunning, T. (2012). *Natural Experiments in the Social Sciences: A Design-Based Approach.* New York: Cambridge University Press.

Duverger, M. (1954). *Political Parties, Their Organization and Activity in the Modern State.* New York: Wiley.

Ebrahim, H. (1998). *The Soul of a Nation: Constitution-Making in South Africa.* Cape Town: Oxford University Press.

Ebrahim, H., K. Fayemi, and S. Loomis (1999). Promoting a Culture of Constitutionalism and Democracy in Africa: Recommendations to the Commonwealth Heads of Government. Technical report, Commonwealth Human Rights Initiative, New Delhi.

Eisenstadt, T. A., A. C. LeVan, and T. Maboudi (2015, August). When Talk Trumps Text: The Democratizing Effects of Deliberation during Constitution-Making, 1974–2011. *American Political Science Review* 109(3), 592–612.

Eisenstadt, T. A., A. C. LeVan, and T. Maboudi (2017a). *Constituents Before Assembly: Participation, Deliberation, and Representation in the Crafting of New Constitutions.* New York: Cambridge University Press.

Eisenstadt, T. A., A. C. LeVan, and T. Maboudi (2017b, June). *Constitutionalism and Democracy Dataset, Version 1.0.* Washington, DC: American University's Digital Research Archive.

Elischer, S. (2013). *Political Parties in Africa: Ethnicity and Party Formation.* New York: Cambridge University Press.

Elkins, Z. (2013). The weight of history and the rebuilding of Brazilian democracy. *Lua Nova: Revista de Cultura e Política* 88, 257–303.

Elkins, Z. (2017). Constitutional Revolution in the Andes. In R. Dixon and T. Ginsburg (Eds.), *Comparative Constitutional Law in Latin America*, pp. 108–125. Northampton, MA: Edward Elgar.

Elkins, Z., T. Ginsburg, and J. Blount (2008). The Citizen as Founder: Public Participation in Constitutional Approval. *Temple Law Review* 81, 361–382.

Elkins, Z., T. Ginsburg, and J. Melton (2009). *The Endurance of National Constitutions.* New York: Cambridge University Press.

Elkins, Z., T. Ginsburg, and J. Melton (2012, October). A Review of Iceland's Draft Constitution. Comparative Constitutions Project, https://webspace.utexas.edu/elkinszs/web/CCP%20Iceland%20Report.pdf.

Elkins, Z., T. Ginsburg, and J. Melton (2014). Characteristics of National Constitutions, Version 2.0. *Comparative Constitutions Project*, www.comparativeconstitutionsproject.org.

Elkins, Z. and A. Hudson (2019). The Constitutional Referendum in Historical Perspective. In D. Landau and H. Lerner (Eds.), *Comparative Constitution-Making*, pp. 142–164. Northampton, MA: Edward Elgar.

Ellis, S. (1993). Rumour and Power in Togo. *Africa* 63(4), 462–476.

Elster, J. (1995). Forces and Mechanisms in the Constitution-Making Process. *Duke Law Journal* 45(2), 364–396.

Elster, J. (1997). Ways of Constitution Making. In A. Hadenius (Ed.), *Democracy's Victory and Crisis: Nobel Symposium No. 93*, pp. 123–142. New York: Cambridge University Press.

Elster, J. (2000). *Ulysses Unbound: Studies in Rationality, Precommitment, and Constraints*. New York: Cambridge University Press.

Elster, J. (2006). Legislatures as Constituent Assemblies. In R. W. Bauman and T. Kahana (Eds.), *The Least Examined Branch: The Role of Legislatures in the Constitutional State*, pp. 181–197. New York: Cambridge University Press.

Elster, J. (2012). The Optimal Design of a Constituent Assembly. In H. Landemore and J. Elster (Eds.), *Collective Wisdom: Principles and Mechanisms*, pp. 148–172. New York: Cambridge University Press.

Englehart, N. A. (2009). State Capacity, State Failure, and Human Rights. *Journal of Peace Research* 46(2), 163–180.

Epstein, L. D. (1967). *Political Parties in Western Democracies*. New York: Praeger.

Everatt, D., K. Fenyves, and S. Davies (1996). *A New Constitution for a New South Africa: Evaluating the Public Participation, Media, Education, and Plain Language Campaigns of the Constitutional Assembly*. Community Agency for Social Enquiry. National Archives of South Africa: CA 8: 1/18/7-1/19/6.

Fabre, C. (2000). *Social Rights Under the Constitution: Government and the Decent Life*. New York: Oxford University Press.

Fallon, R. H. (2005). Legitimacy and the Constitution. *Harvard Law Review* 118(6), 1787–1853.

Figueiredo, A. C. and F. Limongi (2000). Presidential Power, Legislative Organization, and Party Behavior in Brazil. *Comparative Politics* 32(2), 151–170.

Finer, S. E., V. Bogdanor, and B. Rudden (1995). *Comparing Constitutions*. Oxford, New York: Clarendon Press; Oxford University Press.

Fiorina, M. P. (1980). The Decline of Collective Responsibility in American Politics. *Daedalus* 109(3), 25–45.

Fish, M. S. (1998, July). Mongolia: Democracy Without Prerequisites. *Journal of Democracy* 9(3), 127–141.

Fishkin, J. S. (2009). *When the People Speak: Deliberative Democracy and Public Consultation*. New York: Oxford University Press.

Folha de São Paulo (July 27, 1988). Sarney diz na TV que Carta deixa país "ingovernável". *Folha de São Paulo*, A6.

Fox, D. T., G. Gallón-Giraldo, and A. Stetson (2010). Lessons of the Colombian Constitutional Reform of 1991: Toward the Securing of Peace and Reconciliation. In L. E. Miller (Ed.), *Framing the State in Times of Transition: Case Studies in Constitution Making*, pp. 467–482. Washington, DC: United States Institute of Peace.

Franck, T. M. and A. K. Thiruvengadam (2010). Norms of International Law Relating to the Constitution-Making Process. In L. E. Miller (Ed.), *Framing the State in Times of Transition: Case Studies in Constitution Making*, pp. 3–19. Washington, DC: United States Institute of Peace Press.

Frasheri, E. (2011). Transition without Transformation: Legal Reform in the Democratization and Development Process. *Journal of Civil Law Studies* 4(1), 59–112.

French, J. D. (1991). The Origin of Corporatist State Intervention in Brazilian Industrial Relations, 1930–1934: A Critique of the Literature. *Luso-Brazilian Review* 28(2), 13–26.

Fukuyama, F. (1989). The End of History? *The National Interest* (16), 3–18.

Fung, A. (2006). Varieties of Participation in Complex Governance. *Public Administration Review* 66, 66–75.

Fung, A. (2015). Putting the Public Back into Governance: The Challenges of Citizen Participation and Its Future. *Public Administration Review* 75(4), 513–522.

Furley, O. and J. Katalikawe (1997). Constitutional Reform in Uganda: The New Approach. *African Affairs* 96(383), 243–260.

Galligan, D. J. (2013). The Sovereignty Deficit of Modern Constitutions. *Oxford Journal of Legal Studies* 33(4), 703–732.

Garcia-Guadilla, M. P. and M. Hurtado (2000, March). Participation and Constitution Making in Colombia and Venezuela: Enlarging the Scope of Democracy, Paper presented at the Latin American Studies Association, 16 March 2000, Miami.

Gebaly, H. (2012). Constitutional Developments in Egypt in 2011. Venice Commission, Strasbourg, www.venice.coe.int/webforms/documents/?pdf=CDL(2012)004-e.

Gelazis, N. (2001). Institutional Engineering in Lithuania: Stability through Compromise. In J. Zielonka (Ed.), *Democratic Consolidation in Eastern Europe: Volume 1: Institutional Engineering*, pp. 165–185. Oxford: Oxford University Press.

Gerring, J. (2007). *Case Study Research: Principles and Practices*. New York: Cambridge University Press.

Ghai, Y. and G. Galli (2006). Constitution Building Processes and Democratization. In J. Large and T. D. Sisk (Eds.), *Democracy, Conflict and Human Security: Further Reading (Volume 2)*, pp. 232–248.

Ghannouchi, R. (2016). From Political Islam to Muslim Democracy: The Ennahda Party and the Future of Tunisia Essays. *Foreign Affairs* 95(5), 58–75.

Gherghina, S. and M. Hein (2016). Romania. In A. Fruhstorfer and M. Hein (Eds.), *Constitutional Politics in Central and Eastern Europe: From Post-Socialist Transition to the Reform of Political Systems*, Vergleichende Politikwissenschaft, pp. 173–197. Wiesbaden: Springer Fachmedien.

Ginsburg, T. (2003). *Judicial Review in New Democracies: Constitutional Courts in Asian Cases*. New York: Cambridge University Press.

Ginsburg, T., Z. Elkins, and J. Blount (2009). Does the Process of Constitution-Making Matter? *Annual Review of Law and Social Science* 5(1), 201–223.

Ginsburg, T. and A. Z. Huq (2018). *How to Save a Constitutional Democracy*. Chicago: University of Chicago Press.

Gisselquist, R. M. (2008). Democratic Transition and Democratic Survival in Benin. *Democratization* 15(4), 789–814.

Global Citizens Assembly (2019, October). The first Global Citizens' Assembly on Genome Editing, globalca.org/post/first-global-citizens-assembly-genome-editing.

O Globo, (1987a, April 19). Entrevistados querem participar da Constituinte e têm esperança. *O Globo*, 5.

O Globo, (1987b, May 24). Pesquisa mostra que população quer as Forças Armadas na defesa interna. *O Globo*, 9.

O Globo, (1987c, April 26). Pesquisa revela a preferência por sindacto livre. *O Globo*, 12.

O Globo, (1987d, April 19). Pesquisa revela preferencia pelo presidencialismo. *O Globo*, 5.

O Globo, (1987e, July 5). População acha partidos úteis mas quer limitá-los. *O Globo*, 9.

O Globo, (1987f, June 28). População quer ensino obrigatório até 16 anos. *O Globo*, 11.

O Globo, (1987g, June 21). População quer mais direitos para as mulheres. *O Globo*, 8.

O Globo, (1987h, June 14). População quer o salário mínimo 4 vezes maior e negociação das 40 horas. *O Globo*, 8.

Gloppen, S. (1997). *South Africa: The Battle over the Constitution*. Law, Social Change, and Development Series. Brookfield, VT: Ashgate/Dartmouth.

Gluck, J. and B. Ballou (2014, May). New Technologies for Constitution Making. Washington: United States Institute of Peace, Special Report 343, www.usip.org/sites/default/files/SR343_New-Technologies-for-Constitution-Making.pdf.

Gluck, J. and M. Brandt (2015). Participatory and Inclusive Constitution Making: Giving voice to the demands of citizens in the wake of the Arab Spring. United States Institute of Peace, Washington, DC, Peaceworks No. 105, www.usip.org/sites/default/files/PW105-Participatory-and-Inclusive-Constitution-Making.pdf.

Goldfrank, B. (2012). The World Bank and the Globalization of Participatory Budgeting. *Journal of Public Deliberation* 8(2), Online.

Gomes, S. (2006). O Impacto das Regras de Organização do Processo Legislativo no Comportamento dos Parlamentares: Um Estudo de Caso da Assembléia Nacional Constituinte (1987–1988). *DADOS - Revista de Ciências Sociais* 49(1), 193–224.

González, I. (February 21, 2019). Sociedad civil cubana expectante ante referendo constitucional. *Inter Press Service en Cuba*, www.ipscuba.net/politica/sociedad-civil-cubana-expectante-ante-referendo-constitucional/.

Gouws, A. and P. Mitchell (2005). South Africa: One Party Dominance Despite Perfect Proportionality. In M. Gallagher and P. Mitchell (Eds.), *The Politics of Electoral Systems*, pp. 353–373. New York: Oxford University Press.

Graber, M. A., S. Levinson, and M. Tushnet (Eds.) (2018). *Constitutional Democracy in Crisis?* Oxford University Press.

Grönlund, K., M. Setälä, and K. Herne (2010, March). Deliberation and civic virtue: Lessons from a citizen deliberation experiment. *European Political Science Review* 2(1), 95–117.

Guillenchmidt, J., J. Helgesen, W. Hoffman-Riem, J.-C. Scholsem, and J. S. Sørenson (2013, February). *Draft Opinion on the Draft New Constitution of Iceland*. Venice: European Commission for Democracy Through Law, www.althingi.is/pdf/Feneyjanefnd_skyrsla_e.pdf.

Gunther, R. (1985). Constitutional Change in Contemporary Spain. In K. G. Banting and R. Simeon (Eds.), *The Politics of Constitutional Change in Industrial Nations*, pp. 42–70. London: Palgrave Macmillan.

Gunther, R. and L. Diamond (2003, January). Species of Political Parties A New Typology. *Party Politics* 9(2), 167–199.

Gunther, R., J. R. Montero, and J. Botella (2004). *Democracy in Modern Spain*. New Haven, CT: Yale University Press.

Gylfason, T. (2011, October). Crowds and Constitutions, Vox EU, www.voxeu.org/article/crowds-and-constitutions-insights-iceland.

Gylfason, T. (2013a, June). Democracy on Ice: A Post-mortem of the Icelandic Constitution. Open Democracy, www.opendemocracy.net/can-europe-make-it/thorvaldur-gylfason/democracy-on-ice-post-mortem-of-icelandic-constitution.

Gylfason, T. (2013b, March). Putsch: Iceland's Crowd-Sourced Constitution Killed by Parliament Verfassungsblog, www.verfassungsblog.de/en/putsch-icelands-crowd-sourced-constitution-killed-by-parliament/.

Gylfason, T. (2016a). Constitution on Ice. In V. Ingimundarson, P. Urfalino, and I. Erlings-dóttir (Eds.), *Iceland's Financial Crisis: The Politics of Blame, Protest, and Reconstruction*, pp. 203–219. New York: Routledge.

Gylfason, T. (2016b, November). Iceland's New Constitution Is Not Solely a Local Concern. *Challenge* 59(6), 480–490.

Gylfason, T. (2017). The Anatomy of Constitution Making: From Denmark in 1849 to Iceland in 2017. *CESifo Working Paper 6488*, www.cesifo-group.de/ifoHome/publications/working-papers/CESifoWP/CESifoWPdetails?wp_id=19323513.

Habermas, J. (1996). *Between Facts and Norms: Contributions to a Discourse Theory of Law and Democracy*. Cambridge, MA: MIT Press.

Hale, H. E. (2005). Why Not Parties? Electoral Markets, Party Substitutes, and Stalled Democratization in Russia. *Comparative Politics* 37(2), 147–166.

Harris, P. (2010). *Birth: The Conspiracy to Stop the '94 Election*. Cape Town: Umuzi.

Hart, V. (2003). Democratic Constitution Making. United States Institute of Peace, Washington, DC Special Report 107, www.usip.org/pubs/specialreports/sr107.html.

Hart, V. (2010). Constitution Making and the Right to Take Part in a Public Affair. In L. E. Miller (Ed.), *Framing the State in Times of Transition: Case Studies in Constitution Making*, pp. 20–54. Washington, DC: United States Institute of Peace Press.

Hartshorn, I. M. (2017, June). Organized Interests in Constitutional Assemblies: Egypt and Tunisia in Comparison. *Political Research Quarterly* 70(2), 408–420.

Hassan, M. (2013, June). Elections of the People's Assembly, Egypt 2011/12. *Electoral Studies* 32(2), 370–374.

Heilbrunn, J. R. (1993, June). Social Origins of National Conferences in Benin and Togo. *The Journal of Modern African Studies* 31(2), 277–299.

Heilbrunn, J. R. (2019). Presidential Term Limits in Togo: Electoral Accountability Postponed. In A. Baturo and R. Elgie (Eds.), *The Politics of Presidential Term Limits*, pp. 199–220. Oxford: Oxford University Press.

Helgadóttir, R. (2014, October). Which Citizens? – Participation in the Drafting of the Icelandic Constitutional Draft of 2011. *ICONnect: Blog of the International Journal of Constitutional Law*, www.iconnectblog.com/2014/10/which-citizens-participation-in-the-drafting-of-the-icelandic-constitutional-draft-of-2011/.

Heller, P. (2012). Democracy, Participatory Politics and Development: Some Comparative Lessons from Brazil, India and South Africa. *Polity* 44(4), 643–665.

Hetherington, M. J. (2005). *Why Trust Matters: Declining Political Trust and the Demise of American Liberalism*. Princeton, NJ: Princeton University Press.

Hirschl, R. (2004). *Towards Juristocracy: The Origins and Consequences of the New Constitutionalism*. Cambridge, MA: Harvard University Press.

Hochstetler, K. (2000). Democratizing Pressures from Below? Social Movements in the New Brazilian Democracy. In P. R. Kingstone and T. J. Power (Eds.), *Democratic Brazil: Actors, Institutions, and Processes*, pp. 167–184. Pittsburgh, PA: University of Pittsburgh Press.

Holmes, S. (1988). Precommitment and the paradox of democracy. In J. Elster and R. Slagstad (Eds.), *Constitutionalism and Democracy*, pp. 195–240. New York: Cambridge University Press.

Hudson, A. (2018a). When Does Public Participation Make a Difference? Evidence From Iceland's Crowdsourced Constitution. *Policy & Internet* 10(2), 185–217.

Hudson, A. (2018b). Will Iceland Get a New Constitution? A New Revision Process Is Taking Shape. *ICONnect: Blog of the International Journal of Constitutional Law*, www.iconnectblog.com/2018/10/will-iceland-get-a-new-constitution-a-new-revision-process-is-taking-shape/

Huntington, S. P. (1968). *Political Order in Changing Societies.* New Haven, CT: Yale University Press.

Huntington, S. P. (1993). *The Third Wave: Democratization in the Late Twentieth Century.* Norman: University of Oklahoma Press.

Hyden, G. (2010). *Specialist Bodies for Constitution-Making.* Constitution-Making in Focus: Issue Paper. Geneva: Interpeace, https://constitutionmakingforpeace.org/wp-content/uploads/2015/04/InFocus_Hyden_FINAL.pdf.

Statistics Iceland (2010, May), Referendum March 6, 2010, http://statice.is/publications/news-archive/elections/referendum-6-march-2010/.

Statistics Iceland (2011, September), Referendum April 9, 2011, http://statice.is/publications/news-archive/elections/referendum-9-april-2011/.

International Crisis Group (2003, December). Afghanistan: The Constitutional Loya Jirga. International Crisis Group, Kabul/Brussels.

Jacobsohn, G. J. (2012). Making Sense of the Constitutional Revolution. *Constellations* 19(2), 164–181.

James, P. (1997). Drafters of South Africa's New Constitution Adapt to Plain Language. *Clarity* 38, 13–15.

Janda, K. (1970). *A Conceptual Framework for the Comparative Analysis of Political Parties.* Beverly Hills, CA: Sage Publications.

Jarvis, C. J. (2000). The Rise and Fall of the Pyramid Schemes in Albania. *IMF Staff Papers* 47(1), 1, http://elibrary.imf.org/view/IMF001/07256-9781451852127/07256-9781451852127/07256-9781451852127.xml.

Jiménez Martín, C. (2006). Momentos, Escenarios y Sujetos de la Producción Constituyente. Aproximaciones Críticas al Proceso Constitucional de los Noventa. *Análisis Político* 19(58), 132–156.

Johnson, D. E. (2015). Beyond Constituent Assemblies and Referenda: Assessing the Legitimacy of the Arab Spring Constitutions in Egypt and Tunisia The Role of Constitutional Courts in Constitutional Design. *Wake Forest Law Review* 50(4), 1007–1056.

Jornal da Tarde (May 2, 1987). As Minorias fazem suas propostas, e os constituintes quase ignoram homossexuais, negros e indios: uma luta que ainda não sensibilizou os parlamentares. *Jornal da Tarde*, 7.

Jornal do Brasil (May 29, 1985). Apenas 9% dos cariocas sabem o que significa a constituinte. *Jornal do Brasil*, 3.

Jornal do Brasil (1987a, July 23). Emendas populares começam a chegar a constituinte. *Jornal do Brasil*, 2.

Jornal do Brasil (1987b, July 2). UDR leva 30 mil para pressionar constituinte. *Jornal do Brasil*, 2.

Kalyvas, A. (2005). Popular Sovereignty, Democracy, and the Constituent Power. *Constellations* 12(2), 223–244.

Karlsson, M. (2012). Democratic Legitimacy and Recruitment Strategies in eParticipation Projects. In Y. Charalabidis and S. Koussouris (Eds.), *Empowering Open and Collaborative Governance: Technologies and Methods for Online Citizen Engagement in Public Policy Making*, pp. 3–20. Heidelberg: Springer.

Keating, J. (2012, February). Why Does Ruth Bader Ginsburg Like the South African Constitution So Much? *Foreign Policy*, https://foreignpolicy.com/2012/02/06/why-does-ruth-bader-ginsburg-like-the-south-african-constitution-so-much/.

Kelly, S., M. Truong, M. Earp, L. Reed, A. Shahbaz, and A. Greco-Stoner (2013). Freedom on the Net 2013. Freedom House, http://freedomhouse.org/sites/default/files/resources/FOTN%202013_Full%20Report_0.pdf.

Kelsen, H. (1945). *General Theory of Law and State*. Cambridge, MA: Harvard University Press.

Kelsen, H. (1978). *Pure Theory of Law*. Berkeley, CA: University of California Press.

Kende, M. S. (2003). The South African Constitutional Court's Embrace of Socio-Economic Rights: A Comparative Perspective. *Chapman Law Review* 6, 137–160.

Key, V. O. (1961). *Public Opinion and American Democracy* (1st ed.). New York: Knopf.

Kidd, S. (1997). Indigenous Peoples. In P. Lambert and A. Nickson (Eds.), *The Transition to Democracy in Paraguay*, Latin American Studies Series, pp. 114–127. London: Palgrave Macmillan.

Kirkby, C. and C. Murray (2016). Constitution-Making in Anglophone Africa: We the People? In M. Ndulo and M. Gazibo (Eds.), *Growing Democracy in Africa: Elections, Accountable Governance, and Political Economy*, pp. 86–113. Newcastle upon Tyne: Cambridge Scholars Publishing.

Kramon, E. and D. N. Posner (2011). Kenya's New Constitution. *Journal of Democracy* 22(2), 89–103.

Krupavicius, A. (1998). The Post-Communist Transition and Institutionalization of Lithuania's Parties. *Political Studies* 46(3), 465–491.

Kurland, P. B. and R. Lerner (Eds.) (1986). *The Founders' Constitution*. Chicago: University of Chicago Press.

Laakso, M. and R. Taagepera (1979). "Effective" Number of Parties: A Measure with Application to West Europe. *Comparative Political Studies* 12(1), 3–27.

Lambert, P. (2000). A Decade of Electoral Democracy: Continuity, Change and Crisis in Paraguay. *Bulletin of Latin American Research* 19, 379–396.

Lamounier, B. and R. Meneguello (1985). *Political Parties and Democratic Consolidation: The Brazilian Case*. Number 165 in Working Papers. Washington, DC: Latin American Program, The Wilson Center.

Landau, D. (2011). The Importance of Constitution-Making. *Denver University Law Review* 89, 611–633.

Landemore, H. (2012). *Democratic Reason: Politics, Collective Intelligence, and the Rule of the Many*. Princeton, NJ: Princeton University Press.

Landemore, H. (2015). Inclusive Constitution-Making: The Icelandic Experiment. *Journal of Political Philosophy* 23(2), 166–191.

Landemore, H. (2016). What is a Good Constitution? Assessing the Constitutional Proposal in the Icelandic Experiment. In T. Ginsburg and A. Huq (Eds.), *Assessing Constitutional Performance*, pp. 71–98. New York: Cambridge University Press.

Landemore, H. (2017, May). Inclusive Constitution Making and Religious Rights: Lessons from the Icelandic Experiment. *The Journal of Politics* 79(3).

Landemore, H. (April 24, 2019). Can Macron Quiet the "Yellow Vests" Protests with His "Great Debate". *Washington Post*, www.washingtonpost.com/politics/2019/04/24/can -macron-quiet-yellow-vests-protests-with-his-great-debate-tune-tomorrow/.

Landemore, H. (2020a). *Open Democracy: Reinventing Popular Rule for the 21st Century*. Princeton, NJ: Princeton University Press.

Landemore, H. (2020b). When Public Participation Matters: The 2010–2013 Icelandic Constitutional Process. *International Journal of Constitutional Law* 18(1), 179–205.

Lasswell, H. D. and A. Kaplan (1965). *Power and Society: A Framework for Political Inquiry*. New Haven, CT: Yale University Press.

Law, D. S. and M. Versteeg (2011). The Evolution and Ideology of Global Constitutionalism. *California Law Review* 99(5), 1163–1257.

Leon, T. (2008). *On the Contrary: Leading the Opposition in a Democratic South Africa.* Johannesburg: Jonathan Ball.

Lerner, H. (2011). *Making Constitutions in Deeply Divided Societies.* New York: Cambridge University Press.

Lessig, L. (2016, October). A Letter from Iceland: #CanYouHearUs.IS, https://medium.com/@lessig/a-letter-from-iceland-canyouhearus-is-789910d293c0.

Lieberman, E. S. (2003). *Race and Regionalism in the Politics of Taxation in Braziland South Africa.* New York: Cambridge University Press.

Lipset, S. M. (2000). The Indispensability of Political Parties. *Journal of Democracy* 11(1), 48–55.

Lobel, J. (1987). The Meaning of Democracy: Representative and Participatory Democracy in the New Nicaraguan Constitution Essay. *University of Pittsburgh Law Review* 49(3), 823–890.

Lodge, T. (2004). The ANC and the Development of Party Politics in Modern South Africa. *The Journal of Modern African Studies* 42(2), 189–219.

Lord, C. G., L. Ross, and M. R. Lepper (1979). Biased Assimilation and Attitude Polarization: The Effects of Prior Theories on Subsequently Considered Evidence. *Journal of Personality and Social Psychology* 37(11), 2098.

Loughlin, M. (2014). The Concept of Constituent Power. *European Journal of Political Theory* 13(2), 218–237.

Loveman, B. (1994). "Protected Democracies" and Military Guardianship: Political Transitions in Latin America, 1978–1993. *Journal of Interamerican Studies and World Affairs* 36(2), 105–189.

Maboudi, T. (2019). Reconstituting Tunisia: Participation, Deliberation, and the Content of Constitution. *Political Research Quarterly*, 16.

Maboudi, T. and G. P. Nadi (2016). Crowdsourcing the Egyptian Constitution: Social Media, Elites, and the Populace. *Political Research Quarterly* 69(4), 716–731.

Macharia, R. W. and Y. Ghai (2017). The Role of Public Participation in the Two Kenyan Constitution-Making Processes of 2000-2005 and 2010: Lessons Learnt? In T. Abbiate, M. Böckenförde, and V. Federico (Eds.), *Public Participation in African Constitutionalism*, pp. 86–99. London: Routledge.

Mainwaring, S. (1991). Politicians, Parties, and Electoral Systems: Brazil in Comparative Perspective. *Comparative Politics* 24(1), 21–43.

Mainwaring, S. (1992). Brazilian Party Underdevelopment in Comparative Perspective. *Political Science Quarterly* 107(4), 677–707.

Mainwaring, S. (1999). *Rethinking Party Systems in the Third Wave of Democratization: The Case of Brazil.* Palo Alto: Stanford University Press.

Mainwaring, S. and A. Pérez-Liñán (1997). Party Discipline in the Brazilian Constitutional Congress. *Legislative Studies Quarterly* 22(4), 453.

Mainwaring, S. and T. Scully (1995a). *Building Democratic Institutions: Party Systems in Latin America.* Palo Alto: Stanford University Press.

Mainwaring, S. and T. Scully (1995b). Introduction: Party Systems in Latin America. In S. Mainwaring and T. Scully (Eds.), *Building Democratic Institutions: Party Systems in Latin America*, pp. 1–35. Palo Alto: Stanford University Press.

Mansbridge, J. (2003). Rethinking Representation. *American Political Science Review* 97(4), 515–528.

Mansbridge, J. (2014). What Is Political Science For? *Perspectives on Politics* 12(1), 8–17.

Market and Media Research (2012, April). Tveir þriðju styðja tillögur Stjórnlagaráðs, http://mmr.is/frettir/birtar-nieurstoeeur/249-tveir-trieju-styeja-tilloegur-stjornlagaraes.

Martínez Dalmau, R. (2016). Democratic Constitutionalism and Constitutional Innovation in Ecuador: The 2008 Constitution. *Latin American Perspectives* 43(1), 158–174.

Martínez-Lara, J. (1996). *Building Democracy in Brazil: The Politics of Constitutional Change, 1985-95*. St. Antony's Series. New York: St. Martin's Press.

Mattes, R. (2012). Opinion Polls and the Media in South Africa. In C. Holtz-Bacha and J. Strömbäck (Eds.), *Opinion Polls and the Media: Reflecting and Shaping Public Opinion*, pp. 175–197. Houndmills, Basingstoke, Hampshire: Palgrave Macmillan.

McLoughlin, M. A. (1993, May). Letter from M A McLoughlin to Multi-Party Forum, National Archive of South Africa, NEG 4: 1/2/2/1: 1/2/2/104.

Mendes Cardoso, R. (2010). *A Iniciativa Popular Legislativa Da Assembleia Nacional Constituinte Ao Regime Da Constituição de 1988: Um Balanço*. Ph. D. thesis, Pontifícia Universidade Católica do Rio de Janeiro, Rio de Janeiro.

Michiles, C., E. Gonçalves Vieira Filho, F. Whitaker Ferreira, J. G. Lucas Coelho, M. d. G. Veiga Moura, and R. d. P. Santos Prado (1989). *Cidadão Constituinte: A Saga Das Emendas Populares*. Rio de Janeiro: Paz e Terra.

Mijeski, K. J. and S. H. Beck (2011, April). *Pachakutik and the Rise and Decline of the Ecuadorian Indigenous Movement*. Athens, OH: Ohio University Press.

Mikkel, E. and V. Pettai (2004). The Baltics: Independence with Divergent Electoral Systems. In J. M. Colomer (Ed.), *The Handbook of Electoral System Choice*, pp. 332–346. London: Palgrave Macmillan UK.

Millard, F. (2002, September). *Politics and Society in Poland*. London: Routledge.

Moehler, D. C. (2008). *Distrusting Democrats: Outcomes of Participatory Constitution Making*. Ann Arbor: University of Michigan Press.

Molinas, J., A. Pérez Liñán, and S. Saiegh (2004). Political Institutions, Policymaking Processes, and Policy Outcomes in Paraguay, 1954–2003. *Revista de ciencia política (Santiago)* 24(2), 67–93.

Monclaire, S., M. I. S. Magalhães, C. de Barros Filho, and F. Impelizieri (Eds.) (1991). *A Constituição Desejada: SAIC: As 72.719 Sugestões Enviadas Pelos Cidadãos Brasileiros à Assembléia Nacional Constituinte*. Brasília: Centro Gráfico do Senado Federal.

Montlake, S. (March 16, 2020). How to Deal with the Climate Emergency? Ask Your Neighbor. *Christian Science Monitor*, www.csmonitor.com/World/Europe/2020/0316/How-to-deal-with-the-climate-emergency-Ask-your-neighbor.

Morgan, M. I. (1990). Founding Mothers: Women's Voices and Stories in the 1987 Nicaraguan Constitution. *Boston University Law Review* 70(1), 1–110.

Morris, H. (October 24, 2012). Crowdsourcing Iceland's Constitution. *International Herald Tribune*, http://rendezvous.blogs.nytimes.com/2012/10/24/crowdsourcing-icelands-constitution/.

Moyo, J. (March 15, 2013). Zim: Hard-fought "Yes" Campaign Fails to Capture Interest of Voters. *Mail & Guardian Online*.

Mthombothi, B. (March 12, 2017). SA Has World's Best Constitution? Pity People Can't Eat It · · · *Sunday Times*, www.timeslive.co.za/sunday-times/opinion-and-analysis/2017-03-12-sa-has-worlds-best-constitution-pity-people-cant-eat-it/.

Murray, C. (2001). Constitutional Beginning: Making South Africa's Final Constitution, A. *University of Arkansas at Little Rock Law Review* 23, 809.

Murray, C. (2013). Kenya's 2010 Constitution. In P. Häberle (Ed.), *Jahrbuch Des Öffentlichen Rechts*, pp. 747–788. Tübingen: Mohr Siebeck.

Murunga, G. R. (2014). Elite Compromises and the Content of the 2010 Constitution. In G. R. Murunga, D. Okello, and A. Sjogren (Eds.), *Kenya: The Struggle for a New Constitutional Order*, pp. 144–162. London: Zed Books.

Negretto, G. (2020). Constitution-Making and Liberal Democracy: The Role of Citizens and Representative Elites. *International Journal of Constitutional Law* 18(1), 206–232.

Negretto, G. L. (2013). *Making Constitutions: Presidents, Parties, and Institutional Choice in Latin America*. New York: Cambridge University Press.

Negretto, G. L. (2018). Democratic Constitution-Making Bodies: The Perils of a Partisan Convention. *International Journal of Constitutional Law* 16(1), 254–279.

Negri, A. (1999). *Insurgencies: Constituent Power and the Modern State*. Minneapolis, MN: University of Minnesota Press.

Nickerson, R. S. (1998). Confirmation Bias: A Ubiquitous Phenomenon in Many Guises. *Review of General Psychology* 2(2), 175–220.

Nohlen, D. (Ed.) (2005). *Elections in the Americas: A Data Handbook*, Volume 2: South America. New York: Oxford University Press.

Norris, P. (2001). Introduction: The Growth of Critical Citizens? In *Critical Citizens: Global Support for Democratic Government*, pp. 1–30. Oxford: Oxford University Press.

Nzouankeu, J. M. (1993). The Role of the National Conference in the Transition to Democracy in Africa: The Cases of Benin and Mali. *African Issues* 21(1–2), 44–50.

Oddsdottir, K. (2014). Iceland: The Birth of the World's First Crowd-Sourced Constitution. *Cambridge Journal of International and Comparative Law* 3, 1207–1220.

Odoki, B. J. (2001). The Challenges of Constitution-Making and Implementation in Uganda. In J. Olaka-Onyango (Ed.), *Constitutionalism in Africa*. Kampala: Fountain Publishers.

Odoki, B. J. (2005). *The Search for a National Consensus: The Making of the 1995 Uganda Constitution*. Kampala: Fountain Publishers.

Oklopcic, Z. (2018). *Beyond the People: Social Imaginary and Constituent Imagination*. New York: Oxford University Press.

Osiatynski, W. (1997). A Brief History of the Constitution Feature: The 1997 Polish Constitution. *East European Constitutional Review* 6(Issues 2 & 3), 66–76.

Oswin, N. (2007). The End of Queer (as we knew it): Globalization and the Making of a Gay-Friendly South Africa. *Gender, Place & Culture* 14(1), 93–110.

Ottaway, M. and N. J. Brown (2012, March). Egypt's Transition in Crisis: Falling into the Wrong Turkish Model? *Carnegie Endowment for International Peace*, https://carnegieendowment.org/2012/03/30/egypt-s-transition-in-crisis-falling-into-wrong-turkish-model.

Pachano, S. (2012). Estado actual y futuro de la democracia en Ecuador. In A. Dargatz and M. Zuazo Oblitas (Eds.), *Democracias en transformación: ¿Qué hay de nuevo en los nuevos estados andinos?*, pp. 81–102. La Paz, Bolivia: Friedrich Ebert Stiftung.

Paine, T. (1791). *Rights of Man: Being an Answer to Mr. Burke's Attack on the French Revolution*. London: J.S. Jordan.

Papadopoulos, Y. and P. Warin (2007). Are Innovative, Participatory and Deliberative Procedures in Policy Making Democratic and Effective? *European Journal of Political Research* 46(4), 445–472.

Parau, C. E. (2013). Romania's Transnational Constitution. In D. J. Galligan and M. Versteeg (Eds.), *Social and Political Foundations of Constitutions*, Comparative Constitutional Law and Policy, pp. 497–531. New York: Cambridge University Press.

Paredes, Z. and N. Díaz (2007). Los orígenes del Frente Nacional en Colombia. *Presente y Pasado. Revista de Historia* 12(23), 179–190.

Parkin, V. (1991). *Chronic Inflation in an Industrializing Economy: The Brazilian Experience*. New York: Cambridge University Press.

Parliament of South Africa (1995). *Debates of the Constitutional Assembly (Hansard): 24 January to 25 August 1995*. Cape Town: Government Printer.

Parliament of South Africa (1996). *Debates of the Constitutional Assembly (Hansard): 29 March to 11 October 1996*. Cape Town: Government Printer.

Pashko, G. (1993). Obstacles to Economic Reform in Albania. *Europe-Asia Studies* 45(5), 907–921.

Pateman, C. (1970). *Participation and Democratic Theory*. Cambridge: Cambridge University Press.

Pateman, C. (2012). Participatory Democracy Revisited. *Perspectives on Politics* 10(1), 7–19.

Pettai, V. and M. Kreuzer (1999). Party Politics in the Baltic States: Social Bases and Institutional Context. *East European Politics and Societies* 13(1), 148–189.

Pettifer, J. (1996). The Albanian Elections: Electoral Manipulation, the Media and the OSCE. *Mediterranean Politics* 1(3), 388–391.

Pietraru, D. I. (1997). *The Romanian Constitution of 1991: The "Stolen" Constitution*. Ph.D. Thesis, New School for Social Research, New York, https://search.proquest.com/pqdtglobal/docview/304362857/abstract/2D7F444C7DCC4D52PQ/1.

Poplawska, E. (2008). Constitution-Making in Poland: Some Reflections on Popular Involvement. *Zbornik Radova Pravnog Fakulteta u Splitu* 45(2), 279–286.

Prado, N. (1987). *Os notáveis erros dos notáveis: da Comissão Provisória de Estudos Constitucionais*. Rio de Janeiro: Forense.

Preston, J. (January 10, 1987). Ortega Signs Nicaragua Charter, Quickly Suspends Many Rights. *Washington Post*, www.washingtonpost.com/archive/politics/1987/01/10/ortega-signs-nicaragua-charter-quickly-suspends-many-rights/3b89e21c-8188-489e-9274-42ad8e9fde65/.

Přibáň, J. (2004). Reconstituting Paradise Lost: Temporality, Civility, and Ethnicity in Post-Communist Constitution-Making. *Law & Society Review* 38(3), 407–432.

Qvortrup, M. (Ed.) (2014). *Referendums around the World: The Continued Growth of Direct Democracy*. Houndmills, Basingstoke, Hampshire: Palgrave Macmillan.

Rapatsa, M. (2014). Transformative Constitutionalism in South Africa: 20 Years of Democracy. *Mediterranean Journal of Social Sciences*, 887–895.

Rawls, J. (1971). *A Theory of Justice*. Cambridge, Mass: Belknap Press of Harvard University Press.

Reich, G. (2007). Constitutional Coordination in Unstable Party Systems: The Brazilian constitution of 1988. *Constitutional Political Economy* 18(3), 177–197.

Reif, L. C. (2000). Building Democratic Institutions: The Role of National Human Rights Institutions in Good Governance and Human Rights Protection. *Harvard Human Rights Journal* 13, 1–70.

Reilly, B. (2013). Political Parties and Post-Conflict Peacebuilding. *Civil Wars* 15(sup1), 88–104.

Reyntjens, F. (1991). The Winds of Change. Political and Constitutional Evolution in Francophone Africa, 1990–1991. *Journal of African Law* 35(1–2), 44–55.

Richardson, J. (1995). The Market for Political Activism: Interest Groups as a Challenge to Political Parties. *West European Politics* 18(1), 116–139.

Riggs, F. W. (1970). *Administrative Reform and Political Responsiveness: A Theory of Dynamic Balancing*. Beverly Hills, CA: Sage Publications.

Riquelme, M. A. and J. G. Riquelme (1997). Political Parties. In P. Lambert and A. Nickson (Eds.), *The Transition to Democracy in Paraguay*, Latin American Studies Series, pp. 47–64. London: Palgrave Macmillan.

Robertsson, R. (October 21, 2012). Voters in Iceland Back New Constitution, More Resource Control, *Reuters*, www.reuters.com/article/2012/10/21/us-iceland-referendum-idUSBRE 89K09C20121021.

Rosenbluth, F. M. and I. Shapiro (2018). *Responsible Parties: Saving Democracy from Itself*. New Haven, CT: Yale University Press.

Rosenfeld, M. (1998). Constitution-Making, Identity Building, and Peaceful Transition to Democracy: Theoretical Reflections Inspired by the Spanish Example. *Cardozo Law Review* 19, 1891.

Rosenn, K. S. (1990). Brazil's New Constitution: An Exercise in Transient Constitutionalism for a Transitional Society. *The American Journal of Comparative Law* 38(4), 773–802.

Ross, L., D. Greene, and P. House (1977). The "False Consensus Effect": An Egocentric Bias in Social Perception and Attribution Processes. *Journal of Experimental Social Psychology* 13(3), 279–301.

Roznai, Y. (2017). *Unconstitutional Constitutional Amendments: The Limits of Amendment Powers*. Oxford: Oxford University Press.

Rubin, B. R. (2004). Crafting a Constitution for Afghanistan. *Journal of Democracy* 15(3), 5–19.

Rubio-Marín, R. (2020). Women and Participatory Constitutionalism. *International Journal of Constitutional Law* 18(1), 233–259.

Russell, P. H. (2004). *Constitutional Odyssey: Can Canadians Become a Sovereign People?* Toronto: University of Toronto Press.

Saati, A. (2015). *The Participation Myth: Outcomes of Participatory Constitution Building Processes on Democracy*. PhD Thesis, Umeå University, Umeå, Sweden, http://umu.diva-portal.org/smash/get/diva2:809188/FULLTEXT01.pdf.

Saati, A. (2020). Participatory Constitution-Building in Fiji: A Comparison of the 1993–1997 and the 2012–2013 Processes. *International Journal of Constitutional Law* 18(1), 260–276.

Sachs, A. (2009). *The Strange Alchemy of Life and Law*. New York: Oxford University Press.

Sachs, A. (2016, May). The Internal Goals of the South African Constitution Presentation at the University of Johannesburg, Conference on "Has the South African Constitution Performed in the Past 20 Years."

Salazar, P.-J. (2002). *An African Athens: Rhetoric and the Shaping of Democracy in South Africa*. Rhetoric, Knowledge, and Society. Mahwah, N.J.: L. Erlbaum Associates.

Santana, M. A. (2009). Definições e percuso metodológico. In *A Voz e a Letra Do Cidadão*, pp. 17–19. Rio de Janeiro: Museu da República.

Santos Pérez, A. and J. Ibeas Miguel (1995). Elecciones y Reforma Política en Colombia (1990-1991). *Revista de Derecho Político* (40), 341–378.

Sartori, G. (2005). *Parties and Party Systems: A Framework for Analysis*. Colchester: ECPR Press.

Scarrow, H. A. (1967). The Function of Political Parties: A Critique of the Literature and the Approach. *The Journal of Politics* 29(4), 770–790.

Scharpf, F. W. (1997). Economic Integration, Democracy and the Welfare State. *Journal of European Public Policy* 4(1), 18–36.

Scharpf, F. W. (1998). Interdependence and Democratic Legitimation. *MPIfG Working Paper* 98(2), www.mpifg.de/pu/workpap/wp98-2/wp98-2.html.

Bibliography

215

Scharpf, F. W. (1999). *Governing in Europe: Effective and Democratic?* Oxford: Oxford University Press.

Schattschneider, E. E. (1942). *Party Government*. American Government in Action Series. New York: Holt, Rinehart and Winston.

Schmidt, V. A. (2013). Democracy and Legitimacy in the European Union Revisited: Input, Output and "Throughput". *Political Studies* 61(1), 2–22.

Schmitt, C. (2008). *Constitutional Theory*. Durham: Duke University Press.

Seely, J. C. (2009). *The Legacies of Transition Governments in Africa*. New York: Palgrave Macmillan.

Seelye, K. Q. (March 17, 2009). A Different Emanuel for One Church. *The New York Times*, https://thecaucus.blogs.nytimes.com/2009/03/17/a-different-emanuel-for-one-church/.

Segal, L. and S. Cort (2011). *One Law, One Nation: The Making of the South African Constitution*. Pretoria: Jacana Media.

Segura, R. and A. M. Bejarano (2004, June). ¡Ni una asamblea mas sin nosotros! Exclusion, Inclusion, and the Politics of Constitution-Making in the Andes. *Constellations* 11(2), 217–236.

Seidman, G. W. (1994). *Manufacturing Militance: Workers' Movements in Brazil and South Africa, 1970-1985*. Berkeley: University of California Press.

Sekhotho, K. (May 21, 2018). Ramaphosa: Bill of Rights property clause a mandate for radical transformation. Eyewitness News, http://ewn.co.za/2018/05/21/ramaphosa-bill-of-rights-property-clause-a-mandate-for-radical-transformation.

Sieyès, E. J. (1963). *What Is the Third Estate?* London: Pall Mall.

Sigurjonsson, T. O. (2010). The Icelandic Bank collapse: Challenges to governance and risk management. *Corporate Governance* 10(1), 33–45.

Siljanovska-Davkova, G. (2013). Political Parties, Values, and Democratic Consolidation. In S. P. Ramet, O. Listhaug, and A. Simkus (Eds.), *Civic and Uncivic Values in Macedonia: Value Transformation, Education and Media*, pp. 109–133. London: Palgrave Macmillan.

Simeon, R. (1998). *Considerations on the Design of Federations: The South African Constitution in Comparative Perspective*. Kingston, ON: Institute of Intergovernmental Relations, Queen's University.

Simmons, E. S. and N. R. Smith (2017, January). Comparison with an Ethnographic Sensibility. *PS: Political Science & Politics* 50(1), 126–130.

Skidmore, T. E. (1988). *The Politics of Military Rule in Brazil, 1964-1985*. New York: Oxford University Press.

Slater, D. and E. Simmons (2010). Informative Regress: Critical Antecedents in Comparative Politics. *Comparative Political Studies* 43(7), 886–917.

Southall, R. (2013). *Liberation Movements in Power: Party and State in Southern Africa*. Pietermaritzburg: University of KwaZulu Natal Press.

Spitz, R. and M. Chaskalson (2000). *The Politics of Transition: A Hidden History of South Africa's Negotiated Settlement*. Johannesburg: Witwatersrand University Press.

Stacey, R. (2011). Constituent power and Carl Schmitt's Theory of Constitution in Kenya's Constitution-Making Process. *International Journal of Constitutional Law* 9(3–4), 587–614.

Stepan, A. C. (Ed.) (1989). *Democratizing Brazil: Problems of Transition and Consolidation*. New York: Oxford University Press.

Stewart, L. M., S. A. Miller, R. W. Hildreth, and M. V. Wright-Phillips (2014). Participatory Budgeting in the United States: A Preliminary Analysis of Chicago's 49th Ward Experiment. *New Political Science* 36(2), 193–218.

Steytler, N. (2005). Local Government in South Africa: Entrenching Decentralised Government. In N. Steytler (Ed.), *The Place and Role of Local Government in Federal Systems*, pp. 183–212. Johannesburg: Konrad-Adenauer-Stiftung.

Stjórnlagaráð (2011, June). "@dexteryz crowdsourcing is actually a bit of an overstatement. It is more like a fully open and transparenty comity [sic] process." Twitter, https://twitter.com/stjornlagarad/status/79356603983339520.

Stokes, S. C. (1999). Political Parties and Democracy. *Annual Review of Political Science* 2(1), 243–267.

Sunstein, C. R. (1991). Constitutionalism, Prosperity, Democracy: Transition in Eastern Europe. *Constitutional Political Economy* 2(3), 371–394.

Sunstein, C. R. (2001). *Designing Democracy: What Constitutions Do*. New York: Oxford University Press.

Sunstein, C. R. (2003). The Law of Group Polarization. In J. S. Fishkin and P. Laslett (Eds.), *Debating Deliberative Democracy*, pp. 80–101. Malden, MA: Blackwell.

Szeftel, M. (1994). "Negotiated Elections" in South Africa, 1994. *Review of African Political Economy* 21(61), 457–470.

Tarrow, S. G. (2011). *Power in Movement: Social Movements and Contentious Politics*. New York: Cambridge University Press.

Tekin, S. (2016). *Founding Acts: Constitutional Origins in a Democratic Age*. Philadelphia: University of Pennsylvania Press.

Terreblanche, S. (2015). Constraints to Democracy and Public Reasoning in the New South Africa. *Philosophy & Social Criticism* 41(1), 37–45.

The Associated Press (October 16, 1985). Nicaragua Decree Suspends Rights; Cites "Aggression". *The New York Times*, www.nytimes.com/1985/10/16/world/nicaragua-decree-suspends-rights-cites-aggression.html.

The Economist (October 3, 2019). A Belgian Experiment that Aristotle Would Have Approved of. *The Economist*, www.economist.com/europe/2019/10/03/a-belgian-experiment-that-aristotle-would-have-approved-of.

Thiel, H. and R. B. Mattes (1998). Consolidation and Public Opinion in South Africa. *Journal of Democracy* 9(1), 95–110.

Thompson, L. M. (2001). *A History of South Africa* (3rd ed.). New Haven, CT: Yale University Press.

Thoreson, R. R. (2008). Somewhere over the Rainbow Nation: Gay, Lesbian and Bisexual Activism in South Africa. *Journal of Southern African Studies* 34(3), 679–697.

Tilly, C. (1978). *From Mobilization to Revolution*. Reading, MA: Addison-Wesley Pub. Co.

Tilly, C. (2004). *Social Movements, 1768-2004*. Abingdon: Routledge.

Timeslive (June 24, 2018). Over 700,000 Submissions on Land Expropriation Received. *Sunday Times*, www.timeslive.co.za/politics/2018-06-24-over-700000-submissions-on-land-expropriation-received/.

Tripp, A. M. (2010). The Politics of Constitution Making in Uganda. In L. E. Miller (Ed.), *Framing the State in Times of Transition: Case Studies in Constitution Making*, pp. 158–175. Washington, DC: United States Institute of Peace Press.

Tushnet, M. (2012). Constitution-Making: An Introduction. *Texas Law Review* 91, 1983–2013.

Tushnet, M. (2015). Peasants with Pitchforks, and Toilers with Twitter: Constitutional Revolutions and the Constituent Power. *International Journal of Constitutional Law* 13(3), 639–654.

UNHRC (2011, May). Report of the Special Rapporteur on the Promotion and Protection of the Right to Freedom of Opinion and Expression, Frank La Rue. Report A/HRC/17/27,

United Nations Human Rights Council, http://www2.ohchr.org/english/bodies/hrcouncil/docs/17session/A.HRC.17.27_en.pdf.

United States Department of State (1987). *The Sandinista Constitution*. Washington: Office of Public Diplomacy for Latin America and the Caribbean.

Updike Toler, L. (2014). Mapping the Constitutional Process. *Cambridge Journal of International and Comparative Law* 3(4), 1260–1286.

Uslaner, E. M. (2006). Political Parties and Social Capital, Political Parties or Social Capital. In R. S. Katz and W. J. Crotty (Eds.), *Handbook of Party Politics*, pp. 376–386. Thousand Oaks, CA: SAGE.

Valenzuela, A. (1997, January). Paraguay: The Coup that Didn't Happen. *Journal of Democracy* 8(1), 43–55.

Valtysson, B. (2014, January). Democracy in Disguise: The Use of Social Media in Reviewing the Icelandic Constitution. *Media, Culture & Society* 36(1), 52–68.

van Heerden, M. (2007). The 1996 Constitution of the Republic of South Africa: Ultimately Supreme without a Number. *Politeia* 26(1), 33–44.

van Rouveroy van Nieuwaal, E. (1992). The Togolese Chiefs – Caught between Scylla and Charybdis. *Journal of Legal Pluralism and Unofficial Law* 32, 19–46.

Veja (August 5, 1987). Gesto de peso: Quase 2 milhões de pessoas apóiam emendas da CNBB. *Veja*, 43.

Verba, S., K. L. Schlozman, H. Brady, and N. H. Nie (1993). Citizen Activity: Who Participates? What Do They Say? *American Political Science Review* 87(2), 303–318.

Versiani, M. H. (2013). *Linguagens Da Cidadania: Os Brasileiros Escrevem Para a Constituinte de 1987/1988*. Doctoral Dissertation, Fundação Getulio Vargas, Rio de Janeiro, http://bibliotecadigital.fgv.br/dspace/bitstream/handle/10438/10842/Tese%20vers ão%20final%20para%20BIBLIOTECA%20DIGITAL.pdf?sequence=1.

von Savigny, F. K. (1867). *System of the Modern Roman Law*. Madras: J. Higginbotham.

wa Mutua, M. (1997). Hope and Despair for a New South Africa: The Limits of Rights Discourse. *Harvard Human Rights Journal* 10, 63–114.

Waldmeir, P. (1997). *Anatomy of a Miracle: The End of Apartheid and the Birth of the New South Africa*. New York: W. W. Norton.

Waldron, J. (1999). *Law and Disagreement*. Oxford: Oxford University Press.

Walker, L. D. and P. J. Williams (2010). The Nicaraguan Experience: Process, Conflict, Contradictions, and Change. In L. E. Miller (Ed.), *Framing the State in Times of Transition: Case Studies in Constitution Making*, pp. 483–504. Washington, DC: United States Institute of Peace.

Wamai, E. N. (2014). Mediating Kenya's Post-Election Violence: From a Peace-Making to a Constitutional Moment. In G. R. Murunga, D. Okello, and A. Sjogren (Eds.), *Kenya: The Struggle for a New Constitutional Order*, pp. 66–78. London: Zed Books.

Wampler, B. (2007). *Participatory Budgeting in Brazil: Contestation, Cooperation, and Accountability*. University Park, PA: Penn State Press.

Wampler, B. (2008). When Does Participatory Democracy Deepen the Quality of Democracy? Lessons from Brazil. *Comparative Politics* 41(1), 61–81.

Ward, A. (May 3, 2015). Pirate Party Surges in Polls to Become Biggest Political Party in Iceland. *The Independent*, www.independent.co.uk/news/world/politics/pirate-party-surges-in-polls-to-become-biggest-political-party-in-iceland-10222018.html.

Webb, P. (2005). Political Parties and Democracy: The Ambiguous Crisis. *Democratization* 12(5), 633–650.

Weiner, M. and J. LaPalombara (Eds.) (1966). *Political Parties and Political Development*. Number 6 in Studies in Political Development. Princeton, NJ: Princeton University Press.

Weyland, K. (2014). *Making Waves: Democratic Contention in Europe and Latin America since the Revolutions of 1848*. New York: Cambridge University Press.

Wheatley, J. and M. Germann (2013). Outcomes of Constitution-Making: Democratization and Conflict Resolution. In J. Wheatley and F. Mendez (Eds.), *Patterns of Constitutional Design: The Role of Citizens and Elites in Constitution-Making*, pp. 49–68. Routledge.

Widner, J. (2005). Constitution Writing and Conflict Resolution. *The Round Table* 94(381), 503–518.

Widner, J. (2008). Constitution Writing in Post-Conflict Settings: An Overview. *William and Mary Law Review* 49, 1513–1541.

Williamson, J. (2009). A Short History of the Washington Consensus. *Law and Business Review of the Americas* 15(1), 7–26.

Wilson, W. (1885). *Congressional Government: A Study in American Politics*. Boston: Houghton Mifflin.

World Bank (2020). Educational Attainment, at Least Bachelor's or Equivalent, Population 25+, total (%) (cumulative). *The World Bank: DataBank*, https://data.worldbank.org/indicator/SE.TER.CUAT.BA.ZS?end=2018&locations=BR&start=1970.

Wyrzykowski, M. (1997). Introductory Note to the 1997 Constitution of the Republic of Poland Symposium on the Constitution of the Republic of Poland. *Saint Louis-Warsaw Transatlantic Law Journal* 1997, 1–4.

Yang, K. (2016). Creating Public Value and Institutional Innovations across Boundaries: An Integrative Process of Participation, Legitimation, and Implementation. *Public Administration Review* 76(6), 873–885.

Zaiden Benvindo, J. (2016, August). The Brazilian Constitutional Amendment Rate: A Culture of Change? ICONnect: Blog of the International Journal of Constitutional Law, www.iconnectblog.com/2016/08/the-brazilian-constitutional-amendment-rate-a-culture-of-change/.

Index

Milton Keynes UK
Ingram Content Group UK Ltd.
UKHW020836120424
440787UK00021B/137

9 781108 793513